Roman LABA

Ajaccio to Bavella

M-F

GR20 – CORSICA

THE HIGH-LEVEL ROUTE

About the Author

Paddy Dillon is a prolific outdoor writer with over thirty books to his name, as well as dozens of booklets and brochures. He writes for a number of outdoor magazines and other publications, as well as producing materials for organisations such as tourism groups. He lives on the fringe of the Lake District and has walked, and written about walking, in every county in England, Scotland, Ireland and Wales. He has walked in many parts of Europe, as well as Nepal, Tibet, Colorado and the Canadian Rockies.

While walking his routes Paddy inputs his notes directly into a palmtop computer every few steps. His descriptions are therefore precise, having been written at the very point at which the reader uses them. He takes all his own photographs and often draws his own maps to illustrate his routes. He has appeared on television and is a member of the Outdoor Writers' Guild.

Other Cicerone guides by Paddy Dillon

South West Coast Path
Channel Island Walks
Irish Coastal Walks
The Irish Coast to Coast Walk
The Mountains of Ireland
Walking in County Durham
Walking in the Galloway Hills
Walking in the North Pennines
Walking in Madeira
Walking in the Canary Islands – West
Walking in the Canary Islands – East
Walking in Malta
The Cleveland Way and the Yorkshire Wolds Way
The North York Moors
Walking in the Isles of Scilly

GR20 – CORSICA
THE HIGH-LEVEL ROUTE

by
Paddy Dillon

2 POLICE SQUARE, MILNTHORPE, CUMBRIA LA7 7PY
www.cicerone.co.uk

Second edition 2006
ISBN-10 1 85284 477 9
ISBN-13 978 185284 477 6

First published 2001, reprinted 2002
ISBN 1 85284 477 9

A catalogue record for this book is available from the British Library.

Photos by the author.

International Distress Signal
(Only to be used in an emergency)

Six blasts on a whistle (and flashes with a torch after dark) spaced evenly for one minute, followed by a minute's pause.
Repeat until an answer is received. The response is three signals per minute followed by a minute's pause.

The following signals are used to communicate with helicopters

Help Required: raise both arms above head to form a 'V'

Help not required: raise one arm above head, extend other arm downward

Advice to Readers

Readers are advised that while every effort is taken by the author to ensure the accuracy of this guidebook, changes can occur which may affect the contents. It is advisable to check locally on transport, accommodation, shops and so on, but even rights of way can be altered. Paths can be affected by forestry work, landslip or changes of ownership.

The author would welcome information on any updates and changes sent through the publishers.

Front cover: Walkers on the GR20 near Altore on the way to Col Perdu (Stage 4)

CONTENTS

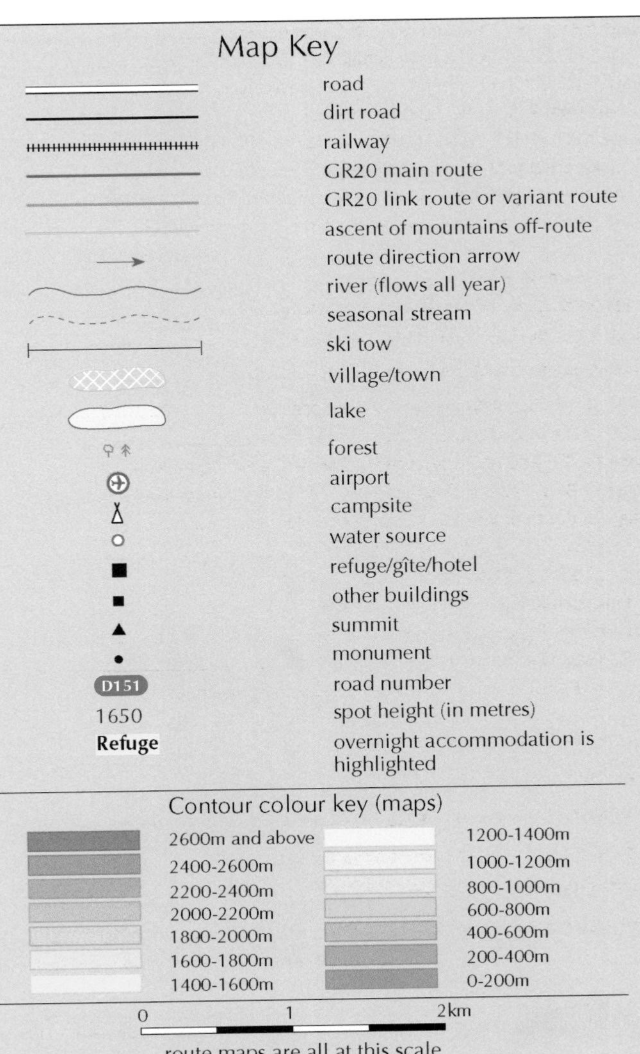
Map Key
road
dirt road
railway
GR20 main route
GR20 link route or variant route
ascent of mountains off-route
route direction arrow
river (flows all year)
seasonal stream
ski tow
village/town
lake
forest
airport
campsite
water source
refuge/gîte/hotel
other buildings
summit
monument
D151
road number
1650
spot height (in metres)
Refuge
overnight accommodation is highlighted
Contour colour key (maps)
2600m and above
2400-2600m
2200-2400m
2000-2200m
1800-2000m
1600-1800m
1400-1600m
1200-1400m
1000-1200m
800-1000m
600-800m
400-600m
200-400m
0-200m
0
1
2km
route maps are all at this scale

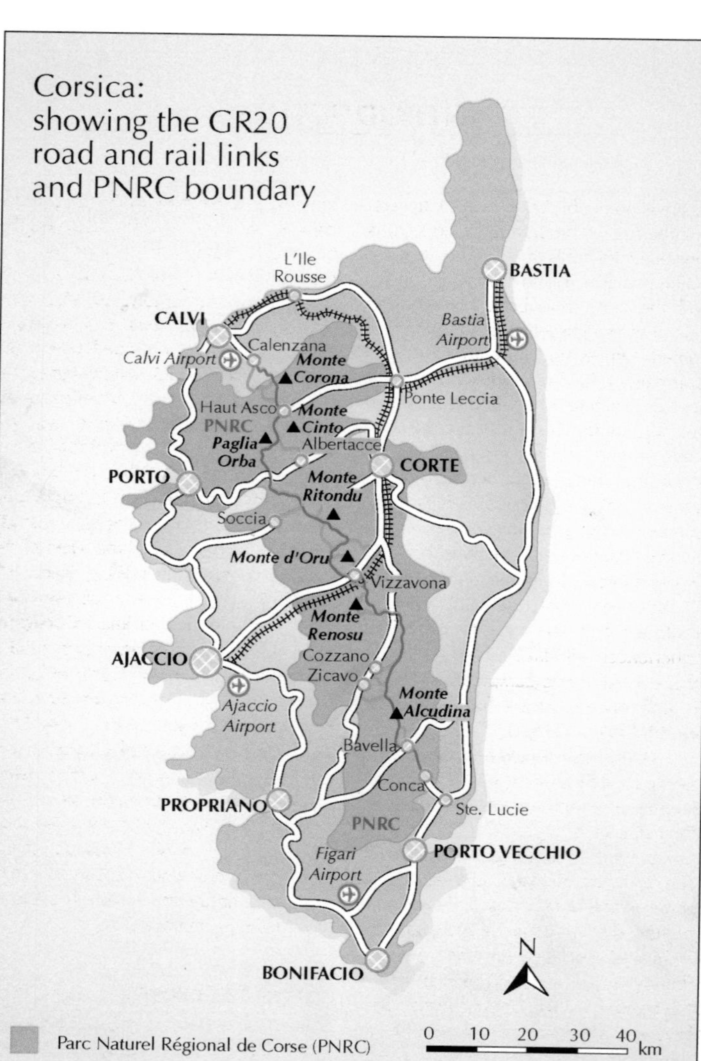
Corsica:
showing the GR20
road and rail links
and PNRC boundary
L'Ile
Rousse
BASTIA
CALVI
Bastia
Airport
Calenzana
Calvi Airport
Monte
Corona
Ponte Leccia
Haut Asco
Monte
Cinto
PNRC
Paglia
Orba
Albertacce
CORTE
PORTO
Monte
Ritondu
Soccia
Monte d'Oru
Vizzavona
Monte
Renosu
AJACCIO
Cozzano
Zicavo
Ajaccio
Airport
Monte
Alcudina
Bavella
Conca
PROPRIANO
Ste. Lucie
PNRC
PORTO VECCHIO
Figari
Airport
BONIFACIO
N
Parc Naturel Régional de Corse (PNRC)
0 10 20 30 40
km

INTRODUCTION

There is no doubt that the GR20, traversing the rugged mountains of Corsica, is one of the top trails of the world. Its reputation precedes it, and most walkers who trek the route describe it afterwards as one of the toughest they have ever completed. Others find they are unable to complete it, having seriously underestimated its nature. The GR20 climbs high into the mountains and stays there for days on end, leading ordinary walkers deep into the sort of terrain usually visited only by mountaineers. The scenery is awe-inspiring, with bare rock and vertical lines in some parts, contrasting with forests, lakes and alpine pastures in other places. Those who walk the route are only too eager to share their experiences with those who haven't, so that everyone who completes the GR20 is probably responsible for two or three more people walking it!

Most people would relish the opportunity to walk among wild mountains, feeling the roughness of the rocks with their fingers, enjoying the clarity of the views under a blazing Mediterranean sun, maybe enlivened with streaks of snow on the higher slopes. There is the perfumed scent of the *maquis*, and the chance to spot eagles in flight. You can do all this, provided you keep an eye on the weather, since Corsica is noted for severe summer thunderstorms, while in winter the mountains are truly alpine. There is the prospect of sleeping in rustic refuges, or even better, sleeping under canvas, peeping out to discover the mountains bathed in moonlight. On moonless nights, you can gaze awestruck at the firmament speckled with millions of pinprick stars. You can enjoy all this and more provided you make careful plans and walk within your limits.

The GR20 is an experience, more than simply a walk, and those who try and rush the route may find they finish with certain regrets. While the 'classic' route can be covered in a fortnight, discerning walkers will be happy to include variations – maybe climbing some of the nearby mountains, or visiting nearby villages. The main route allows little opportunity to meet ordinary Corsicans, but a detour into a village, or better still, a night or two spent with a Corsican family, will enhance the quality of the walk. Take the time to sample local foodstuffs, including the meat and cheese that is made in the mountains, maybe washed down with a homemade wine, but always be aware of where your next fill of water is available. Corsican food is generally simple and wholesome – ideal for a trek through the mountains, and all part of the joy of travel!

GEOLOGY

Corsica is often referred to as 'the Granite Isle', and it is easy to dismiss the whole island simply as one enormous granite massif, but this would be wrong. Corsica is geologically divided into two parts by a line running very roughly from L'Ile Rousse on the north coast, through Corte in the middle of the island, to Favone on the east coast.

Everything west of this line is referred to as 'Hercynian Corsica', named after a mountain-building era that occurred between 345 and 225 million years ago. The bedrock in this, the greater part of Corsica, is essentially a massive granite intrusion. It was pushed into the Earth's crust under immense pressure and temperature, so that the rock was in a molten state. As it cooled over a long period of time, coarse crystals formed, chiefly of quartz, feldspar and mica. Geologists sub-divide the granite according to its mineral composition, which varies from place to place, especially around the northwest of the island. Granophyres and quartz porphyries are common, and conspicuous linear dykes have been intruded into some rocks. The mountains that were raised during the Hercynian era are long gone, and the granite mountains of Corsica are merely their deepest roots.

Everything east of the dividing line is referred to as 'Alpine Corsica', simply because the rock types were pushed up during the later era of mountain building that was associated with the creation of the Alps. There are several rock types, including schists of uncertain age that have been folded and metamorphosed time and again. There are also layers of limestone and sedimentary rocks that were formed on the seabed, before buckling under immense pressure to form mountains. Fossils contained in these rocks reveal that they were formed in the Upper Carboniferous, Liassic and Eocene periods – with respective ages from around 300, 150 and 50 million years ago.

The Ice Age, which ended only around 10,000 years ago, had a profound effect on the mountains of Corsica. The mountains were high enough to ensure that snow never melted from year to year, but increased in depth so that glaciers could form, grinding out deep corries and carving steep-sided valleys into the mountainsides. During a much wetter period than at present, powerful rivers scoured the valleys deeper, and spread fans of alluvial rubble further downstream, and around the coast. During harsh winters in the mountains, conditions are again reminiscent of the Ice Age, when the high corrie lakes freeze completely and deep snowdrifts are heaped up against the cliffs. By the time Man discovered Corsica, the island valleys were well wooded, though parts of the coast and the high mountains were bare rock, much as they are today.

BRIEF HISTORY

Those who walk the GR20 may feel that they are completely bypassing anything of historical interest on Corsica. Transhumance, the seasonal movement of livestock to summer pastures in the mountains, followed by a retreat to the low ground before the onset of winter, has been practised in Corsica for thousands of years. The island has been invaded dozens of times by all kinds of armies, and native Corsicans have often fought to resist each successive attempt at colonisation. However, high in the mountains, there are few ancient monuments or proud fortifications, nor are there any museums to visit. The GR20 is essentially a tough mountain walk almost completely divorced from the history and culture of the island. History, by and large, was wrought elsewhere on the island, and the best you can do is at least be aware of some of the key events and turbulent times that Corsica has experienced.

7000BC The first human settlers probably reached Corsica from Tuscany during the Palaeolithic era. They were hunter/gatherers who lived in caves and other natural shelters, using only basic stone tools and items of pottery.

6600BC 'Bonifacio Woman', a Neolithic woman whose skeleton was discovered near Bonifacio, is the earliest human being discovered on Corsica. Soon afterwards, people began the tradition of transhumance, involving the seasonal movement of animals to summer pastures in the mountains, retreating to the coast and lower valleys in the winter. As semi-nomads, shepherds and herdsmen built themselves temporary shelters.

4000BC The climax of the Megalithic era, during which huge stone monuments, menhirs and dolmens, were raised around the island. Human society was clearly well organised to enable people to build such structures, and the period of construction spanned several centuries.

1500BC Invaders known as the Toréens, named after the stone towers they erected, landed at Porto Vecchio and gradually spread through Corsica. The earlier inhabitants, however, continued to raise their own stone monuments even into the Iron Age.

565BC Greek refugees from Phocaea established a colony at Alalia, where Aléria now stands. They were traders who planted olives and vines, but were troubled by attacking Carthaginians and Etruscans.

535BC The Greeks abandoned their colony, and the Etruscans who occupied the site were later displaced by the Carthaginians.

259BC Roman soldiers were sent to Corsica to prevent the Carthaginians advancing through the Mediterranean. Native Corsicans joined forces with the Carthaginians to hold the Romans at bay, so the Roman conquest took 40 years to subdue the island. Roman power remained dominant for over 500 years, and while ports were constructed, little change took place in the interior. The Roman strategy was essentially to prevent any other power from occupying the island, which was conveniently close to Rome.

303AD Christianity had been brought to Corsica, and the beheading of Santa Restituda gave the island its first Christian martyr. As the Roman empire began to wane, Vandals began to raid coastal settlements and were well established on the island in the middle of the 5th century.

534AD Byzantine forces launched an invasion of Corsica and made it part of their empire. However, they in turn suffered a series of raids, notably from the Ostrogoths, and later from the Lombards.

725AD The Lombards took control of Corsica, but by this time the Saracens were sending raiding parties to the island, harrying coastal settlements.

754AD Pépin le Bref, King of the Franks, offered to give Corsica to the Pope after freeing it from Lombard control. The process took 20 years, and it was Pépin's son, Charlemagne, who finally handed the island to the Pope. However, the Saracens continued raiding the island and at times almost completely overran it.

825AD Ugo della Colonna is reputed to have driven the Saracens from Corsica at the request of the Pope, but tales are legendary and it is difficult to separate the man from the myth. Seigneurial families, who were split by long-standing rivalries, dominated life on the island. The feudal system ensured that common folk were treated quite harshly, leading to some internal conflicts.

1077 The Pope appointed the Bishop of Pisa to administer Corsica, and for a time the island enjoyed a period of peace.

1133 The Genoese, who were rivals to the Pisans, successfully lobbied the Pope for a share of Corsica, and the island was divided between Pisa and Genoa. The Genoese gradually undermined Pisan control on the island.

1284 The Genoese finally defeated the Pisans at the Battle of Meloria, and began to erect considerable fortifications around Corsica. Resentment was rife, as many Corsicans were simply evicted from their properties and forced into servitude. The Pope handed Corsica and Sardinia to the Aragonese, but the Genoese refused to relinquish control, setting the scene for decades of conflict.

1420 An Aragonese force managed to take control of most of Corsica and a Viceroy ruled the island until 1434, when the Genoese beheaded him.

1453 The Genoese appointed a powerful financial body, the Office de St Georges, to administer Corsica. They installed a military regime, strengthened fortifications around the island, developed agriculture and raised taxes.

1553 Corsica was invaded by French troops, in which a colonel called Sampiero Corso, also known as 'the Fiery', and 'the Most Corsican of Corsicans', scored notable victories over the Genoese. Although Corsica was regarded then as a French possession, it was handed back to the Genoese under the Treaty of Cateau-Cambrésis. Sampiero Corso made another bid at conquest in 1564, but this was ultimately unsuccessful. The Genoese remained troubled by Saracen raids and therefore further strengthened the fortifications around the island. The lot of common Corsicans remained dire.

1730 When an old man refused to pay his taxes, increasing numbers of

Corsicans joined him in refusing to pay theirs also, and this led to a rebellion against Genoese rule. In 1732, Austrian soldiers were dispatched to the island to restore order, and were soundly defeated at the Battle of Calenzana. The Genoese, however, quickly and brutally regained control.

1736 Obviously in need of a leader, many Corsicans flocked to support a German adventurer called Théodore de Neuhoff, who was proclaimed Théodore I, King of Corsica. Although he promised military support against the Genoese, it was not forthcoming, and Corsicans had to struggle on by themselves against their brutal colonisers.

1738 The Genoese accepted an offer of military assistance from the French. By 1741, the French considered that they had put down the rebellion and departed, only to return when trouble flared up again in 1748.

1754 Pascal Paoli, one of the most famous names in Corsican history, led a rebellion that briefly allowed a Corsican state to be established, with its centre of control in the mountain citadel of Corte. Democracy, education and justice were central to Paoli's administration, but the Genoese again looked to France to regain control over the island. In the event, the French ended up taking control of Corsica away from both the Genoese and native Corsicans.

1769 The beginning of French rule in Corsica was followed closely by the French Revolution, which was wholeheartedly supported by Corsicans. Pascal Paoli enjoyed a brief period of favour with the French, and when he lost their favour, Corsicans proclaimed him 'Father of the Nation'.

1794 A British force attacked Calvi, where Nelson lost his eye, and an Anglo–Corsican state was proclaimed. Sir Gilbert Elliot was installed as viceroy, angering supporters of Paoli. Some Paoli supporters later joined forces with the French, so that the British eventually departed from Corsica.

1796 French rule was restored on the island, but there was widespread discontent, even though a famous son of Corsica, Napoleon Bonaparte, was crowned Emperor in 1804. It seems that Napoleon did little for his native island, and prevented native Corsicans from taking positions of control.

1801 Corsica found itself under military rule under General Morand, followed in 1811 by General César Berthier.

1814 British soldiers responded to an appeal from the inhabitants of Bastia, but were quickly withdrawn from Corsica following the abdication of Napoleon.

1815 Corsica's establishments and infrastructure were improved, with the construction of roads and a railway, schools and industry, but this did little to stem massive emigration from the island. In fact, Corsica's population was halved, and the island had a reputation as a place of crime and violence.

1909 A plan was proposed for the development of Corsica, but this suffered a setback due to the First World War. Thousands of Corsican soldiers enlisted in the army and died in battle, cutting further into the island's population.

1940 Mussolini had been interested in Corsica for some time, before helping to land some 90,000 Fascist and Nazi troops on the island. Many Corsicans waged a guerilla war on the occupiers, coining the term 'Maquis' for the Resistance, after the impenetrable scrub covering much of the island. The Allies armed the guerillas by dropping caches of weapons onto remote places on the island. At the end of the war, the Americans sprayed DDT on the island to rid it of the scourge of malaria that had affected it for thousands of years.

1962 The 'events in Aleria', as they came to be known, started with *pieds-noirs* Algerians and a scandal in wine-making processes, and ended with a militant Corsican sit-in and the deaths of two policemen. Discontent had been brewing for some time around the island, and indeed, had its roots in centuries of domination and oppression. Corsican nationalism took on many forms, from street protests and political posturing, to crime and assassination, with bombing campaigns throughout the 1970s. Calls for autonomy have at least resulted in the Collectivité Territoriale de Corse having a distinct language and culture of its own, and a greater control over its affairs than any other region of France.

2003 France offered Corsica greater autonomy, but when this was put to the vote in a referendum, the plan was narrowly defeated by 51% to 49%.

A turbulent history indeed, and one that is set to run and run. It is a great pity that walkers on the GR20 will barely be aware of any of it!

TRAVEL TO CORSICA

Shop around the travel agents or browse the websites to find appropriate flight, coach, rail and ferry schedules, as well as the best prices. When choosing outward and return dates, it is wise to build in a couple of extra days in case of any delays, or in case inclement weather or fatigue cause alterations to your original carefully planned walking schedule.

By Air

By far the easiest way to reach Corsica is to fly, and in terms of walking the GR20 it is best to fly to Calvi airport. Other airports in Corsica are at Bastia, Ajaccio and Figari. There are flights from all over Europe, but none by true budget operators. The closest is Air Berlin, **www.airberlin.com**, from Germany to Calvi, or GB Airways, **www.gbairways.com**, from London Gatwick to Bastia. EasyJet, **www.easyjet.com**, operates flights from a few British airports to Nice, from where CCM Airlines, **www.ccm-airlines.com**, flies to all four Corsican aiports. Charter flights operate to all the airports, but are usually available for trips of only one or two weeks' duration. Check Western Air, **www.westernair. co. uk,** for details.

Looking to the jagged peaks beside the Brèche de Capitellu from the rocky shore of Lac de Capitellu (Link from Bocca a Soglia to Bergeries de Grotelle).

Scheduled flights to Corsica may involve a change of aircraft at Nice or Marseille, or even a change of airport in Paris, between Charles de Gaulle and Orly, for which there are regular bus transfers. Scheduled flights with good connections are operated by Air France, **www.airfrance.com**. Most short flights between southern France and the four Corsican airports are operated by CCM Airlines, but bookings are handled through Air France.

By Road and Rail

Those travelling overland through France by car, coach or train will find that ports such as Nice or Marseille provide the most straightforward ferry connections to Corsica. Check with Eurolines, **www.eurolines.com**, or Eurostar, **www.eurostar.com**, to find good coach or rail connections to the ports.

The view from the old course of the GR20 after crossing Punta Culaghia, looking towards Punta Stranciacone.

Travelling overland to Nice or Marseille to catch an onward CCM Airlines flight to Corsica could also be considered.

By Sea

Ferries from ports such as Nice and Marseille serve the four main Corsican ports of Ajaccio, Bastia, Calvi and Porto Vecchio, but some ferries serve L'Ile Rousse and Propriano. There are also ferries to Corsica from other ports in France and Italy. When linking overland travel with ferry timetables, be sure to check schedules and timetables carefully, with due regard to check-in times, to ensure a smooth transfer. The main ferry operators are SNCM, **www.sncm.com**, and Corsica Ferries, **www.corsicaferries.com**. Two minor operators are CMN, **www.cmn.fr**, and Moby Lines, **www.mobylines.fr**.

Taking or Hiring a Car

Taking a car to Corsica is not a particularly good idea, except for back-up purposes, and even then its use will be limited. Apart from the beginning and end of the GR20, the route is accessible at only six other points for vehicles. Walkers would still need to carry the bulk of their food and gear, while the back-up driver would need to pursue other interests for the days between each road access point. Cars can be hired at the airports and ferryports.

TRAVEL AROUND CORSICA

By Train

Travel by train is remarkably simple. There is in effect only one line between

Ajaccio and Bastia, with a branch line running to Calvi. The junction is at Ponte Leccia, and the railway crosses the course of the GR20 at its midpoint at Vizzavona. The line is operated jointly by CFC and SNCF, **www.ter-sncf.com**, and there is no harm picking up a timetable whether you plan to use the railway or not. Bear in mind that timetables do change during the course of the summer, and while trains run every day, there are likely to be variations on Sundays. Travel by train is remarkably scenic, but it can be hot and uncomfortable at times, and while trains usually set off on time, they stop frequently and often arrive late at their destinations.

By Bus

If travelling by bus, it is essential to check and double-check timetables. There are several bus operators, many services that operate only for a brief summer season, and no central authority issuing information. A useful website is **www.corsicabus.com**, and a brief one-page summary of bus services is available from tourist information offices.

When you wish to catch a bus, be sure to turn up early and ask someone *exactly* where the departure point for the bus is located, as bus stops are rare. Bear in mind that some buses look very plain, and it may not be immediately obvious that they are being used for public transport. Most coaches are comfortable and air-conditioned, but some services are operated using more basic minibuses.

Buses usually leave on time, but delays are commonplace, so beware if you are trying to achieve a fairly tight connection somewhere along the way. Individual bus services and contact details are mentioned as appropriate throughout this guidebook. Some short shuttle-bus services are referred to as *navettes,* and this term is also used for complimentary transport offered by accommodation providers.

By Taxi

Taxis are available at all the airports and ports, in all the main towns, and in many villages and rural locations. The telephone numbers of certain taxi companies and individuals are given throughout this guidebook, since they may offer the only chance to reach or leave some of the places along or near the GR20. Fares may be metered or fixed, though you may be able to agree a price. Most drivers charge extra in the evenings and on Sundays, and there may be a small charge for your baggage too. For short journeys, when you want to keep moving, a taxi is good value, but for a long transfer round the island, expect it to be very expensive, bearing in mind that you may have to contribute towards the driver's long journey home. A general rule of thumb is that a long taxi journey will cost 10 times more than the bus fare.

HOW TO REACH THE GR20

From Calvi

Simply leave the airport and grab the first available taxi. Ask to be taken to Calenzana. One look at your big rucksack and the driver will guess you are walking the GR20. He may refer to the route with a word that sounds like *jairvan* – get used to the sound! If you have already arranged accommodation in Calenzana, leave it to the driver to take you there. The telephone numbers of some of the taxi drivers are given in the section about Calenzana and the start of the GR20.

If you reach Calvi by ferry, either take a taxi to Calenzana, or wait for a bus operated by Beaux Voyages, tel. 04 95 65 11 35 or 04 95 65 08 26. Buses, taxis and trains all operate close to the Place de la Porteuse d'Eau, which is near the railway station in Calvi and only a short walk from the port. If you wish to walk only half of the GR20 from Vizzavona, then it is easy to catch the CFC/SNCF train, tel. Calvi 04 95 65 00 61. The tourist information office is nearby at Port de Plaisance, tel. 04 95 65 16 67.

From Bastia

There are daily buses between the airport and Bastia, operated by the Société des Autobus Bastiais, tel. 04 95 31 06 65. Alternatively, use Les Taxis de l'Aéroport, tel. 04 95 36 04 65. Buses from Bastia to Calvi run daily, except Sundays, and are operated by Beaux Voyages, tel. 04 95 65 11 35 or 04 95 65 08 26. Buses from Bastia to Vizzavona and Ajaccio run daily through July and August, then Monday to Friday for the rest of the year, and are operated by Eurocorse Voyages, tel. Bastia 04 95 31 73 76. Use Les Rapides Bleus Corsicatours, tel. Bastia 04 95 31 03 79, to reach Ste Lucie de Porto Vecchio for Conca, if walking the GR20 south to north. Buses run daily from mid-June to mid-September, but not on Sundays for the rest of the year.

CFC/SNCF trains run daily from Bastia to Calvi, Vizzavona and Ajaccio, tel. Bastia 04 95 32 80 61. If your flight to Bastia is delayed, a taxi ride to nearby Casamozza might allow you to catch a bus or train that has already departed south from Bastia. If arriving by ferry to Bastia, a short walk straight inland from the ferry terminal leads to the bus terminus, behind the *mairie*, and railway station. The tourist information office is on the Place St Nicolas, tel. 04 95 54 20 40.

From Ajaccio

There are daily buses between the airport and Ajaccio, operated by TCA, tel. 04 95 23 29 41. Alternatively, use a taxi to get into town – there are several operators to choose from. Those arriving by ferry berth at the Gare Routière, which is a combined ferry and bus terminal. There are no direct buses from Ajaccio to Calvi, so it may be best to catch a CFC/SNCF train, tel. Ajaccio 04 95 23 11 03. The railway station is only a few minutes' walk along the Quai l'Herminier.

Buses serve places on the southern half of the GR20. Use Eurocorse Voyages, tel. 04 95 21 06 30, to reach Vizzavona daily through July and August, and Monday to Friday throughout the rest of the year. Use Autocars Santoni, tel. 04 95 22 64 44 or 04 95 21 29 56, to reach Zicavo, daily except Sundays, throughout the year. Use Autocars Balesi Evasion, tel. 04 95 70 15 55, to reach Bavella, daily except Sundays through July and August, then Monday to Friday through the rest of the year. Use Autocars Ricci, tel. 04 95 51 08 19, to reach Bavella, daily through July and August. Use Eurocorse Voyages, tel. Ajaccio 04 95 21 06 30, to reach Porto Vecchio for onward travel to Conca, if walking south to north, Monday to Saturday from July to mid-September. The tourist information office is on Boulevard Roi Jérôme, tel. 04 95 51 53 03.

From Figari or Porto Vecchio

Those who arrive at Figari airport can catch the airport bus, tel. 04 95 71 00 11, or use Taxi Figari, tel. 04 95 71 04 45 or 04 95 71 10 10, to reach Porto Vecchio. If arriving by ferry, it is a simple matter to walk into Porto Vecchio to catch a bus. Use Les Rapides Bleus Corsicatours, tel. Porto Vecchio 04 95 70 10 36, to cover the distance from Porto Vecchio to Ste Lucie de Porto Vecchio, if heading for Conca to walk the GR20 from south to north. Stay on the bus to Bastia for onward connections by bus or train. Use Autocars Balesi Evasion, tel. 04 95 70 15 55, to reach Bavella, daily except Sundays through July and August, then Monday to Friday through the rest of the year. Use Eurocorse Voyages, tel. Porto Vecchio 04 95 70 13 83, to reach Ajaccio for onward connections by bus or train. The tourist information office is on the Rue du Dr du Rocca Serra, tel. 04 95 70 09 58.

To and From the GR20

Contact numbers for trains, buses and taxis are given at appropriate points along the course of the GR20 in this guidebook. Only a handful of roads are crossed by the GR20, and not all of them are used by buses, but there may also be links with nearby villages that have bus services. Where these are available they are noted in the guidebook. Note that there are few buses running on Sundays, so check timetables carefully or contact the operators.

WHEN TO WALK THE GR20

May

Walking the GR20 is not recommended until at least the beginning of June, although sometimes it is possible to start in the middle of May. Last minute bookings can be made if you hear that the route is clear of snow, but those who plan their travel well in advance are taking a big chance, and deep snow could still affect the higher parts of the route. Think about packing an ice axe and crampons.

Walking at this time means that the refuges, although open, will not be staffed and therefore will have no food supplies. *Bergeries* that offer food and drink along the way will not be open, so you will have to carry most of your food. Even bus services crossing the route will be fairly limited.

June

Walking the route in June avoids the really crowded summer months. The refuges will be staffed, and they'll sometimes be full too, but they won't be under the intense pressure seen during the peak summer season. Food supplies will be available at practically every night's stop, and the *bergeries* that offer alternative food, drink and accommodation should be open.

Bear in mind that snow will still be lurking in some of the more sunless gullies. Days will be warm, but not too hot. Some bus services may not be fully operational.

July and August

These are the peak summer months on the GR20. Expect large numbers of walkers and the refuges to be full. Consequently, all services are in full swing and it is easy to obtain food and drink along the way. Bear in mind that some seasonal water sources dry up. Should it be necessary to leave or join the route at any point, the full summer range of bus services will be available.

This is also the hottest time of the year, with an increasing risk of thunderstorms. There have been devastating forest fires in the past around this time, closing parts of the route to walkers.

September

Numbers of walkers are gradually reduced and there is more chance of securing a bed in the refuges, which remain staffed and supplied with food and drink. Some of the *bergeries* offering food and drink may close towards the end of the month, and some of the bus services crossing the route are withdrawn.

The days are cooler than the peak summer season, but remain warm and clear. After June, this is the best month to walk.

October

Those starting to walk the GR20 and aiming to complete it by the middle of the month might be lucky enough to miss the first snowfalls in the mountains, though a few warmer clothes may be necessary. It is not advisable to complete the route much later than this, and the onset of winter virtually closes the route to ordinary walkers.

Obtaining food and drink along the way is more difficult, so you will need to carry much more, and there are fewer bus services crossing the route. The refuges remain open, but are unstaffed, unsupplied, and may have their internal water supplies disconnected. Some of them may become completely buried beneath snow in the depths of winter.

This picture was taken towards the end of May and the GR20, up the gully, is full of snow.

This picture was taken towards the end of July and the snow has gone from the gully.

HOW TO WALK THE GR20

The Main Route

The most straightforward way to walk the GR20 is north to south, on the main red/white flashed waymarked trail from Calenzana to Conca, taking about two weeks to cover the distance. Be sure to build in a couple of spare days just in case they are needed.

GR20 Nord

It is possible to walk the northern section of the trail from Calenzana to Vizzavona in just over a week, maybe nine or ten days, and experience the most rugged highlights of the route. For those who are confident of their abilities, this is worth considering if time is limited.

GR20 Sud

Those who are wary of the level of difficulty involved on the higher parts could sample a week on the southern section from Vizzavona to Conca and reserve judgement on the northern section. This stretch also has its tough moments from time to time, so be warned!

South to North

Although most people walk the GR20 from north to south, experiencing the toughest sections first, it is also possible to walk from south to north, thereby gradually building up to the most rugged and spectacular parts of the route. Currently, about 5% of walkers trek the whole of the GR20 in this direction, though maybe 30% trek half the route south to north.

Alternatives

Note that there are sometimes high- and low-level alternatives along the way. This provides walkers with a choice of route. Sometimes the main route is the low-level one, and sometimes the high-level route can be a bit easier than the low-level route. Alternative routes are fully described in this guidebook in exactly the same detail as the main route.

Links

Walkers who complete the whole of the GR20 generally have only one regret – that they didn't visit some of the villages off-route. This guidebook includes off-route links with a handful of villages, so that at least a little Corsican culture can be enjoyed. The links highlight possibilities for leaving the route if time is limited, mentioning onward transport services.

Mountains

The hardiest enthusiasts could walk the whole of the GR20 and include a handful of mountain peaks along the way. Some of the prominent peaks close to the route can be climbed with a little scrambling. Those walking the GR20 and climbing a few extra peaks should allow about three weeks. Details of the more popular extra ascents are given in this guidebook, including some of the highest mountains in Corsica.

Guided Walking Holidays

A number of companies offer guided walks along the GR20. Approach them with caution, as commercial operators cannot book beds in refuges for their clients, and so may require participants to carry all of their gear for much of the

Those who follow only the classic course of the GR20 often regret not visiting villages or climbing mountains. This is the summit of Monte Renosu (Stage 11, high-level).

time. Others will book whatever other accommodation they can, and take care of baggage transfer, but at the cost of missing some stretches of the GR20.

Many operators organise their trips from south to north, maybe starting at Bavella and finishing at Vizzavona, Haut Asco or Bonifatu. Few operators package the classic GR20 route from Calenzana to Conca, and to avoid disappointment you should question them carefully to find out if they are offering the sort of trip you really want.

HOW TO USE THIS GUIDE

This book contains all the information needed to follow the GR20. The classic route from north to south is described from start to finish in 15 stages, and details of high- and low-level alternative routes are given, as well as a few notes on the ascent of nearby prominent peaks. It is therefore possible to pick and choose which sections to complete, and to compare and contrast any alternatives that are presented. You will probably use only half the book.

Information on the route is given near the start of the route description. Distances are given in kilometres and miles, but for the most part these are irrelevant. What really counts is the nature of the terrain – the gradients on the ascents and descents, and the conditions underfoot. The total ascent and descent for each stage is presented in metres and feet. Route profiles show altitude on the vertical axis at 500m intervals and distance on the horizontal axis at 1km intervals. Conditions underfoot are noted in the actual route descriptions. The main features on the sketch maps are shown in bold type in the route descriptions, making it easier to monitor progress along the route.

Most walkers measure their progress simply by time, and timings for various stages of the GR20 have been promoted so often that they might as well be carved in stone. In some instances, they are at least carved in wood on signs! As most walkers are using the same times, they are given in more or less the same form in this book, in the route descriptions and in the summary tables in Appendices 1 and 2. *Use these timings as a basic guide.*

Those who complete the route a little faster in the first couple of days are likely always to be a little ahead. Walkers who are a long way behind the given times should work out by how much, then apply that to their onward progress. Note that the times are walking times, *and take no account whatsoever of breaks for lunch, rests or taking pictures.* Over roughly two weeks you will probably cover a distance of about 190km (118 miles) and climb some 12,500m (41,000ft) in total.

It is a slow and often difficult walk, but one where the scenery is so magnificent that you wouldn't want to be anywhere else. The best advice is to take it steadily. Don't rush the route or overexert yourself. Aim to enjoy the experience and give the walk as long as it needs for a successful completion.

The French Foreign Legion, who are based in Corsica, generally take a week to complete the GR20. The record for covering the distance non-stop is currently 37 hours 7 minutes, set by Jean François Luciani.

MAPS OF THE GR20

The route of the GR20 is well marked throughout. While walking without maps can never be recommended, it is true to say that the waymarking is so good that walkers might never need to refer to a map for directions. However, this would mean walking in complete isolation from the surroundings, never knowing the names of nearby mountains and valleys, never knowing in advance the shape of the terrain, and never knowing of other route options. To walk without a map is to walk with no real knowledge of your surroundings.

The best maps of the route are produced by the IGN (Institut Géographique National) at a scale of 1:25,000. These maps have blue covers and belong to a series known as Top 25. Order these in advance of your visit from map suppliers such as Stanfords (12–14 Long Acre, London WC2E 9BR, tel. 0207 836 1321), The Map Shop (15 High Street, Upton-upon-Severn WR8 0HJ, tel. 01684 593146) or Cordee (3a De Montford Street, Leicester LE1 7HD, tel. 0116 254 3579). Six sheets are needed to cover the entire route, as follows:

- 4149 OT Calvi
- 4250 OT Corte and Monte Cinto
- 4251 OT Monte d'Oro and Monte Rotondo
- 4252 OT Monte Renoso
- 4253 OT Petreto-Bicchisano and Zicavo
- 4253 ET Aiguilles de Bavella and Solenzara

The popular Didier-Richard series, at a scale of 1:50,000, covers the GR20 on two sheets. The relevant numbers are: 20 Corse Nord and 23 Corse Sud. It is also useful to carry a small reference map covering the whole of Corsica, partly to give an overview of the GR20, but also in case you decide to move off-route and travel on buses or trains to other parts of the island. The IGN Mini Corse map is recommended, at a scale of 1:250,000.

The maps in this guidebook are basically diagrammatic, at a scale of 1:50,000. Transferring the route from these maps to one of the recommended walking maps should be fairly straightforward. The gradient profiles provide an immediate visual appreciation of all the ups and downs along the way.

MOUNTAIN WEATHER

Mountain ranges have a habit of creating their own weather conditions. The mountains of Corsica boast several summits over 2000m (6560ft). In the summer months the sun beats down relentlessly on bare granite slopes, raising the temperature of the air and creating great updraughts. This draws in cool, moist air from the Mediterranean, leading to condensation, cloud cover, rain and fearsome thunderstorms. The usual pattern is for the day to start sunny and clear, with cloud building up in the afternoon. Whether the cloud eventually results in rain or thunderstorms depends on the amount of build-up. The mountain ridges are very exposed in severe weather conditions and sudden lightning strikes have claimed walkers' lives.

Even without thunderstorms the heat alone can be severe at times, causing problems of thirst, dehydration, sunburn and sunstroke. Seasonal streams dry up

This picture was taken in November and if snow covers the markers, the route becomes very difficult to trace (Stage 13).

completely, so that a full day's ration of water needs to be carried. The recommended minimum is two litres, but three or four may be needed, so take careful note of the availability of water sources in the middle of the day, where these are available. At either side of the peak summer period walkers can take advantage of cooler, clear conditions.

The onset of winter sees snow covering the paths, obliterating walking trails and waymarks, making most slopes too dangerous for walking. Conditions may be truly Alpine. In general, consider the GR20 closed to ordinary walkers from mid-October to mid-May, though much depends on the severity of the winter months. Bear in mind that it can snow in the mountains in summer, though this is very rare and any snow cover will be very short-lived.

Weather forecasts, known as *meteos,* should be obtained on a daily basis at the refuges along the way. Those walking the GR20 early or later in the season should take a small radio to keep in touch with the weather forecasts, as no one will be posting information while the refuges are unstaffed.

PATH CONDITIONS

For the most part the GR20 is a narrow, stony, rocky mountain trail. Walkers usually trek in single file, and give way to walkers coming in the opposite direction. However, it is often a well-trodden and well-marked trail, so that anyone keeping their eyes on the route will have no trouble following it. The standard form of waymarking quickly becomes familiar. One red and one white stripe of paint, parallel to each other, are daubed at intervals on rocks, trees, boulders and other immovable objects. There are a few signposts, generally at the refuges, and at prominent intersections with other routes.

There are alternative routes and link routes from the GR20, and these are usually marked with yellow stripes of paint at intervals. The GR20 occasionally intersects with other long-distance routes crossing Corsica from coast to coast, and these are marked with orange stripes. Anyone walking for more than a few minutes without any sign of waymarking has probably gone off course, because generally there are abundant markers.

If the route in this guidebook is at variance with the waymarking, then it may well be that the route has been changed. This happens occasionally and it is best to follow the new markers, but if possible, ask someone else coming in the opposite direction what the extent of re-routing is.

Snow cover can linger well into the summer, but the amount of snow and the length of time it lies depend on many factors. Apart from the obvious risks of snow and ice being slippery underfoot, there is also the problem of painted waymark flashes being buried, so that walkers find themselves unsure about the intricacies of route-finding in complex terrain. If there is too much snow cover, an ice axe and crampons become necessary.

The standard red and white flashes of the GR20 make route-finding easy through the mountains.

MOUNTAIN RESCUE

Every year there is at least one casualty along the course of the GR20 and a number of accidents. On the whole, these incidents don't happen where you might expect them, but seem to be the result of a moment of carelessness or lack of concentration. Watch where you are putting your feet when you are walking, as the ground is often rough and rocky or covered in stones and boulders. Walkers scrambling up or down rock slabs and gullies should be careful how they move, and not make a move unless it can be reversed. Take special care if snow and ice lingers into the summer. If there is an unusual amount, an ice axe and crampons may be needed. Avoid getting into dangerous situations, as the terrain is unforgiving.

A walker suffering a serious fall or injury will have to be rescued. The international distress signal is given opposite the contents page. The mountain rescue service is a paid-for service, and costs can be incredibly high. Take out an appropriate insurance policy to cover for such an eventuality. Some cheap policies may class a walk along the GR20 as a 'hazardous pursuit', in which case you may not be covered. The BMC Trek policy, however, classes it as an ordinary walk, **www.thebmc.co.uk/insurance**.

Getting a message out in an emergency is not always easy. Mobile phones simply don't work along many parts of the GR20. When the refuges are staffed, most of them have radio contact with the outside world, and there are usually little helipads alongside. If it is possible to get a message out via one of the refuges, then help will be quickly forthcoming.

In a very few places, such as the Cirque de la Solitude (Stage 4), chains or cables have been installed for protection.

Without a mobile phone signal, it might prove necessary to descend to a road and find a telephone, bearing in mind that delays can be crucial. The appropriate telephone numbers are police 17, ambulance 18 or the European emergency number of 112. Any of these services can alert the mountain rescue and take appropriate action, but try not to get into a situation in the first place where rescue is needed.

For less urgent health matters there is a pharmacy at Calenzana, and beyond that you would have to leave the GR20 and head for one of the larger villages or towns. If you need any regular medication, take plenty with you, or be prepared to leave the route. If a doctor or a trip to a hospital is required, European citizens should present their European Health Insurance Card, which has replaced the old E111 certificates, and which may help to offset the cost of certain treatments.

KIT CHECK

Most walkers on the GR20 carry far too much equipment. Think very carefully about the gear you plan to carry, and ruthlessly pare it to the bare minimum. The GR20 is a tough, steep and rocky trail that is generally walked in blazing sun, so it is unwise to carry a heavy load, which will sap your energy and slow you down.

Neither is there any need to carry much food, so long as you don't mind paying handsomely to buy food that has been carried up to the refuges. There is no need to carry heavy gear when so much lightweight gear is available. If you are travelling at a quiet time of year and can rely on getting a bed in the refuges, you can dispense with all your camping gear and carry the lightest possible sleeping bag. Nor is there any great need to carry more than one complete change of clothing, since clothes can be washed and dried along the way. Keep your pack light and aim to enjoy the walk!

ESSENTIALS

- Good footwear – either lightweight boots or shoes, for those absolutely confident about wearing them.
- Sock combination – try something like Bridgedale ATs, with a dedicated Coolmax liner sock.
- Clothing combination – polyester or polycotton, which is better than all-cotton for comfort.
- Sun protection – those who burn easily should use light-coloured long sleeved/legged clothing and a sun hat.
- Sunscreen – the sun can be very strong in the mountains and your skin can be burnt quite easily.
- Waterproofs – a lightweight jacket is sufficient; trousers aren't necessary, but carry them if preferred.
- Windproofs – a lightweight jacket is useful, but may be classed as optional, and your waterproof might suffice.
- Rucksack – should be big enough to carry everything, and no more, and of course it should be comfortable.
- Sleeping bag – a lightweight one is sufficient, as it will never get too cold in the summer months.
- Tent – a lightweight one; it may not be used all the time and the weather in summer is often good.
- Survival bag – just in case it is needed, and maybe for a bit of protection underneath your tent.
- Mattress – campsites are usually hard and stony, so use something like a Therm-a-rest mattress.
- Water carrier – with a capacity of at least two litres, and preferably a Platypus-type with a drinking hose.
- Torch – there are plenty of tiny, high-power torches to choose from, and take a spare battery.
- Wash kit – toothbrush, soap, towel, toilet paper, etc., and maybe a biodegradable travel wash for clothes.
- First aid kit – a compact one for the usual cuts, sprains, blisters, burns, breaks, stings, pains, etc.
- Money – take enough cash for the duration, as further supplies are only available off-route.
- Maps – IGN maps of a scale and quality to see clearly what is happening along the route and off-route.
- Ice axe – an essential item if there is any chance of snow or ice cover early or late in the season.

NON-ESSENTIALS

- Camera – for recording the sights and experiences of this remarkable journey, but keep it lightweight.
- Stove and cookset – to cook outside refuges, but fuel may not always be available along the way.
- Mobile phone – may be unusable for much of the time, and there won't be much chance to recharge it.
- Sunglasses – can be very useful in blazing sunshine, but are ultimately a matter of personal preference.
- Walking poles – can be very useful, especially a pair of them, but are a matter of personal preference.
- Shoes/sandals – for comfort while strolling around in the evenings after completing each day's walk.
- Radio – for keeping in touch with the outside world; really tiny ones weigh as little as 25g.
- Rope – only for the really insecure on the rocky parts, or if there is any chance of extensive snow cover.
- Books – either field guides to Mediterranean flora and fauna, or the latest novel choice for the evenings.

SERVICES ON THE GR20

Some say that the GR20 starts in Calenzana, passes through Vizzavona at the halfway stage, and ends in Conca. That is an over-simplification, and in fact a good half-dozen villages lie only two or three hours off the GR20. There are some good lodgings that lie even closer to the route, so don't imagine that the GR20 involves a complete commitment to a mountainous environment for a week at a time.

Fussy walkers should bear in mind that *basic* is *standard* along the main route, and even camping spaces tend to be hard and dusty, with limited facilities. Anything above basic is the exception. There are a few *gîtes d'étape*, which are similar to hostels, and even fewer hotels on or near the route.

Refuges

For walkers staying strictly on the classic GR20, most services revolve around mountain refuges situated at intervals along the way. These are provided by the Parc Natural Régional de Corse (PNRC), and are open throughout the year, but are only staffed by a *gardien* between June and September. The refuges remain open through winter, but are unstaffed, and services such as gas, electricity and water may be disconnected. Basic unisex bunk accommodation and foam mattresses are provided, often with a couple of electric lights operated using solar-charged batteries. There is a kitchen/dining room with tables, pots and pans, knives and forks, crockery and basic gas cookers (indoors and outdoors).

Inside the Refuge de Tighjettu (Stage 4), which is one of the more spacious refuges provided by the PNRC.

There is always a water supply, either inside or outside the building. Toilets and showers may be primitive, and where limited to one of each, there can be queues at busy periods. Showers are solar-heated, but often run cold, while the toilets are usually squat-type and occasionally out of use. You need to bring your own toilet paper.

Nearly all the refuges provide at least a basic hot meal and stock basic supplies of food and drinks, and the choice varies from place to place. Walkers who will eat anything will not need to carry any food supplies beyond a snack for lunch. Although it is possible to walk the whole of the GR20 and stay indoors every night, bear in mind that it is not possible to reserve a place at the refuges, and at busy times it's a case of 'first come first served'. You cannot book them in advance and you cannot rely on a bed being available. The refuges hold between 15 and 40 people, but as many as 300 may descend on them in the peak season!

Refuges are non-smoking and dogs are not allowed indoors. Quiet is maintained from 2200 and walkers are asked to vacate the buildings before 0900. However, some walkers like to go to bed early and rise as early as 0300! Carry a tent and sleeping bag as back-up, and packing a stove and pans avoids queues in the refuge kitchens.

To stay at a refuge, simply present yourself to the *gardien* and tell them whether you wish to stay in the refuge or camp nearby. They will charge you accordingly – €9.50 for a bed in the refuge or €4.00 to camp (at the time of writing) – and give you a ticket, and maybe a label to fix to your tent. Keep hold of these, as you may be required to present them as proof that you have paid. When the refuges are unstaffed in the winter, you can leave a fee in an honesty box.

Bergeries

Apart from the refuges, there are also *bergeries* along the way – working summer farms that sometimes supply basic foodstuffs to passing walkers, and some of which bring in extra supplies of food and drink for sale. A couple of *bergeries* have basic bar–restaurant facilities, and may allow camping, or even provide fixed tents for hire. Commercial guided walking holiday operators often book *bergerie* accommodation on and off the course of the GR20, since they cannot book accommodation in refuges for clients.

Simple summer farms, or bergeries, *may sell food and drink to walkers, or allow overnight camping nearby (Stage 6).*

Camping

For those carrying a tent, camping is available near all the refuges and some of the *bergeries, gîtes* and hotels, but only very rarely in other places. It is generally forbidden to camp wild throughout the Parc Natural Régional de Corse (PNRC), no matter how tempting a site might look. Bear in mind that the ground reserved for camping is usually bare, hard, stony and dusty, so pack a sleeping mattress, such as a *Therm-a-Rest* or similar. Those who camp near the refuges have access to the toilets, showers and outside stoves and cooking areas, but they should check with individual *gardiens* to see if they can use the stoves, pans, crockery and utensils inside the refuges.

Luxury Lodgings

Apart from the refuges, there are a few hotels and *gîtes d'étape* along the GR20. Walkers can indulge themselves at these places, enjoying more comfortable rooms and hot showers, and eating in restaurants or dining rooms. It is possible to phone ahead and book accommodation at most of these places, and telephone numbers are given throughout this guidebook.

Village Life

Detours off-route for accommodation, food and drink in nearby villages are heartily recommended, as the course of the GR20 allows little interaction with native Corsicans. Information is provided about spurs and loops taking in a handful of fine little villages, listing their facilities and transport links.

Back-up

For walkers wanting vehicle back-up for their walk, road access is possible at the start, finish, and at six points in between: Calenzana, Haut Asco, Hôtel Castel di Vergio, Vizzavona, Bergeries d' E Capanelle, Bocca di Verdi, Village de Bavella and Conca. The back-up driver would need to find some other occupation for the long days between supplying walkers' needs, but there is plenty of interest around Corsica.

FOOD, DRINK AND FUEL

The amount of food and drink, and what sort of supplies to carry, is entirely a matter of personal preference. Food and drink are available at almost every refuge along the way (but only when they are staffed from June to September), as well as at *gîtes* and hotels, so there is no need to carry anything apart from a lunch pack and emergency rations each day.

Walkers who will eat anything, and who don't mind paying over the odds for food that has been carried on horseback to the refuges, or dropped from helicopters, can travel extremely lightweight. Fussy feeders, however, may not find much to their taste, and may find supplies rather limited in some places. It won't be *haute cuisine*, and fresh food is a rarity at remote refuges, though it may be obtained by moving off-route to a nearby village.

When cooked meals are available, as they are at almost every refuge, *gîte* and hotel, be sure to order one as soon as possible. Some places require a couple of hours advance notice, and may even need to be told the night before if you wish to have a breakfast prepared, even though it may be nothing more than bread, jam and coffee. Prepared meals are of course expensive, partly because everything has been carried into the mountains, but if you don't feel like cooking or washing up, then they are good value.

Those who wish to carry food supplies should think lightweight, and choose freeze-dried and high-energy foods to keep their pack weight down. When given the chance to obtain more substantial fare, it makes sense to eat heavy, fresh foodstuffs on the spot and carry lighter items away with you. Carrying glass bottles can be dangerous and messy if they break. Drinks in plastic bottles or cans are safer, but the containers need to be disposed of at the refuges. Take careful note of re-supply points along the way, and strike a balance between rationing supplies and eating to reduce the pack weight. Remember that while supplies can be obtained at frequent intervals along the GR20, this is drastically reduced outside the peak summer season. Beware of lightweight foods laced with monosodium glutamate, masquerading as a taste enhancer. This substance requires large quantities of water to enable it to be flushed out of the body, and can promote a raging thirst. Unfortunately, more and more processed and dehydrated foods contain it.

Those who have special dietary requirements, or suffer from serious food allergies, would be well advised to have someone re-supply them at intervals along the trail, rather than run the risk of finding no suitable food available. Corsican food, or at least that which is generally available in remote refuges, tends to be based around pork products and cheeses, with many foodstuffs containing plenty of sugar, nuts or salt. Packets and tins of food are likely to be

Always be aware of where your next water source is located, and guard against dehydration at all times.

brands that you haven't seen before, which is fine for those who like to experiment and sample new foodstuffs, but a nightmare for others!

Water is available at all the refuges and most *bergeries* along the route. It is spring water, straight from the mountainside, and considered safe to drink without boiling or treating, unless advised otherwise. Water from streams may be seasonal at best, and may need treating if used over-much by animals or for bathing.

Bottled water is scarce in the mountains, but the two main Corsican brands are St Georges and Zilia. There is a canned drink called Corsica Cola, for those who like a variation on a theme! Corsican beer, or *bièra Corsa*, on sale in the mountains includes Pietra, Serena, Torra and even a brand of chestnut beer, or *bière chataigne*. Wine is sometimes on sale, either from labelled or unlabelled bottles.

Fuel can be a problem along the GR20. Those who fly to Corsica will not be allowed to carry fuel, so will need to buy it on arrival. The most common types are *alcohol à bruler,* which is the nearest equivalent to methylated spirits, and Camping Gaz cylinders. If you are doing your own cooking, you will need a stove that uses one or the other. To get further supplies of fuel, you will have to keep asking at the refuges and other stores along the way, in the hope that some of them have what you need. When there is a sudden rush on fuel stocks, it can take a while for remote places to re-supply. In the meantime you would have to use the gas stoves at the refuges. Lighting fires is forbidden along the GR20, as signs along the way will remind you.

LANGUAGE

The Collectivité Territoriale de Corse has a distinct language and culture of its own, and a greater control over its affairs than any other region of France. The native island language is Corsican, which has its roots in the Tuscan dialect of Italy. However, French is spoken throughout Corsica and this is probably the language that walkers will use most. Many Corsicans are also fluent in Italian, but it is best to assume that English is not widely understood by the islanders.

Most placenames on maps and signposts, and in this guidebook, are in fact Corsican words, though often there is a variant French form, and there is a lot of variety in spellings in some locations. Thus Corsicans use words like *bocca* where the French would use *col.* Corsicans often use the letter 'u' as the last vowel in many words. The Corsican guttural compound 'ghj' is entirely unknown in French. These traits make it easier to distinguish between the two languages. (The Corsican name for the GR20, incidentally, is 'Fra li Monti', meaning 'Through the Mountains'.)

No one expects visitors to learn Corsican, but a few words of French are useful. You may start by greeting everyone you meet with a hearty *bonjour,* only to find out later that none of them speak French! In fact, walkers from a dozen nationalities or more are likely to be met along the route, and English quickly becomes a common trail language. A knowledge of French, however basic, and a willingness to use the language is a distinct bonus. While walking the GR20, only a minimal amount of French is needed, but anyone travelling elsewhere around the island will require a much wider vocabulary. See Appendix 3 on page 233 for a basic selection of useful words and phrases.

CURRENCY

Cash is king on the GR20, so be sure to have plenty of *euros* when you start the walk. Mountain refuges *and bergeries* along the way will only accept cash for accommodation, food and drink. In fact, they must accumulate countless thousands of euros between them! Hotels may take credit cards, but payment by that method is only possible two or three times. There are no banks along the GR20, and more money is available only by moving off-route to one of the larger towns.

The rate of exchange between sterling and the euro is variable, but, at the time of writing, generally hovers around £1.00 buying between €1.45 and €1.50. The standard price of an overnight in the PNRC refuges is €9.50 per person, and €4.00 per person for camping near the refuges (valid in 2005, but will rise slightly in successive years). Expect a *demi pension* (dinner, bed and breakfast) rate in a *gîte d'étape* to be around €30 per person, and *demi pension* in a hotel to cost upwards of €50 per person.

Make sure you pack enough money for the duration of your trip through the mountains. Expect food and drink along the GR20 to be expensive – it has, after all, been brought a long way into the mountains, either by helicopter or on horseback. A basic refuge meal can cost up to €10, while a meal in a good hotel or restaurant could cost up to €30.

FLOWERS AND WILDLIFE

Corsica is like most other long-established islands – it has a flora and fauna with a wealth of unique subspecies. It is unrealistic to think that you can walk the GR20 and also study the range of flora and fauna in any depth, but it is also amazing just how many things will gain your attention along the way. Be ready for surprises, such as finding a long line of pine processionary caterpillars shuffling through the forest.

Maquis

The tangled ***maquis*** vegetation for which Corsica is renowned looks colourful and smells wonderful – a heady mix of perfume and herby aromas. The classic *maquis* species will be seen very little, however, because the route rises so quickly into the mountains and stays there for so long. The mountain scrub is largely composed of ***calycotome***, or spiny broom, and a ground-hugging form of **juniper** – they are both as prickly as gorse. Bushy growths of **alder scrub** are also present, indicating a little more moisture in the ground.

Spiny broom, or calycotome, is a very common plant in the scrub cover on the high mountains

An uncommon wild olive tree might be spotted, while cultivated olives are seen at Calenzana and Conca.

The arbutus, or strawberry tree, is found in the lower valleys off-route and bears red fruit in the autumn.

Trees

Tree cover in mountain valleys is dominated by tall, straight **laricio pines**, **maritime pines**, **birch** and **beech**. There are a few localised patches of **holm oak**, **mountain ash**, **sycamore** and **arbutus**. While **chestnuts** may be one of the most important trees in Corsica, very few of them are seen in the mountains, but they are usually found by moving off-route to villages. Some areas of forest have been devastated in recent years by forest fires.

Flowers

On the higher mountains there are interesting communities of plants. **Violets** and **thyme** can be abundant, and Alpine species include **saxifrages** and **Alpine avens**. As the snow melts in early summer, look out for delightful **Corsican crocuses**. Colourful **orchids**, big clumps of **euphorbia** and poisonous **hellebores** are also found. **Corsican aconites** grow only on the Plateau du Cuscione, alongside streams draining the closely cropped grasslands. Look out for curious parasitic plants. **Mistletoe** often thrives on laricio pines, while dense mats of **dodder** spread over spiny broom.

Mammals

Wild animals in the mountains are rarely spotted. There are herds of ***mouflon*** – wild, long-horned, short-haired sheep that graze on almost inaccessible ledges. Hundreds of them live on the island's mountains. **Wild boar** are shy and seldom seen – a more common sight is herds of **feral pigs**, ranging from black to piebald and pink. **Pigs**, **cattle** and **goats** graze at prodigious heights in the mountains and can be found even on high rocky ridges. Shepherds keep track of them by listening for the bongling bells on lead animals. **Foxes** are present, but keep very much to themselves. You may catch a glimpse of the shy, nocturnal, dormouse-like ***loir*** in the evenings.

Pigs are turned loose to forage for food through the summer and are rounded up before winter.

Cattle have been grazed high in the mountains of Corsica for thousands of years.

Lizards and Amphibians

Lizards can be spotted every day that the sun shines brightly, and walkers may also catch a glimpse of the larger, slow-moving **salamander**, its black body speckled with yellow blobs to ward off would-be predators. A curious newt-like creature called the ***euprocte*** lives and spawns in most streams on the island, even high in the mountains.

Fish

Fishermen are seen from time to time on the larger streams or chancing their arms at one of the lakes, generally fishing for **trout** or **eels**. (Sometimes fishermen stay at the refuges, giving walkers a chance to talk to them about their passion.)

Birds

The lucky few may spot an **eagle** circling overhead, and other birds of prey such as **buzzards** and **peregrines** can be seen. **Ravens** are completely at home in the mountain fastnesses, and almost everyone will tell you about the **Corsican nuthatch**, which creeps head-first down tree trunks in search of insects, but is rarely seen. Most of the time, the birds seen and heard are likely to be little **pipits**, with a delightful range of colours, notes and songs, flitting across the mountainsides as you approach.

Field Guides

A couple of good field guides devoted to birds and plants of the Mediterranean are useful for those prepared to carry the extra weight. There are specific guides to Corsican species, but these are available only in French. Most bookshops on the island stock a variety of field guides as well as plenty of colourful books about the mountains.

ADVICE IN A NUTSHELL

Don't walk too early or too late in the year.
Make sure you are fit and well prepared.
Keep your pack weight as low as possible.
Be sure to carry enough food and water.
Walk slowly and steadily with care.
Be aware of your options each day.
Obtain a weather forecast each day.
Consider using two walking poles.
Use a high-factor sunscreen and wear a hat.
Learn at least a few words of French.

POINTS TO BEAR IN MIND

It is a tough walk but not a rock climb.
The mountain refuges are always open.
The refuges have well-equipped kitchens.
The refuges can quickly fill to capacity.
Facilities outside the peak season are scarce.
Snow can lie well into June and even July.
Mobile phones only rarely get a signal.
Waymarking is usually very good.
Most other walkers are going your way.
English is not widely spoken in Corsica.

FOOD SUPPLIES AND SERVICES

Almost all the refuges offer meals and supplies.
Some *bergeries, gîtes* and hotels sell supplies.
Supplies are very limited outside the summer.
Order cooked meals as soon as you arrive.
Order a prepared breakfast the night before.
Supplies of fuel can be difficult to obtain.
Some buses only run in July and August.
Long taxi rides are very expensive.
Banks and ATMs are a long way off-route.
Basic services are *standard* on the GR20.

Calenzana and the Start of the GR20

Calenzana is often overlooked by walkers who are in a hurry to start the GR20. Try and spend at least a night there, if not a whole day, before starting the walk. Just outside the village is the Romanesque Chapelle di Santa Restituda, burial place of a revered Corsican martyr. Santa Restituda was beheaded for her Christian faith in the year 303AD, during the reign of the Roman Emperor Diocletian. Her marble sarcophagus is in the crypt of the chapel and was restored in 1951. The site has long been a place of pilgrimage, and although the chapel has been rebuilt and renovated many times, it contains some 11th-century stonework and 13th-century frescoes. The Festa di Santa Restituda takes place late in May alongside the old chapel, featuring a fairground with all the usual stalls and amusements, as well as food and drink.

The baroque Église St Blaise stands in the middle of Calenzana, dating from 1691, though it took several years to complete. In 1732 the village rose up against the Genoese rulers of Corsica, who retaliated by sending in a force largely comprising Austrian soldiery. The villagers fought with whatever they could lay their hands on, from agricultural implements to beehives, killing some 500 troops. The soldiers were buried beside the church in a plot that became known as the Cimetière des Allemands. The church bell tower was planted there in 1862. There are other little chapels in the village, including an ancient brotherhood chapel at A Casazza, while U Pala was the ancient palace of the Bishops of Sagone.

Calenzana has a fairly small range of services, yet manages to cope admirably with large numbers of visitors and GR20 walkers. There are a few accommodation options, a selection of bars and restaurants, shops selling food and drink, as well as a post office. A larger range of services, including banks with ATMs, is available in nearby Calvi.

Accommodation There is only a small range of accommodation in Calenzana. At the budget end, and the first place on the left at the entrance to the village, is the Gîte d'Étape Municipal, tel. 04 95 62 77 13 or 04 95 62 70 08. It has small dormitories offering 30 beds, with space for camping alongside. Further into the village is the 10-room Hôtel Monte Grosso, tel. 04 95 62 70 15. The 13-room Hôtel Bel Horizon is in the middle of the village, opposite the church, tel. 04 95 62 71 72. Anyone looking for a wider range of accommodation could spend their first night at Calvi, which is a busy and attractive little port.

Food and Drink There is a well-stocked Spar shop at the bottom end of Calenzana – fill your rucksack with last-minute items at this point. Further up through the village is the little Restaurant l'Olmia, opposite the Hôtel Monte Grosso. Just uphill, Le GR20 Bar Restaurant has obviously been named to catch the attention of walkers! The Bar Picciu Glacier and Restaurant Pizzeria Prince Pierre are found before the church.

The Gîte d'Étape Municipal offers basic accommodation and a campsite near the start of the GR20 in Calenzana.

The Bar Restaurant La Calenzana is to the left of the church, while the Bar Le Royal is to the right, opposite the bell tower. To sample local meat, cakes, honey or wine, simply follow little signs to the appropriate outlets. An excellent stock of local produce can be found at l'Atelier du Village at the top end of Calenzana. Eat a hearty meal and enjoy as much fresh produce as possible before leaving Calenzana.

Transport A bus service between Calvi and Calenzana is operated by Beaux Voyages, tel. 04 95 65 11 35 or 04 95 65 08 26. It runs once or twice a day, except Sundays. There are no buses between Calvi Airport and Calvi, or from the airport to Calenzana, but taxis meet all incoming flights. In Calvi, taxis are usually found on the Place de la Porteuse d'Eau, near the railway station. If there are no taxis at the airport or railway station, then phone Radio Taxis Calvais, tel. 04 95 65 30 36. Those walking the GR20 in reverse, who need to get away from Calenzana at the end, should call Calenzana Taxis, tel. 04 95 62 77 80, mobile 06 08 16 53 65.

STAGE 1

Calenzana to Refuge d'Ortu di u Piobbu (high-level)

The first day's walk on the GR20 can be a shock to the system. You leave Calenzana with everything on your back, probably in hot weather, with a question mark over the availability of water along the way. You learn which plants in the *maquis* are the thorniest. Lizards scuttle for cover as you approach. The ascent is unremitting – uphill all the way. You climb higher than anywhere in Britain, then climb even further, scrambling across a rocky mountainside with a big pack on your back. You carefully ration your water and wonder if it will last. When you finally reach the refuge, you take the accommodation and services as you find them, knowing there is nowhere else you can go. This day is a fine introduction to the rigours and the delights of the GR20 – it's your baptism of fire!

Distance	12km (7½ miles)
Total Ascent	1550m (5085 feet)
Total Descent	235m (770 feet)
Time	7 hours
Maps	IGN 4149 OT and 4250 OT
Terrain	Mixed, including steep slopes of *maquis,* forest and rocky mountainsides. This is a tough day's walk because of the relentless ascent, and scrambling is needed at times. Take it slow and steady – many walkers overtax themselves and finish the day exhausted and dehydrated.
Shelter	Shade is available in isolated stands of forest along the way. There is a drystone windbreak shelter on Bocca a u Salto. The higher parts are exposed in wind and rain.
Food and Drink	All necessary last-minute food supplies are available in Calenzana. There are a couple of streams on the ascent, but they dry up in the summer. The Refuge d'Ortu di u Piobbu serves meals and sells basic provisions.

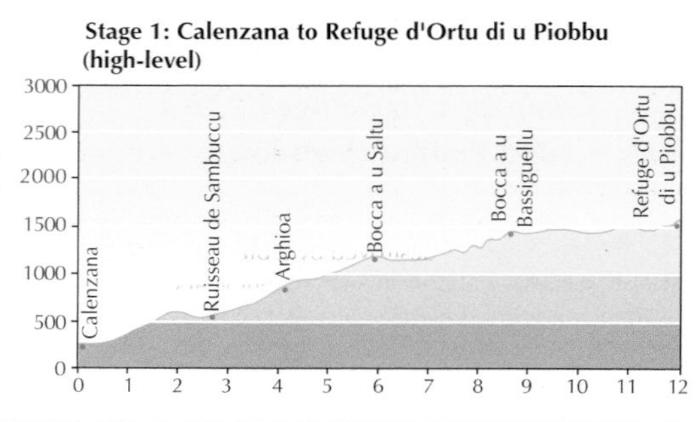

Walk up through **Calenzana** from the Municipal Gîte d'Étape and campsite, passing the Spar shop at 255m (835ft) – the last chance to get a good range of supplies together. Follow the road up through the village to pass the Hôtel Monte Grosso. At Le GR20 Bar Restaurant come the first **signposts** for the GR20 and Tra Mare e Monti (TMM), and there is a choice of waymarked routes leading up through town.

The Frontstreet Route

Pass Le GR20 Bar Restaurant and follow the road past the Bar Picciu Glacier and Pizzeria Prince Pierre to reach the Hôtel Bel Horizon and the **Église St Blaise** in the middle of the village. The road swings right, climbing above the church and passing a car park on a leafy square. The route is well signposted, passing **l'Atelier du Village** and leading to the Place Commune and **Place Saint Antoine**.

The Backstreet Route

Turn right at Le GR20 Bar Restaurant, then left, as signposted along and up a narrow concrete backstreet called **A Torra**. Walk straight up through a narrow crossroads, as signposted, into the **Place Saint Antoine**. The Oratoire St Antoine de Padoue is at the start of the GR20, for those wishing to offer a little prayer for the successful completion of their walk (St Anthony of Padua is, after all, patron saint of lost causes!).

A few concrete steps climb up from a **GR20/TMM sign**, then a cobbly path leads through a deep earthen groove overhung by trees. When the path emerges from the trees it reaches an area of bare granite at **Colletola** and turns right to follow a low drystone wall further uphill. Dense growths of sticky leaved cistus press in on both sides as the path climbs up an eroded groove in the bedrock, and there are ruined **drystone walls** on either side. ▶

There is a view back to Calenzana, as well as to the neighbouring village of Moncale, while Calvi and Lumio are seen near the coast as you climb further.

The slope is exposed to the sun and there are the charred remains of trees destroyed by a big fire in 1982. The area has seen smaller blazes in subsequent years.

There is a stand of tall, charred laricio pines on the broom-covered slope, then later a **water source** on the left, before some charred chestnut trees. The path rises fairly gently, passing a couple more chestnut trees and a few pines, zigzagging up to a signpost at a **junction of paths** at 550m (1805ft). (There is a worn patch on the hillside, about an hour from Calenzana, where walkers can't resist dropping their packs and taking a break.) The GR20 heads uphill to the left, marked by red and white paint flashes. The Tra Mare e Monti heads off to the right, marked by orange paint flashes.

At this point a choice must be made between the high-level route and the low-level variant. See the next section for a description of the low-level route.

An hour after leaving Calenzana, the GR20 and the Tra Mare e Monti part company at a junction on the hillside.

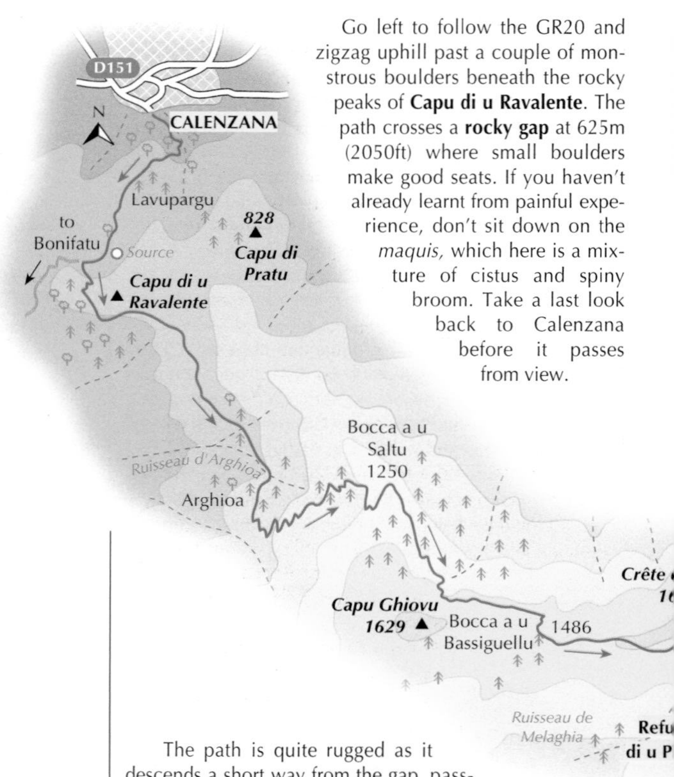

Go left to follow the GR20 and zigzag uphill past a couple of monstrous boulders beneath the rocky peaks of **Capu di u Ravalente**. The path crosses a **rocky gap** at 625m (2050ft) where small boulders make good seats. If you haven't already learnt from painful experience, don't sit down on the *maquis,* which here is a mixture of cistus and spiny broom. Take a last look back to Calenzana before it passes from view.

The path is quite rugged as it descends a short way from the gap, passing beneath an **overhanging rock** with holm oaks growing in crevices. The surface is easier underfoot as the path contours along an old terrace high on the slope. Straggly barbed wire fencing runs alongside to the right, and the *maquis* is an exotic mix of aromatic species. The path rises to a few chestnut trees that draw moisture from a seasonal stream, the **Ruisseau de Sambuccu**, and it is clear that they have suffered a severe burning in the past. *Bergeries* can be seen on the valley sides, and the bongling bells of cattle or goats grazing in the *maquis* may be heard. ◀

The low-level track leading to Bonifatu can also be seen. Hopefully you won't be wishing you were on it at this late stage!

As it leaves the chestnut trees, the path is in an eroded **rocky groove**, but it levels out as it runs across the slope. The barbed wire fence is still visible on the right. Another stream called the **Ruisseau d'Arghioa** is crossed where tall laricio pines grow, and the path on either side of the watercourse is quite rocky. This is a fine place to fill up with water early in the summer, but it quickly dries away, leaving this whole stage waterless. Above the stream there is a pleasant grassy ledge at **Arghioa,** overlooking the valley from an altitude of 800m (2625ft). Walkers who reach this point within 1½ hours of leaving the GR20/TMM trail junction are doing fairly well.

A zigzag path leads up past young pines and heather scrub on a steep and stony slope. The path is well graded and well marked at all the crucial turnings, though there are a couple of other paths that lead away on either side. Note the clumps of hellebores growing profusely in places. There is a rocky stretch where the path crosses a streambed at a higher level, then it swings right near a **rocky pinnacle**. There are more zigzags and a few tight squeezes where young pines and tall heather grow thickly between tall laricio pines on the higher slopes. Another series of zigzags leads above young pines and spiny broom scrub to reach a grassy gap, the **Bocca a u Saltu**, at 1250m (4100ft). Walkers should reach this point 1½ hours after leaving Arghioa. There is a small drystone windbreak shelter to the left and the rocky spires of **Capu Ghiovu** to the right. Monte Corona is seen rising beyond the next gap.

Watch carefully as the GR20 markers lead away from the gap. The path runs downhill around the **base of a cliff**, then rises gently between tall laricio pines. A bouldery zigzag path climbs up to a rocky slope, then a series of **short scrambles** must be completed. Watch carefully for the markers, which always indicate the easiest course. The pitches are very short and there are plenty of holds, but walkers carrying a full pack on their first full day will find getting their balance right more of a problem. There is very little sense of exposure because of the tall trees alongside, and there is often good shade as the slope faces north. ▶

Looking around, it is often possible to spot long-horned *mouflon* grazing along some of the ledges.

Impressive rock scenery on the slopes of Capu Ghiovu features some short stretches of scrambling.

There is another easy stretch of path and another bouldery ascent, then **more scrambling** on a more open slope of rock. A short **cable** marks the point where the route straddles a rock ridge and enters a gully, and there may be a drop of water here early in the summer. After more uphill scrambling, the path drops to pass beneath a **spire of rock** pierced with a hole, then crosses a bouldery slope. There are a couple of **rocky notches** to cross, with some grotesque outcrops of rock high above, and plenty of prostrate juniper and clumps of hellebore on the ground. An eroded groove leads up to another gap, the **Bocca a u Bassiguellu**, which has patches of grass and scrub at 1486m (4875ft). The scrambling from gap to gap should take 1½ hours, depending on how cautiously you proceed.

Turn left to follow the path gently uphill past some tall pines. There is a sudden fine view of distant mountains, and their profiles will become familiar over the next few days. An easy, level stretch of path runs below the **Crête de Fucu**, where the juniper gives way to spiny broom. The refuge is visible across the valley. Young pines press in on either side and there are bouldery areas to cross. The path rises across slopes of broken rock, and is well wooded in places with birch and alder. There is a rugged little climb around the head of the valley, with a turn to the right and left, before you reach the **Refuge d'Ortu di u Piobbu**, within 1½ hours of leaving the Bocca a u Bassiguellu.

REFUGE D'ORTU DI U PIOBBU

The PNRC Refuge d'Ortu di u Piobbu is perched at 1570m (5150ft), occupying the site of a former *bergerie,* on a tongue of sloping, open land surrounded by high mountains, overlooking a forested valley. It has two dormitories offering 30 beds, a kitchen/dining room and the *gardien*'s quarters. Hot meals, food supplies and drinks are on sale. A toilet and shower stand away from the building, and there are spaces spreading downhill to accommodate tents. Although there is water in the refuge and a water trough near the refuge, the water is not suitable for drinking. Water should be drawn from a source signposted 200m beyond the refuge.

STAGE 1

Calenzana to Refuge d'Ortu di u Piobbu (low-level)

If the first day's high-level walk along the main GR20 route seems daunting, then maybe you should ask yourself why you are here in the first place! However, there can be good reasons for choosing to start with this low-level variant. Foul weather on the first day, when you just want to get on with the walk, could lead to choosing this easier alternative. Searing heat could lead to choosing a route with a bit more water and shade, and this low-level route enjoys good forest cover in its latter stages. Bear in mind that the distance is almost double that of the main GR20 route, and there is actually a little more ascent involved, even if the paths are easier. A cursory glance at the map reveals that it is actually easier to walk all the way from Calenzana to the Refuge de Carozzu in a day, thus stealing a whole day's lead on the high-level walkers, but this really does smack of cheating!

Distance	20km (12½ miles)
Total Ascent	1610m (5280 feet)
Total Descent	295m (970 feet)
Time	7¾ hours
Maps	IGN 4149 OT and 4250 OT
Terrain	Some short, steep slopes of *maquis* at first, followed by broad tracks and a road later. A long climb on rugged forest paths leads finally to the refuge.
Shelter	Shade is sparse for the first half of the walk, then there is more tree cover beyond Bonifatu.
Food and Drink	Water may be found in streams in the Forêt de Sambuccu, but water from la Figarella Rivière should be treated. The Auberge de la Forêt at Bonifatu provides accommodation and meals, and there is a nearby water source. Water may be found in a stream on the ascent to the Refuge d'Ortu di u Piobbu.

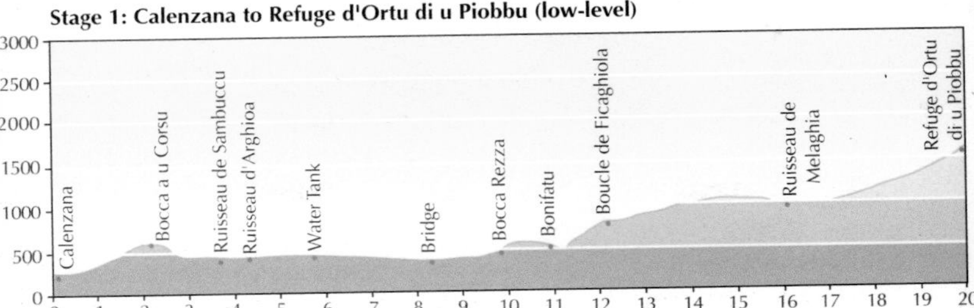

Walk up through **Calenzana** from the Municipal Gîte d'Étape and campsite, passing the Spar shop at 255m (835ft) – the last chance to get a good range of supplies together. Follow the road up through the village to pass the Hôtel Monte Grosso. At Le GR20 Bar Restaurant come the first **signposts** for the GR20 and Tra Mare e Monti (TMM), and there is a choice of waymarked routes leading up through town:

The Frontstreet Route

Pass Le GR20 Bar Restaurant and follow the road past the Bar Picciu Glacier and Pizzeria Prince Pierre to reach the Hôtel Bel Horizon and the **Église St Blaise** in the middle of the village. The road swings right, climbing above the church and passing a car park on a leafy square. The route is well signposted, passing **l'Atelier du Village** and leading to the Place Commune and **Place Saint Antoine**.

The Backstreet Route

Turn right at Le GR20 Bar Restaurant, then left, as signposted along and up a narrow concrete backstreet called **A Torra**. Walk straight up through a narrow crossroads, as signposted, into the **Place Saint Antoine**. The Oratoire St Antoine de Padoue is at the start of the GR20, for those wishing to offer a little prayer for the successful completion of their walk (St Anthony of Padua is, after all, patron saint of lost causes!).

A few concrete steps climb up from a **GR20/TMM sign**, then a cobbly path leads through a deep earthen groove overhung by trees. When the path emerges from the trees it

There is a view back to Calenzana, as well as to the neighbouring village of Moncale, while Calvi and Lumio are seen near the coast as you climb further.

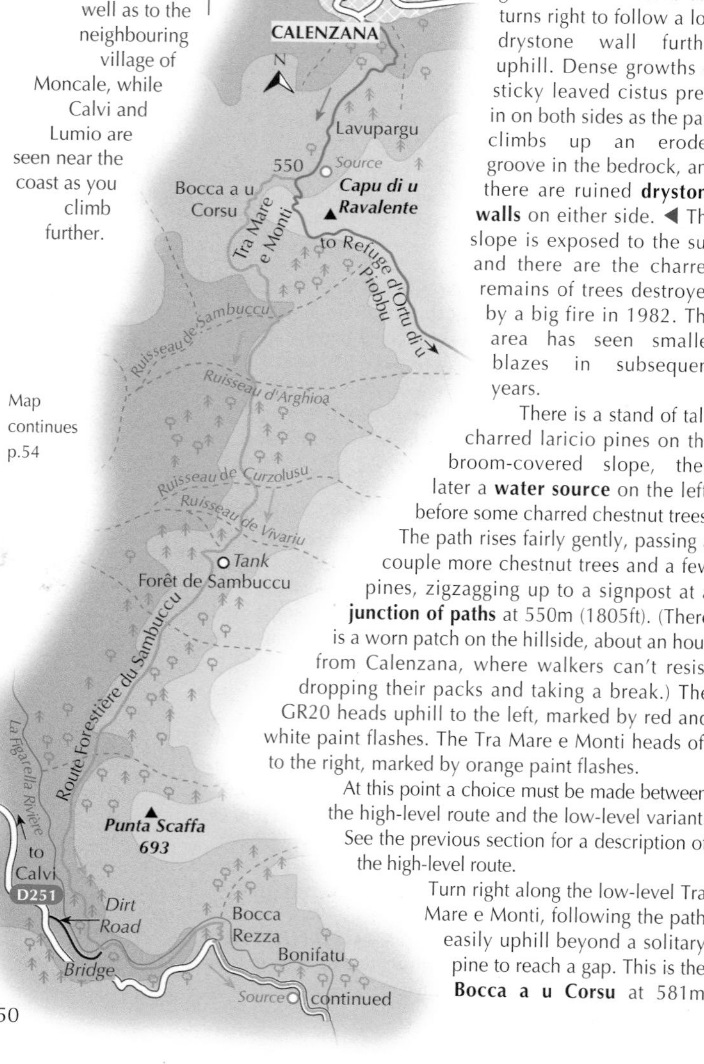

Map continues p.54

reaches an area of bare granite at **Colletola** and turns right to follow a low drystone wall further uphill. Dense growths of sticky leaved cistus press in on both sides as the path climbs up an eroded groove in the bedrock, and there are ruined **drystone walls** on either side. ◀ The slope is exposed to the sun and there are the charred remains of trees destroyed by a big fire in 1982. The area has seen smaller blazes in subsequent years.

There is a stand of tall, charred laricio pines on the broom-covered slope, then later a **water source** on the left, before some charred chestnut trees. The path rises fairly gently, passing a couple more chestnut trees and a few pines, zigzagging up to a signpost at a **junction of paths** at 550m (1805ft). (There is a worn patch on the hillside, about an hour from Calenzana, where walkers can't resist dropping their packs and taking a break.) The GR20 heads uphill to the left, marked by red and white paint flashes. The Tra Mare e Monti heads off to the right, marked by orange paint flashes.

At this point a choice must be made between the high-level route and the low-level variant. See the previous section for a description of the high-level route.

Turn right along the low-level Tra Mare e Monti, following the path easily uphill beyond a solitary pine to reach a gap. This is the **Bocca a u Corsu** at 581m

(1906ft), where grass and thistles spread in a circle beyond a signboard, with the more dense cistus at a distance. Enjoy the views of the surrounding mountains and the valley of la Figarella Rivière, where the route is heading next.

Follow the path downhill through the *maquis,* walking on bare rock or stones. The path is enclosed between **low drystone walls**, though they are only glimpsed from time to time. Follow a deep groove in the crumbling granite bedrock, where the *maquis* sometimes presses in on the path. An olive tree stands beside a huge boulder beside the **Ruisseau de Sambuccu**, which may offer a trickle of water early in the summer.

The way ahead is clear, taking advantage of an old **cultivation terrace**. A wall and fence are visible to the left from time to time. The arbutus scrub is still quite tall and dense, and must be brushed past in places. Zigzag a short way up to the left to cross the **Ruisseau d'Arghioa**, then follow the path gently uphill, emerging on a tight loop on a much broader **track**. This point, at 454m (1490ft), should be reached about 1½ hours after leaving the GR20/TMM trail junction. Walkers on the high-level GR20 are directly uphill to the east.

Walk straight onwards, following the track gently uphill. The hillside is terraced and was once under cultivation, but now there are young pines and plenty of arbutus scrub. There are two **fords** paved with stone, and one of them offers a particularly attractive shady waterhole in times of flow. The track rises to a hairpin bend and a junction with another track beside a circular concrete **water tank**. ▶

There is a wide, flat, grassy area offering a good viewpoint over the valley. Any rifle shots that might be heard are probably from a firing range on the other side of la Figarella Rivière.

Turn right at the track junction to follow a broad track, the **Route Forestière du Sambuccu**. There is a TMM signpost and the way is flashed with orange paint. Dense growths of arbutus rise on either side throughout the gradual descent. Walk straight onwards at a junction of tracks and cross a stream. The track runs fairly close to the broad and bouldery bed of **la Figarella Rivière**. ▶

The landscape looks quite devastated – there are solitary pines, charred or fallen trunks, and blasted outcrops of granite.

A curiously eroded outcrop, full of deeply weathered hollows, is passed just before a **concrete bridge** spans the river at 360m (1180ft). Walkers should reach the bridge after following the track for 1¼ hours. Take a break at the bridge and enjoy the mountains, which seem much closer now, and consider the flow of the river.

Cross a metal suspension bridge below the Auberge de la Forêt before the climb to the Refuge d'Ortu di u Piobbu.

To follow the **riverside path** ▶, turn left after crossing the bridge. It can be quite bouldery underfoot at times, and a bewildering mixture of vegetation grows alongside. In hot weather, some of the pools in the river look particularly inviting. The path is quite rugged in places, and a series of **zigzags** finally climbs up from the river, on a slope of arbutus trees. A road is reached on a bend at **Bocca Rezza**, at 510m (1673ft), so watch for traffic when turning left.

After rare occasions of heavy rain, the riverside path can flood in places, in which case it is better to follow the track up to a nearby road to reach Bonifatu.

The **Maison Forestière du Bonifatu** is visible, perched on a brow overlooking the river, with towering mountains all around. The road leads past the buildings and crosses a bridge over the **Torrent le Terrible**, where there is a shady picnic area and **water source**. Stay high above a terraced car park to pass the **Auberge de la Forêt**. This point should be reached, at an altitude of 540m (1770ft), about an hour after leaving the bridge over la Figarella Rivière.

AUBERGE DE LA FORÊT

The Auberge de la Forêt, tel 04 95 65 09 98, is a bar–restaurant with a small 5-room hotel and 22-bed *gîte d'étape,* with camping spaces also available. Walkers who have had enough and can't face a hot afternoon climbing could enjoy a good meal and a comfortable night here at Bonifatu instead. A limited range of food supplies are available for self-caterers. Although tour coaches regularly run to Bonifatu, there is no bus service. Radio Taxis Calvais, tel 04 95 65 30 36, offer a link with Calvi.

To continue, note that the Refuge d'Ortu di u Piobbu is 3 hours away, while the Refuge de Carozzu is 2½ hours away. Obviously, it would be possible to steal a whole day's lead on the high-level walkers, but the route description assumes that you will be heading for the Refuge d'Ortu di u Piobbu, so walk down through the **car park** as signposted. Yellow paint flashes reveal a zigzag path down to the river. Cross a metal **suspension footbridge** and follow a woodland path to a **junction**. Turn right as signposted for the Boucle de Ficaghiola, following both yellow and red paint marks.

A **bouldery path** rises in tight, well-graded zigzags that are never very difficult despite the steepness of the slope. ▶

The woods are mixed pines and holm oak, with an understorey of arbutus, tall heather, broom and brambles. Wildlife in the area includes wild boar, *mouflon*, the bearded vulture and the Corsican nuthatch.

There are glimpses back down to Bonifatu, but for the most part the woods are dense. The path levels out among pines at 743m (2438ft) on the **Boucle de Ficaghiola**. Turn left, as flashed with yellow and signposted for the GR20. Keep zigzagging uphill, where there are fewer trees and more scrub as a rocky ridge is gained. Watch for another **path junction** – the Boucle des Finocchi is signposted straight ahead in red, so turn right to follow another path flashed with yellow paint. Zigzag up the rugged ridge, then contour at roughly 1050m (3445ft) along the valley side. A gentle descent leads through scorched pines to a **stony track**. Turn left to follow the track,

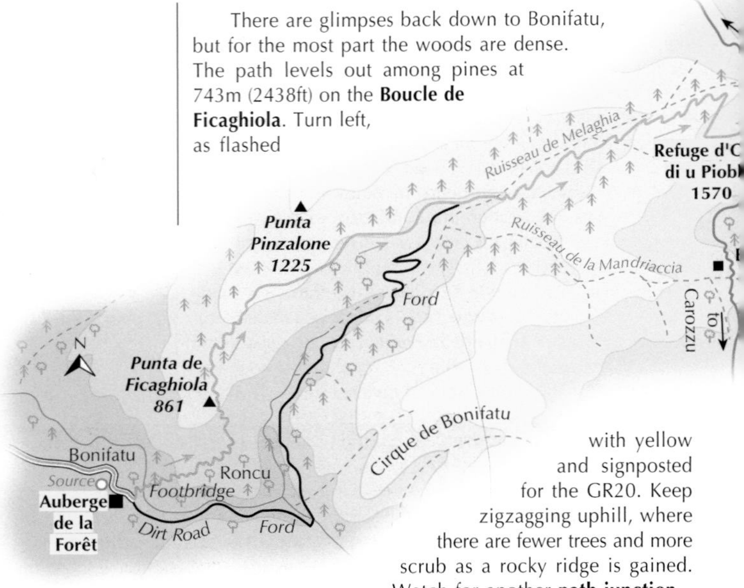

Ruisseau de Melaghia
Refuge d'C
di u Piob
1570
Punta
Pinzalone
1225
Ruisseau de la Mandriaccia
Ford
to Carozzu
N
Punta de
Ficaghiola
861
Cirque de Bonifatu
Bonifatu
Source
Roncu
Footbridge
Auberge
de la
Forêt
Dirt Road
Ford

A clear waymarked path cuts across the mountainside and leads into the valley of the Ruisseau de Melaghia.

and there is soon an option to follow another yellow-flashed path running parallel, though both lines quickly lead to a ford in the bouldery streambed of the **Ruisseau de Melaghia**.

A **signpost** across the river appears to point into a heap of boulders, and gives an allowance of 1½ hours to reach the refuge. Yellow paint flashes indicate the way through the boulders and along a **rough path** flanked by tall heather and bracken. The trees in the forest are mostly laricio pines at this level, above the 1000m (3280ft) contour. The path crosses a **streambed** that carries water early in the season, then the terrain underfoot is rather easier.

The path rises up a steep slope clothed in tall pines, but it has been engineered in zigzags to ease the gradient. Looking up the slope, **bare rock faces** can be seen, and the path swings right and cuts across the foot of the cliffs. There is a pronounced swing to the left afterwards and the path zigzags up onto the **rocky crest** high above the valley. After passing a tall, dead pine in an area of younger pines, the refuge can be glimpsed above. Walk up out of the forest and follow a braided, stony path further uphill. There is spiny broom on the ground, and the path is flashed in yellow, leading directly to the **Refuge d'Ortu di u Piobbu**.

REFUGE D'ORTU DI U PIOBBU

The PNRC Refuge d'Ortu di u Piobbu is perched at 1570m (5150ft), occupying the site of a former *bergerie,* on a tongue of sloping, open land surrounded by high mountains, overlooking a forested valley. It has two dormitories offering 30 beds, a kitchen/dining room and the *gardien*'s quarters. Hot meals, food supplies and drinks are on sale. A toilet and shower stand away from the building, and there are spaces spreading downhill to accommodate tents. Although there is water in the refuge and a water trough near the refuge, the water is not suitable for drinking. Water should be drawn from a source signposted 200m beyond the refuge.

Ascent of Monte Corona from Refuge d'Ortu di u Piobbu

Those who reach the Refuge d'Ortu di u Piobbu and are fighting fit might like to climb Monte Corona, on whose slopes the refuge has been built. Alternatively, for anyone who wants to enjoy a bit of a break at the refuge, yet still complete a short walk, the ascent could make a fine half-day walk. The mountain can be climbed lightweight, which will make a big difference to your progress. There is a waymarked zigzag ascent from the refuge to the Bocca di Tartagine, then follow a series of cairns up the rugged ridge to the stony summit and enjoy the views. This is a fairly easy ascent and it might give you a taste for more serious ascents further along the course of the GR20. See map p.55.

Distance	5km (3 miles) there and back
Total Ascent	575m (1885 feet)
Total Descent	575m (1885 feet)
Time	2½ hours there and back
Map	IGN 4250 OT
Terrain	Wooded slopes give way to scrub-covered slopes, which can be rocky or stony in places, but are not particularly difficult.
Shelter	There is shade in the woods near the start, but the upper parts of the mountain are open and exposed to sun, wind and rain.
Food and Drink	There is no water on the ascent. Food and drink are available at the Refuge d'Ortu di u Piobbu.

Walk straight uphill from the **Refuge d'Ortu di u Piobbu**, picking a way along narrow paths and aiming for the left-hand side of the birch woods higher up the slope. A path marked with flashes of **yellow paint** enters the woods and zigzags uphill. There is one **rocky stretch** where there is a view back to the refuge. The zigzags swing more to the left, and on leaving the birchwoods cross a slope of alder and juniper scrub, with stony patches in between. Next, reach the gap at the **Bocca di Tartagine**, at an altitude of 1852m (6076ft). There is a view across the Tartagine valley to Monte Padru, while **Capu a u Dente** raises its rocky towers to the left.

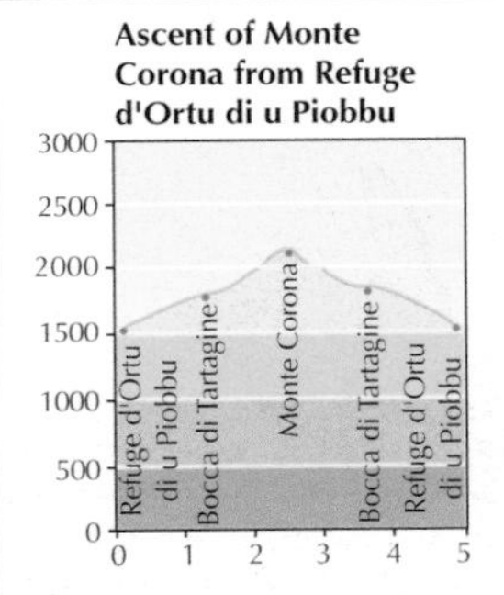

Turn right to leave the gap, following a rugged ridge southwards towards Monte Corona. There is a vague zigzag path marked by **cairns**, threading its way up a steep slope of alder scrub. Grapple with boulders and outcrops of rock at a higher level, and keep an eye peeled to spot more small cairns. On reaching a higher part of the ridge, there is a **stony path** away to the right that continues climbing. The summit of **Monte Corona** is a stony dome crowned with a cairn at 2144m (7034ft).

There are fine views of the surrounding mountains, and walkers can try to pick out the course of the GR20 to the south, until Monte Cinto and Paglia Orba block the view. Calvi can be seen to the northwest, and there is also a bird's-eye view down to the refuge. Looking along the ridge, you may wonder if it is worth walking straight towards the neighbouring peak of Capu Ladroncellu to rejoin the GR20. When heading back down the mountain to the refuge, be careful not to be drawn off-course to the left, which leads into an awkward area of alder scrub.

The Refuge d'Ortu di u Piobbu makes a convenient base for a relatively easy climb to Monte Corona.

Looking from the Refuge d'Ortu di u Piobbu to the rugged Capu a u Dente beyond the Bocca di Tartagine.

STAGE 2

Refuge d'Ortu di u Piobbu to Refuge de Carozzu (high-level)

The high-level route from the Refuge d'Ortu di u Piobbu is a tough day's walk, especially after the exertions of the first day. It involves walking round a rugged shoulder to reach a valley, then spending the morning climbing to the Bocca Piccaia at the head of the valley. The view from the gap is magnificent, providing the day is clear – full of spires and towers of rock. The route traverses round the flanks of the mountains, and although it starts easily it becomes quite difficult, with numerous short rocky ascents and descents. There is another chance to enjoy exceptional views before a long, steep and stony descent to the Refuge de Carozzu at the end of the day. (If this day's walk sounds too tough, refer to the next section for a low-level alternative.)

Distance	8km (5 miles)
Total Ascent	750m (2460 feet)
Total Descent	1050m (3445 feet)
Time	6½ hours
Map	IGN 4250 OT
Terrain	Rugged wooded slopes at the start and open mountainsides afterwards. The slopes can be steep and rocky, and a series of short scrambles must be completed on many of the higher parts. Paths leading downhill at the end of the day are steep and stony, running into woodlands.
Shelter	The early and later parts of the walk are through woods that offer a certain amount of shade, but most of the route is across exposed rocky mountainsides.
Food and Drink	Water is available on crossing the first two valleys, at the Ruisseau de la Mandriaccia and at a source near Leccia Rossa. Meals and supplies of food and drink are available at the Refuge de Carozzu.

Leave the **Refuge d'Ortu di u Piobbu** as signposted for Carozzu, entering a birch wood and crossing the stream used

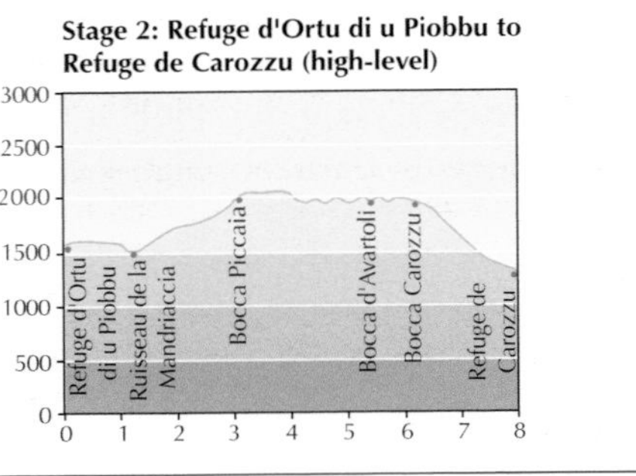

as a **water source** for the refuge. The path climbs steep and rocky terrain, and there are a couple of fine views back towards the refuge through gaps in the trees. After contouring more easily around a slope, reaching 1627m (5338ft), the path descends a steep and rugged slope where the slender birch trees are dwarfed by a few large laricio pines. Pass close to the **Bergeries de la Mandriaccia**, then drop downhill to cross the **Ruisseau de la Mandriaccia** at 1510m (4955ft). This is usually a good source of water until midsummer, though it occurs early in the day, only an hour into the walk, and you may prefer to wait until reaching the next source. ◀

The wooded valley is overrun by ants, so stopping or sitting for any length of time is not recommended.

Watch carefully for the paint flashes as the path climbs up a steep and **bouldery slope** covered in trees. The path leads up towards a sloping cliff and for the most part walkers pick their way along the base of the cliff between the trees and the **bare rock walls**. There are more open views as the path climbs higher through the valley and the trees begin to thin out. Stay near the base of the cliff until the path climbs to cross a streambed at **Leccia Rossa** in an extensive area of alder scrub. This is a good source of water, until it dries up, and is reached around 1620m (5315ft). Take a drink and also drink in the surroundings, marvelling at the towers of rock on either side of the valley.

Climb uphill after crossing the stream, mostly scrambling on bare **rocky stairways,** watching for a painted indicator reading 'Source 200m GR'. A bouldery path leads down through the alder scrub to reach a small **water source**, but be sure not to be drawn off-course along an older waymarked route, which misses the source. Watch carefully for more paint flashes as the path steers through the scrub, then scramble up the bouldery, rocky slopes of the valley. There is a series of zigzags, and early in the summer wonderful displays of Corsican crocuses. A final steep and bouldery slope leads to a gap at the head of the valley, called **Bocca Piccaia**, around 1950m (6400ft).

The rocky peaks of Punta Piccaia and Capu Ladroncellu flank

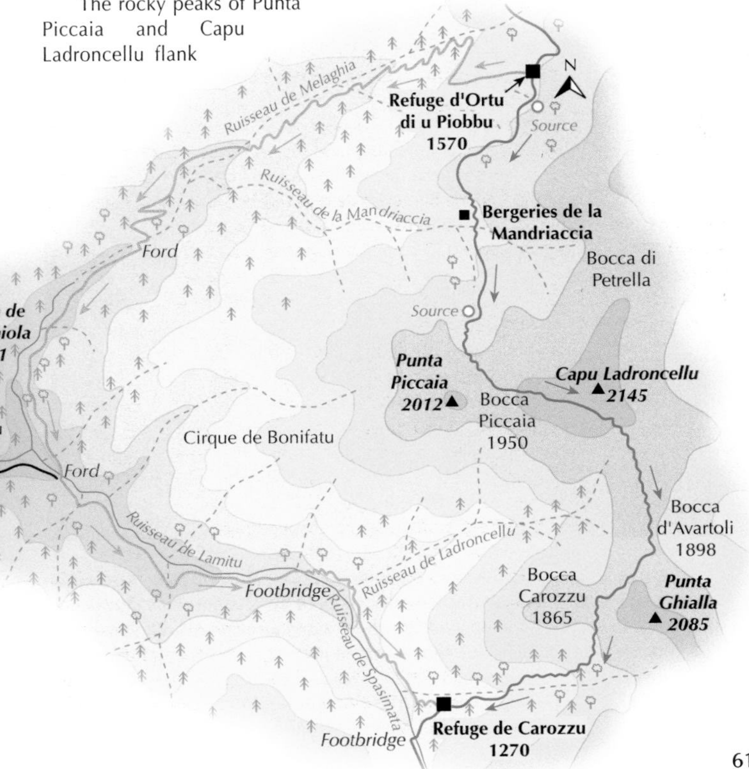

The GR20 picks its way between birch woods and sloping slabs as it climbs from the Ruisseau de la Mandriaccia.

the gap, but your attention is more likely to be focused on the awesome drop down into the Ladroncellu valley, which is surrounded by rugged mountains and filled with amazing pinnacles and towers of rock. If the walkers ahead of you looked rooted to the spot as they reached this gap, you now understand why! Those who reach this gap 2½ hours after leaving the Ruisseau de la Mandriaccia are doing well.

Turn left to climb along the ridge, grappling with the rock in places and gradually rising towards **Capu Ladroncellu**. Don't climb to the summit, as the path heads off to the right before that point, cutting across slopes of **broken rock and scree** on the upper part of the mountain, around 2020m (6625ft). Juniper and spiny broom scrub bind the loose stones together. After passing an **overhanging rock** the path begins a sustained descent that can be steep and rocky in places, down to around 1900m (6235ft). After crossing a **scree slope** covered in juniper scrub, there is a short climb through an awkward arrangement of **jammed boulders**.

The path beyond the jammed boulders is a rocky roller coaster as it continues its traverse of the mountain. Walkers have to grapple with the rock, and there must be at least 100m (300ft) of extra ascent and descent on this stretch, involving a few awkward moves. Even when the route reaches the **Bocca d'Avartoli**, there are still plenty of ups and downs. It is a particularly tiring part of the GR20. Watch carefully for the markers, as the path switches from side to side while traversing the gap. The altitude on the lowest part of the Bocca d'Avartoli is 1898m (6227ft), and it will probably take around an hour to reach the gap from the Bocca Piccaia.

A lone laricio pine grows from a rocky ridge, seen on the way down towards the Refuge de Carozzu.

The path seems to continue easily across the steep upper slopes of **Punta Ghialla**, but there is a short **rock gully** that has to be negotiated by scrambling up and down yet again. Corsican crocuses abound early in the summer as the path traverses the slope at the base of a cliff. The route drops down on the next gap, which is known as the **Bocca Carozzu**, or Bocca Inuminata, around 1865m (6120ft). Walkers should reach this gap ¾ hour after leaving the Bocca d'Avartoli. ◀

This is a last chance to look back across the pinnacles and towers of rock around the Ladroncellu valley to the Bocca Piccaia, where this amazing scenery was first witnessed.

Turn left to leave the **Bocca Carozzu**, walking down a steep scree path running through juniper and spiny broom scrub. Further downhill the route is **rocky and bouldery** as it weaves through alder scrub. As the path gradually swings right around a bend in the valley the Refuge de Carozzu becomes visible, but it is still quite a long way below. Take care following the path, as there are some side-spurs that don't lead anywhere.

Walk past birch and pines, then cross a **bouldery streambed**. The path becomes gentler as it descends through a birch wood, crossing another **streambed**, and although there are stony clearings along the way, the refuge remains concealed almost until it is reached. It will take around 1¼ hours to complete the descent from the gap to the **Refuge de Carozzu**.

REFUGE DE CAROZZU

The PNRC Refuge de Carozzu is situated in an amazing location, at 1270m (4165ft) on the only flat bit of ground in sight. It is hemmed in by tall mountains arranged around the Cirque du Bonifatu, yet features a view that extends down through the forested valley to the rugged little mountains near Calvi. A wooden terrace is positioned in front of the building so that weary wayfarers can rest and watch the sun go down at leisure, and marvel at the pines that cling to sheer rock all around. The building has a dormitory with 30 beds, a kitchen/dining room and the *gardien's* quarters. Toilets, showers and water taps are located nearby. Meals, food and drink supplies are on sale. There are camping spaces in the woods, where abundant insect life flourishes!

STAGE 2

Refuge d'Ortu di u Piobbu to Refuge de Carozzu (low-level)

The low-level variant between the Refuge d'Ortu di u Piobbu and the Refuge de Carozzu would suit walkers who have overtaxed themselves on their first day on the high-level GR20. If the weather turns abysmal, some may prefer to take the lower route in order to keep moving, hoping for better weather later. The low-level route simply heads down a rocky crest and zigzags down rugged paths and tracks through a forested valley. After fording a river, the ascent to the Refuge de Carozzu is along a rough and narrow path, emerging suddenly into magnificent mountain surroundings at the end of the day. (See map on p.61.) Walkers who use this low-level route as well as the low-level route on the first day are warned that without experiencing the high mountains, they are in for something of a shock quite soon!

Distance	12km (7½ miles)
Total Ascent	660m (2165 feet)
Total Descent	960m (3150 feet)
Time	4½ hours
Map	IGN 4250 OT
Terrain	Forested valleys with good paths and tracks. Generally easy walking, though with some steep zigzags in places and some narrow, rocky paths.
Shelter	Forest shade is available for most of the descent and ascent.
Food and Drink	Rivers in the valleys run throughout the year, though the water may need treating, and some tributaries may dry up. The Auberge de la Forêt is off-route at Bonifatu, providing accommodation, food and drink. Meals and supplies of food and drink are available at the Refuge de Carozzu.

Leave the **Refuge d'Ortu di u Piobbu** by walking downhill, looking for yellow flashes of paint along a stony, braided path through spiny broom. Ahead is a rocky outcrop – keep left of it to continue down a **rocky crest**. The path enters an area of young pines, then as it approaches a tall, dead pine, it swings right and runs downhill along the **base of a cliff**. Further downhill, it swings left and descends in easy zigzags down a steep slope covered in tall laricio pines, boulders and bracken. The path crosses a **streambed** that carries water early in the season, then becomes more rugged and eventually runs through tall heather and boulders to reach a bouldery ford on the **Ruisseau de Melaghia**. The altitude here is around 1000m (3280ft).

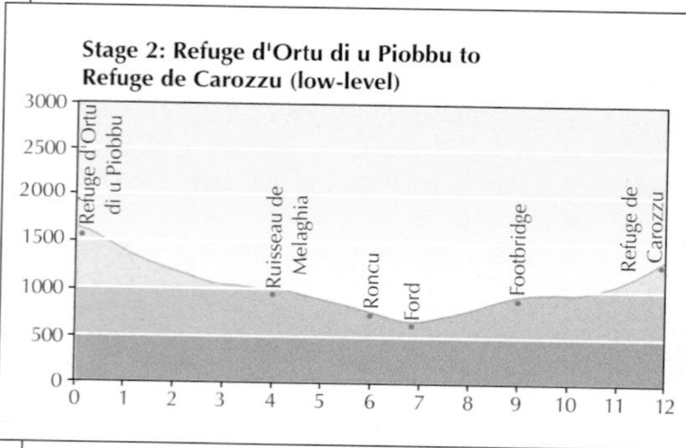

After fording the river, a rugged **forest track** continues gently downhill, later signposted 'Carozzu par le Roncu'. Laricio pine gives way to maritime pine, holm oak and arbutus. ◀

There are a couple of points where, looking back up the valley, it is possible to spot the Refuge d'Ortu di u Piobbu, with Monte Corona rising above it.

The track zigzags down to the **Ruisseau de Melaghia** again. Cross at a flat concrete ford, or use boulders just upstream if the water is more than boot depth.

Continuing down the track, there are views of wooded valleys converging, and while you may hear **waterfalls**, it is actually difficult to see them through the foliage. The track is surfaced in concrete where it has been cut from a cliff, and the cliff overhangs the track in places. There is another slab of concrete, then the rough and bouldery track lands beside a bouldery river below **Roncu**. Ford the river by hopping from boulder to boulder, though after heavy rain it could be a difficult crossing. The end of a **dirt road** on the other bank should be reached some 2½ hours after leaving the Refuge d'Ortu di u Piobbu, and the altitude is around 620m (2035ft). ◀

Walkers needing a quick exit for any reason should note that the dirt road can be used to reach Bonifatu and the Auberge de la Forêt.

To continue with the walk, go past a **signboard** that indicates the path leading to the Refuge de Carozzu. Allow about 2 hours for the walk up to the refuge from this point. The path is quite rough and rocky at first, even though it has been specially constructed and fixed to a rocky ledge above the river. Avoid a right turn signposted for the Boucle de Candia. The **Ruisseau de Lamitu** can be seen, or at least heard, down to the left, as views are often obscured by pines, holm oak, arbutus and tall heather trees.

The path beside the Ruisseau de Lamitu is well wooded, but occasionally there are glimpses of the mountains.

Photographers will find that good views are available from the middle of the bridge, but it probably wobbles too much to allow pictures to be taken successfully.

A **streambed** is crossed that carries water early in the summer, then later a larger **streambed** is crossed where water is more likely to be flowing. The path becomes much easier underfoot, almost level in places, then a rough stretch leads up to a suspension footbridge over the **Ruisseau de Spasimata**.

Take a break at this point, as the gorge is remarkably rugged and soaring peaks of pink granite rise all around. ◀

Tall laricio pines grace the slopes, and the peaks at the head of the valley may be streaked with snow early in the summer. Rock pools may prove irresistible on a hot day. After crossing the footbridge, a **rugged path** continues further up the valley side, with occasional glimpses of the rocky riverbed, its waterfalls, cascades and pleasant pools.

Were it not for a dense holly bush beside the table, this would be a perfect place to take a break and admire the rocky slabs and the fine tower of rock high above.

Cross the bouldery **Ruisseau de Ladroncellu** and follow the rugged path further uphill. There are zigzags, tightly hemmed in by trees, cutting out views of the valley for a while, then the path leads across the base of awesome **rock slabs** to reach another inflowing river. Cross the river and follow the zigzag path uphill, passing a stone **picnic table**, dated 1938, on the way. ◀

The path drifts away from the river and passes a **stone hut** with a corrugated iron roof. Signs forbid camping at this point, and those who get a shock seeing this rude hut are assured that it is not the refuge! The path zigzags further uphill through tall laricio pines and, by keeping left, the **Refuge de Carozzu** appears quite suddenly in a clearing.

REFUGE DE CAROZZU

The PNRC Refuge de Carozzu is situated in an amazing location, at 1270m (4165ft) on the only flat bit of ground in sight. It is hemmed in by tall mountains arranged around the Cirque du Bonifatu, yet features a view that extends down through the forested valley to the rugged little mountains near Calvi. A wooden terrace is positioned in front of the building so that weary wayfarers can rest and watch the sun go down at leisure, and marvel at the pines that cling to sheer rock all around. The building has a dormitory with 30 beds, a kitchen/dining room and the *gardien*'s quarters. Toilets, showers and water taps are located nearby. Meals, food and drink supplies are on sale. There are camping spaces in the woods, where abundant insect life flourishes!

STAGE 3

Refuge de Carozzu to Haut Asco

This is a tough day's walk and there are no easier alternatives. Only minutes after leaving the Refuge de Carozzu there is a steep and rugged descent into the Spasimata gorge. After crossing a suspension footbridge, walkers have to pick their way up the Spasimata Slabs. Although cables have been fixed to the rock, most of the slabs are unprotected. Be warned that the slabs can be slippery when wet, and even a light frost will make them treacherous. A steep and rocky ascent, sometimes holding snow well into the summer, leads to a high rocky gap. After a traverse across the steep face of Muvrella to reach another gap, there is a bird's-eye view of the ski-station at Haut Asco. The descent is very steep and rugged, taking longer than you might imagine to complete, but on reaching the ski-station you are rewarded with abundant food and drink, and a choice of accommodation.

Distance	6km (3¾ miles)
Total Ascent	860m (2280 feet)
Total Descent	710m (2330 feet)
Time	5½ hours
Map	IGN 4250 OT
Terrain	The steep and bare Spasimata Slabs need special care, especially when wet, and should be avoided when icy. A long, steep and rugged ascent is followed by a long descent on rocky and stony slopes.
Shelter	There are tall trees offering shade at the start and finish, but the highest parts are across open and exposed rocky mountainsides.
Food and Drink	Water is available in rivers on the early part of the ascent, but there is none on the higher parts or on the descent. Haut Asco offers plenty of food and drink, and the opportunity to replenish food supplies.

Leave the **Refuge de Carozzu** as signposted for Asco and Bonifatu. After only a few paces reach a **path junction** in the trees and turn left as signposted for Asco. Birch trees give

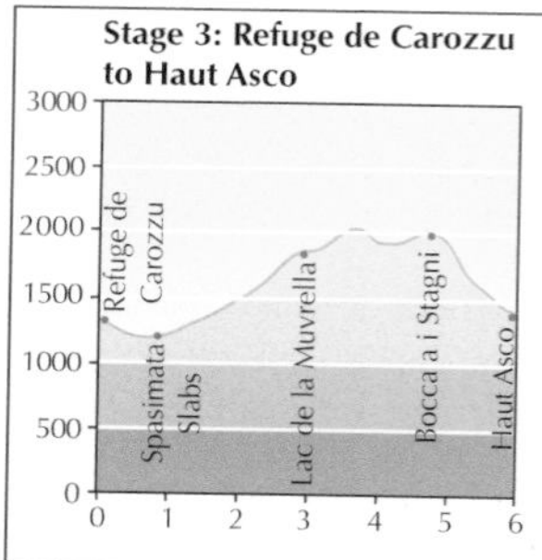

way to stately laricio pines, maritime pines and arbutus scrub. A **cable** protects one part of the route, where inclined slabs of rock are crossed. A rugged stretch of path leads down to the **Ruisseau de Spasimata**, where a metal suspension footbridge spans the river. It is a very wobbly bridge, especially if you are carrying a big pack. The altitude is around 1220m (4000ft). The pool beneath the bridge is a popular bathing spot for weary walkers in hot weather, and indeed, many motorists climb from the road end at Bonifatu to reach it.

A bouldery path climbs to the left, then the trees thin out and walkers start crossing the sloping **Spasimata Slabs** high above the river. Some of the slabs are protected with **cables**, but only on this first stretch of the route. In dry conditions the cables are superfluous, but in wet weather the slabs can be greasy and the cables prove more useful. Do not cross the slabs if there is snow or ice present. ◀

Find a safe stance and marvel at your surroundings – sheer rock walls and pinnacles rise all around, and a few isolated laricio pines appear to grow from solid rock on the cliffs.

Care is needed on the Spasimata Slabs, which can be slippery when wet and should be avoided when icy.

There may be an inflowing watercourse and a little shade in hot weather, then more **slabs** have to be climbed, this time without the benefit of cables. Look out for unusual plants cowering in cracks, especially saxifrages. After passing a tall, dead laricio pine, you may feel that there are no more slabs. In fact, there is one final series, then turn a bend in the valley and enjoy a fine view of a **waterfall** down to the left, which may be the last place to obtain water. The path climbs into a wooded side-valley, steep and stony underfoot, with juniper scrub all around. Watch as the path suddenly switches to the right, climbing uphill beside a **rocky rib**. Also look out for a small, cool cave on the right, offering shade on a hot day.

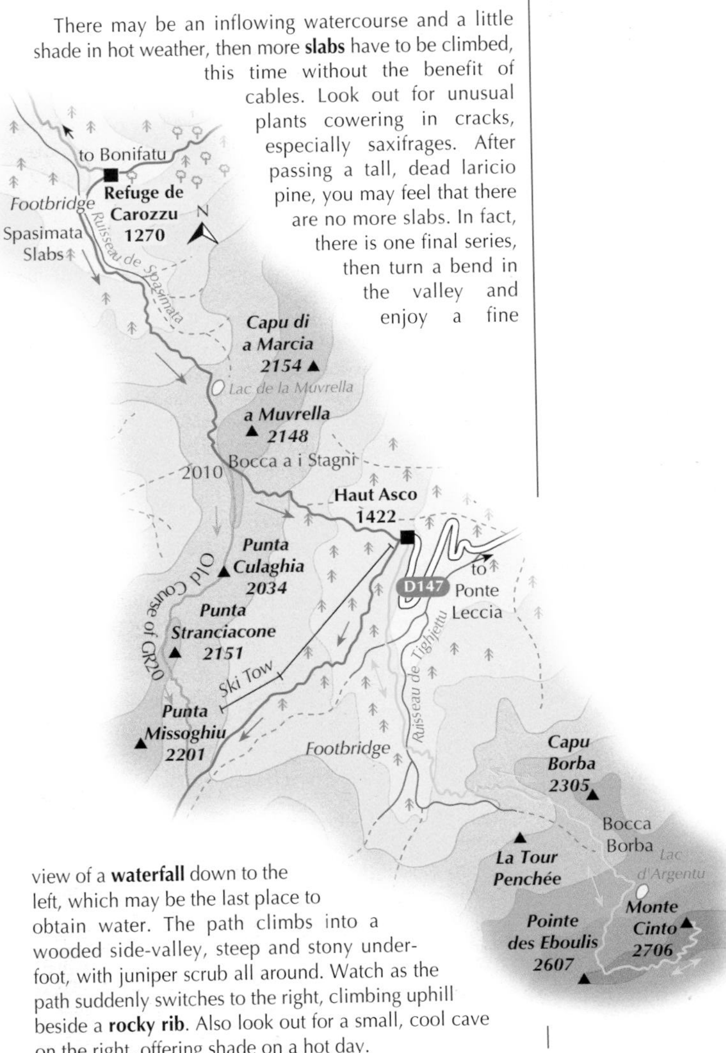

The path roughly contours across the valley side, passing through alder scrub where slender mountain ash also grows. After crossing the valley, climb a path that is alternately **rocky and stony**. Watch for the markers and generally walk between the tree scrub and the **rock walls** to the left. Keep climbing until directed up onto a **rocky ridge**, then walk above a little rocky hollow containing **Lac de la Muvrella** at 1860m (6100ft). The water here is stagnant and should not be used for drinking. Big boulders around the lake offer shade and it might be a good place for a break before tackling the next part of the climb. Walkers should reach the lake some 3 hours after leaving the Refuge de Carozzu.

Note that the next stretch can be covered in snow well into the summer. It is a north-facing **gully** full of boulders and broken rock. Zigzag up through the gully to reach a narrow, **rocky gap** around 2000m (6560ft). The towering peak of **a Muvrella** partly overhangs the gap, on the left-hand side, and walkers can take a break to admire this nearby feature, as well as the more distant view. Turn right to leave the gap and scramble round a **rocky corner**, then turn sharp left and head downhill across the slope, scrambling on rock at times, as well as across slopes of juniper and alder scrub. Be sure to keep left at a path junction to reach another narrow gap, the **Bocca a i Stagni**, around 2010m (6595ft). Walkers should reach this gap within an hour of leaving Lac de la Muvrella. (See the section after 'Ponte Leccia' for details of the old course of the GR20, which leaves this gap and avoids Haut Asco completely.)

Cross the gap and walk down a **steep and stony path**, watching carefully for markers, especially when there are rocky sections to be negotiated. The route shifts from side to side across the **rocky valley**, and although the complex of buildings at Haut Asco are visible, they don't seem to move any closer! In fact, it takes about 1½ hours to complete the descent. In the lower part of the valley the buildings are lost from sight, and the path runs along the base of a **sheer cliff**, where there is usually good shade. A final bouldery slope covered in laricio pines leads down to a wide **dirt road** beside some chalets. Turn left, then right as indicated by paint flashes, to drop down to the buildings at **Haut Asco**.

HAUT ASCO

The Haut Asco ski-station is located at 1422m (4665ft), and it is difficult to imagine the winter ski season while the valley acts as a heat trap in the summer. Many walkers who reach this point, especially those who have been struggling, yearn to take a day off. Those with more time and energy to spare can contemplate an ascent of Monte Cinto (see the second next section for details). A few walkers, sadly, will have had enough and feel unable to face another day on the trail, and will be looking for a quick exit down the valley.

Accommodation There is a choice of accommodation at Haut Asco. The most luxurious lodgings are at the fairly basic Hôtel le Chalet, tel 04 95 47 81 08, which has 22 rooms and also operates a *gîte d'étape* with 25 beds. The PNRC Refuge Asco-Stagnu is a fine building offering 32 beds. Camping is available around the foot of the ski-lifts and campers can pay for the use of some of the facilities provided by the hotel or refuge.

Food and Drink Most walkers will be happy to frequent the bar and restaurant at the Hôtel le Chalet, sampling good Corsican food and drink, and may feel tempted to take a day off and indulge themselves further. A more limited choice of snack food and drinks is available at Snack l'Altore across the car park. When the time comes to leave, food supplies can be obtained either from the hotel bar, or from the GR20 Ravitaillement shack operated by the *gardien* of the Refuge Asco-Stagnu.

Transport Haut Asco is at the end of the 30km (19 mile) long D147 that links with regular bus and rail services at Ponte Leccia. A taxi along this road would cost a fortune. During the peak summer season there are two *navette* services per day, except Sundays, linking with trains at Ponte Leccia and operated by Autocars Grisoni Voyages, tel 04 95 38 20 74 or mobile 06 07 47 55 87 or 06 73 86 16 52. These services also allow walkers to enjoy a mini-break at the precariously stacked mountain settlement of Asco village, overlooking the dramatic Gorges de Asco.

PONTE LECCIA

Those who leave the GR20 at Haut Asco will need to link with onward bus and rail services at Ponte Leccia, or spend the night in the village. The place is surprisingly busy, as most of the traffic around the northern half of Corsica passes through it at some point, and people often change buses and trains there. The main historical attraction is the graceful, 17th-century Genoese four-arched stone bridge from which the village takes its name, while the Domaine Vico vineyard is popular with visitors. There is a post office and a bank with an ATM. Those who wish to sample other outdoor activities around Corsica should visit In Terra Corsa, located beside the railway station.

Accommodation There are only two places to stay in Ponte Leccia. Le Stuart Hôtel, tel 04 95 47 61 11, is close to the Genoese bridge and has 18 rooms. The Hôtel Las Vegas, tel 04 95 47 61 59, has eight rooms and is along the main road in the direction of Corte.

Food and Drink Ponte Leccia straggles along busy main roads lined with a handful of bars and restaurants, a few shops and a supermarket, so there is no shortage of food and drink.

Transport Eurocorse Voyages run buses from Ponte Leccia to Bastia, Vizzavona and Ajaccio all year round except Sundays, tel 04 95 21 06 30, 04 95 31 73 76 or 04 95 70 13 83. Beaux Voyages run buses between Calvi and Bastia, passing Ponte Leccia, all year round except Sundays, tel 04 95 65 11 35 or 04 95 65 08 26. The CFC/SNCF railway at Ponte Lecchia links with the same places as the buses every day. Pick up a timetable from the station, or tel 04 95 46 00 97, 04 95 23 11 03, 04 95 32 80 61 or 04 95 65 00 61.

The 17th-century stone arches of the Genoese bridge spanning Le Golo Fleuve in Ponte Leccia.

Old Course of the GR20

Originally, the GR20 omitted Haut Asco and stayed high in the mountains to cross Punta Culaghia and rub shoulders with the rocky towers of Punta Stranciacone. At the time, there was a refuge at Altore, but this was burnt to the ground, apparently to 'encourage' walkers to visit Haut Asco and boost business prospects for the ski station in the summer months. The old course of the GR20 is still a clear path, and strong walkers can cover the distance from the Refuge de Carozzu to the Refuge de Tighjettu, omitting the descent to Haut Asco and subsequent re-ascent, in a day. This means negotiating the Cirque de la Solitude in the hottest part of the day, when energy levels are declining. There is a saving over the two days, when compared to the main route, of 1.5km (1 mile) and 200m (655ft) of ascent. (See map on p.71.)

Route Description

Instead of crossing the **Bocca a i Stagni** at 2010m (6595ft), keep walking straight along a narrow path, noting how the old GR20 markers have been obscured with grey paint. This only affects the first few markers, but the old red and white paint flashes are rather faded later. The path runs close to the crest, and you can look down on Haut Asco from **Bocca Culaghia**, at 1957m (6421ft). Continue down a **sloping rock terrace** to avoid a rocky summit, then follow the marked path into a rugged jumble of **boulders**. Watch carefully for the way up through the boulders and pass through a couple of **narrow rocky gaps** on the crest. Walk up a bouldery slope, onto bare rock, and head for the summit of **Punta Culaghia** at 2034m (6673ft). There are splendid views of the surrounding mountains, particularly Punta Stranciacone ahead.

The view from the old course of the GR20 looking towards Punta Stranciacone.

Walk down to a **gap** at 1980m (6496ft) and follow an easy path across a slope of scrub. As the path climbs it passes through a **rocky notch**. Traverse along the foot of some cliffs, passing beneath two huge towers of rock on **Punta Stranciacone**. Climb to a rugged **gap** and drop straight down the other side, where a steep and **stony path** runs down into alder scrub. The gradient eases as the path swings to the right, rejoining the main course of the GR20 around 1830m (6000ft). Turn left to follow the route up to **Altore**.

Ascent of Monte Cinto from Haut Asco

If the thought of climbing the highest mountain in Corsica appeals, then allow all day and complete the ascent from Haut Asco. Monte Cinto rises to 2706m (8878ft) and presents a fine challenge in addition to completing the GR20. Although the route described is the usual *tourist* ascent, it is quite arduous, involving scrambling on rock and climbing steep slopes of scree or boulders. Clear weather is needed to make the most of the ascent, not only for views of the surrounding mountains, but also for the immediate scenery, which is often quite breathtaking. Leave all your heavy gear at Haut Asco and climb the mountain with a light day-sack, though it will still take most of the day. (See map on p.71.)

Distance 12km (7½ miles) there and back
Total Ascent 1450m (4760 feet)
Total Descent 1450m (4760 feet)
Time 7 hours there and back
Map IGN 4250 OT
Terrain A forested valley walk gives way to easy scrambling on a steep and rocky slope. The higher parts of the valley feature steep and bouldery slopes, leading eventually to a high ridge. More easy scrambling over slabs and boulders leads to the summit of Monte Cinto.
Shelter Some shade in the forest at first, but none on the open slopes of the mountain. Monte Cinto is very exposed to wind and rain, in which conditions an ascent is not recommended. Its slopes can hold snow well into summer.
Food and Drink Available at Haut Asco at the start and finish. Water can be obtained from a couple of streams on the ascent.

Cross the car park in front of the Hôtel le Chalet to leave **Haut Asco** at 1422m (4665ft). A large sign points the way to Monte Cinto and the path passes a wooden building hidden in the trees. Note the **red paint marks** that show the way to Monte Cinto, as well as the orange flashes that mark the way

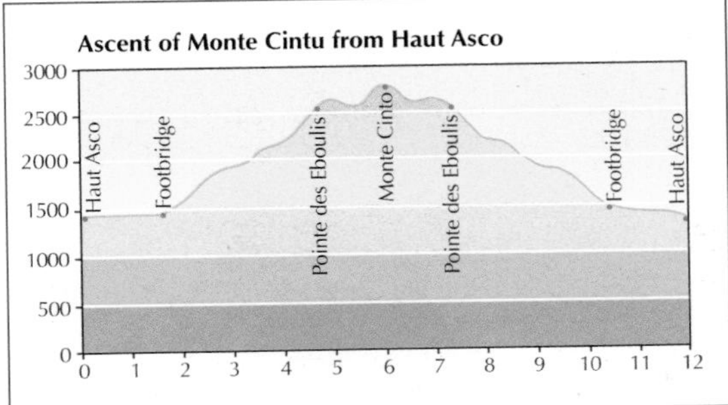

to the neighbouring peak of Punta Minuta. A narrow path leads past laricio pines, roughly contouring across the slope. Pass a small **water source**, then cross a bouldery stream at a series of cascades and continue gently downhill towards the **Ruisseau du Tighjettu**. Walk upstream roughly parallel to the river, leaving the shade of the pines and walking through juniper, alder and spiny broom scrub on rocky ground. Turn left as marked for 'Cinto' and cross a wooden **footbridge** over the Ruisseau du Tighjettu, at 1488m (4882ft). Pause to admire the fine array of peaks around the head of the valley.

The walk becomes more difficult as it follows the **red paint marks** in zigzags up a **steep and rocky slope**. Be wary of any wet patches, where the rock can be greasy underfoot. Those who start the ascent early in the day might find good shade on the slope before the sun strikes the rock. **White paint flashes** indicate left and right turns, so take careful note of them. The route eventually swings round to the left to enter a high, rocky valley surrounded by towers of rock, including the ominous overhanging **La Tour Penchée**.

The path is quite rough and stony, and there are some short sections across **bare rock**. Look ahead to spot small cairns and look for evidence of a trodden path. Climb up a **scree slope** at the foot of massive buttresses of rock on the left-hand side of the valley, walking through juniper and alder scrub. Reach a place below **Capu Borba** where there is a cave under a boulder on the right, offering a bit of shade and an excuse to stop and study the rocky peaks encircling the valley. There are cairns leading across a rocky lip nearby, but don't follow them.

The ominous leaning tower of La Tour Penchée is seen to good effect on the way up and down Monte Cinto.

Keep crunching up a **scree path** and let the higher line of cairns lead you across a level, stony hollow around 2150m (7050ft), below the gap of **Bocca Borba**. Water is available off to the left, where a stream splashes downhill before vanishing into the stones. Monte Cinto rises steep and rocky above, and looks unassailable. The north-facing slopes can hold a considerable amount of snow even in summer, so proceed with caution. The **line of cairns** swings round to the right – look ahead to spot each one in turn, as well as **red paint marks** and a trodden path.

Watch for the charming little **Lac d'Argentu** off-route to the left. As the slope becomes steeper and rockier, a variety of paths begins to branch out and climb towards the high crest of the mountain. Choose whichever suit you best, but avoid those that run dangerously close to rocky edges. The crest is at a general level of 2600m (8530ft) near the **Pointe des Eboulis** and there are fine views southwards. ▶

Lac du Cinto, to the southwest, may be frozen well into the summer.

Turn left on the crest and look for more cairns and **red paint marks**, which lead along a course generally below the crest, on the southern side. A summit is reached at 2651m (8698ft), where a **sign** points out that Monte Cinto is still further along the crest, just in case you happen to reach this point in mist and assume you are already on top! Walkers must follow the **arrow** pointing right, then pick a way below the crest, crossing areas of **big boulders** below a gap, before a zigzag scramble leads up a steep, bouldery, rocky slope to the summit of **Monte Cinto** at 2706m (8878ft).

Take in the extensive views, with particular reference to the high mountains already passed, and those still to be passed, on the GR20. Also, take care how you pick your way back down the rocky slopes to Haut Asco. It may take about 4½ hours to climb to the summit, while the descent could be completed in only 2½ hours. There is the added incentive that the descent ends at a bar!

On reaching the crest of the range, Monte Cinto is further along the ridge and is reached by easy scrambling.

STAGE 4

Haut Asco to Auberge U Vallone

This is the day that many walkers on the GR20 dread. Indeed, some have been known to slip away down the road from Haut Asco rather than face the traverse of the Cirque de la Solitude. While there is no doubt that the Cirque demands respect, and needs to be treated with care and caution, the difficulties of the traverse tend to be overstated. It is true that if all the helpful chains were removed, it would indeed be a rock climb, but only of a *moderate* grade. With all the chains, and even a short metal ladder, it is no more arduous than any of the scrambles endured so far, just more sustained. Anyone who has come this far on the GR20 will almost certainly be able to traverse the Cirque, and will probably look back on the experience with a measure of pride. If you don't like the look of the place, you can always turn back, but at least take a peek!

Distance	9km (5½ miles)
Total Ascent	1000m (3280 feet)
Total Descent	1000m (3280 feet)
Time	6½ hours
Map	IGN 4250 OT
Terrain	A relatively easy path climbs in stages towards the Col Perdu. The steep, rocky and bouldery confines of the Cirque need care and caution, but assistance is provided by a number of chains and a ladder. The descent to the Refuge de Tighjettu is steep, stony and rocky in places, though the continuation to the Auberge U Vallone is easier.
Shelter	Apart from limited tree cover at the start, there is little shelter. The traverse of the Cirque de la Solitude is not recommended in wet weather and should be avoided altogether if there is snow or ice present.
Food and Drink	Have a good breakfast at Haut Asco. Water can be obtained at a source near a small lake above the old Altore refuge site. The Refuge de Tighjettu and the Auberge U Vallone offer meals and keep stocks of food and drink.

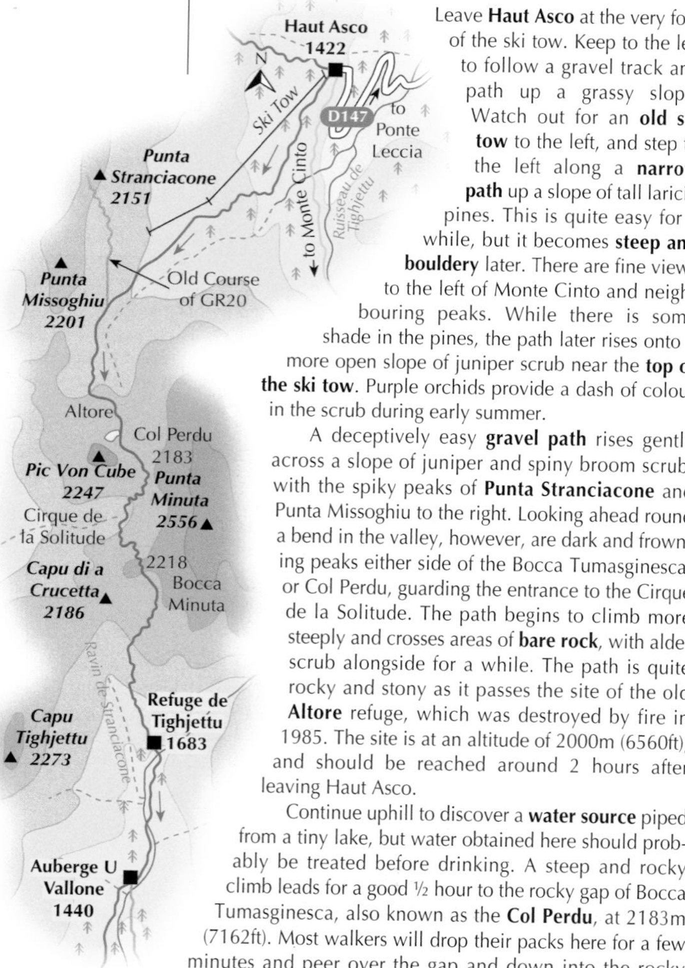

Leave **Haut Asco** at the very foot of the ski tow. Keep to the left to follow a gravel track and path up a grassy slope. Watch out for an **old ski tow** to the left, and step to the left along a **narrow path** up a slope of tall laricio pines. This is quite easy for a while, but it becomes **steep and bouldery** later. There are fine views to the left of Monte Cinto and neighbouring peaks. While there is some shade in the pines, the path later rises onto a more open slope of juniper scrub near the **top of the ski tow**. Purple orchids provide a dash of colour in the scrub during early summer.

A deceptively easy **gravel path** rises gently across a slope of juniper and spiny broom scrub, with the spiky peaks of **Punta Stranciacone** and Punta Missoghiu to the right. Looking ahead round a bend in the valley, however, are dark and frowning peaks either side of the Bocca Tumasginesca, or Col Perdu, guarding the entrance to the Cirque de la Solitude. The path begins to climb more steeply and crosses areas of **bare rock**, with alder scrub alongside for a while. The path is quite rocky and stony as it passes the site of the old **Altore** refuge, which was destroyed by fire in 1985. The site is at an altitude of 2000m (6560ft), and should be reached around 2 hours after leaving Haut Asco.

Continue uphill to discover a **water source** piped from a tiny lake, but water obtained here should probably be treated before drinking. A steep and rocky climb leads for a good ½ hour to the rocky gap of Bocca Tumasginesca, also known as the **Col Perdu**, at 2183m (7162ft). Most walkers will drop their packs here for a few minutes and peer over the gap and down into the rocky recesses of the **Cirque de la Solitude**. True, it looks intimidating, but not as intimidating as the pointed Pic Von Cube or Punta Minuta that rise high above the gap to right and left.

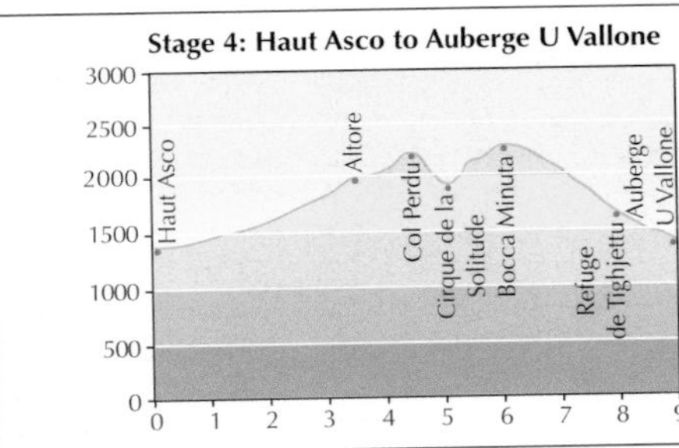

You may question other walkers as they prepare to enter the Cirque, or better still, talk to walkers who are emerging, having just completed the traverse in the other direction. In the end, you have to decide for yourself whether or not to proceed. There is no need for ropes or any other rock-climbing equipment – you just need to be fairly fit and agile, with a good head for heights, aided by dry weather. Anyone who has got this far on the GR20 should be able to complete the traverse. If there are long queues, it may be necessary to wait in line. Walkers with rock-climbing skills will find it easier to pick their own way along alternative lines to pass any bottlenecks.

Watch very carefully for the **paint flashes** as you step left into the Cirque. There is a very steep and rocky zigzag before reaching a **short chain**. Hang onto the chain, or simply scramble down the rock and hold the chain at a couple of more crucial points. At the end of the chain drift to the right down into a **rocky gully**, then later move to the left across to a couple of dark dykes, using them as steep, uneven, **rocky stairways**. Step back to the right across to the **gully** as marked and continue down what is basically a steep **boulder scree**. Take care not to send any boulders crashing down on walkers below, and hope that walkers above have the same concern for your own welfare. Continue to watch for the **paint flashes**, which later lead left around a mass of **bulbous rock** and down into the Cirque to around 1980m (6495ft).

The paint flashes show the way up a vegetated **sloping ledge** to start the ascent from the Cirque. A monstrous pillar of rock away to the right constantly frowns on you as you climb. Carefully follow the markers for the best footing, then

Deep snow cover at the end of May, above a tiny lake at Altore, on the climb towards the Col Perdu.

continue up a bouldery gully. A short, eight-runged **iron ladder** gives assistance up a little rockstep, then follow **two long lines of chains** as they zigzag up a series of **slabs**. Don't hang onto the chains and heave yourself bodily up the slabs, which will only make you tired. Instead, scramble up the slabs, holding the chains only when necessary, and generally let the course of the chains dictate your route upwards. Once at the top end of the chains, there is a scramble up a **bouldery gully**, then continue left across other **rock slabs** without any chains to hold onto.

Carefully follow the markers across the rock, and across a **bouldery slope**, to reach a little **gap** next to a prominent pinnacle of rock. Either pause here to watch other walkers negotiating the Cirque, or simply continue straight up a steep and **bouldery gully** as marked to reach the **Bocca Minuta**. This gap is at an altitude of 2218m (7277ft), and is flanked by the rocky peaks of Punta Minuta and Capu di a Crucetta. Most walkers will leave the Cirque some 2 hours after entering it. It's all over, so take one last look back!

To descend from the **Bocca Minuta**, follow a stony path in a wide sweep across the slopes of Punta Minuta, gradually steepening as the slope features more and more **boulders and bare rock**. The juniper, alder and spiny broom scrub barely manage to find rootholds on this steep and rocky mountainside, and in some places walkers need to look carefully for the paint flashes to be led down the easiest way as the route skips from terrace to terrace. There is a glimpse of the roof of the **Refuge de Tighjettu**, but the building is not really visible again until you land at the door, some 1½ hours after leaving the Bocca Minuta.

REFUGE DE TIGHJETTU

The PNRC Refuge de Tighjettu isn't built in the usual stone *bergerie* style, but is a curious timber chalet construction, at 1683m (5255ft), partly supported on stilts. It enjoys a fine view down the valley and is couched on a rugged spur between the Ravin du Stranciacone and the Ravin de Valle di Stagni. The building has three dormitories with 39 beds and a large kitchen/dining area. The *gardien*'s quarters are part of the building. Meals are available and there is a good stock of food and drink. The showers are underneath the refuge, where there is a good sheltered space with a wash place, and there is a separate toilet block just downhill. Small camping spaces are dotted around the steep slope below the refuge.

Some walkers will be happy to stop at the **Refuge de Tighjettu**, while others will prefer to put in another ½ hour and stay further down the valley. Walk downhill from the refuge, keeping to the right of the toilets, then swing left along a rocky path to pass a couple of tall **laricio pines**. Follow a stony, bouldery path down through juniper and spiny broom scrub, or walk across bare rock, and cross the **Ravin de Valle di Stagni** at a cascade. Continue along the path, taking the time to look back at the refuge clinging to the steep and rocky slope. Cross the **Ravin du Stranciacone**

Walkers deep in the Cirque de la Solitude look ahead to spot the course of the GR20 climbing steeply uphill.

and walk further down through the valley into an area of young pines. Keep to the marked path to reach the Bergeries de Ballone, also known as the **Auberge U Vallone**, at 1440m (4725ft).

AUBERGE U VALLONE

The Auberge U Vallone has a basic bar–restaurant and offers meals, snacks, drinks and the opportunity to buy food supplies to take away. Camping is permitted around the area, but there are also fixed tents for hire, and a large tent full of bunk beds used as a very basic *gîte d'étape*. There is a shower, a toilet and a water source. Walkers can sit at tables and chairs on a terrace and admire the surrounding mountains as they eat and drink, with the bongling bells of grazing cattle sounding all around. Rock pools in the river are most welcome on a hot day. There is an easy route leading from the *auberge*, down through the valley to the little villages of Calasima, Pietra and Albertacce (see the next section for details).

Link from Auberge U Vallone to Albertacce

Walkers occasionally leave the GR20 from the Auberge U Vallone. Some feel that they have seen the toughest four days of the route, and that the rest is going to be an anticlimax. They are wrong! Others, having suffered in the Cirque de la Solitude, wish to see no more of the GR20, which is a pity. A rugged path leaves the *bergerie* to link with a dirt road through a forested valley, which quickly gives way to a tarmac road leading to Calasima – the highest village in Corsica. The road leads through another small village, Pietra, before zigzagging down to Albertacce. Walkers who object to road walks can phone for a taxi to cover the distance from Calasima to Albertacce.

Distance	13km (8 miles)
Total Ascent	60m (195 feet)
Total Descent	625m (2050 feet)
Time	4 hours
Map	IGN 4250 OT
Terrain	Forested slopes and rugged paths give way to easy road walking across open, scrubby slopes. Over half the route is on a tarmac road.
Shelter	There is initially shade in the forest, but much of the road crosses open, scrubby slopes.
Food and Drink	There are water sources at Calasima. A couple of restaurants and a couple of snack bars are located in Albertacce.

Leave the **Auberge U Vallone** and walk down a path flashed with yellow paint to find a ford across the **stream**. Follow the rough and stony path down past laricio pines to join a rugged track at a **metal hut**. Vehicles may be parked here and are used to supply the *bergerie*. Follow the track gently downhill at first, then more steeply to cross a **bridge** over a

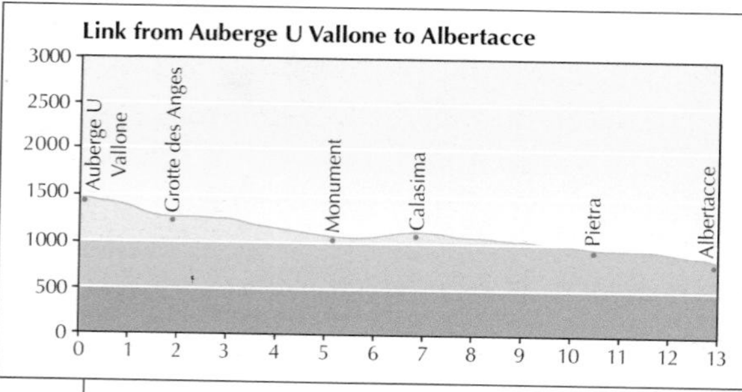

Note a memorial off to the right, in the shape of an aircraft propeller, commemorating three people killed while fighting a forest fire in 1979.

stream. Walk down to a turning space below a concrete **water tank**, then step to the right, off the track, to follow a **rugged path** marked with yellow paint. The path hits a bend further down the **stony track**. Do not follow the track, but look for the continuation of the path among tall laricio pines. Yellow marks on trees show the way past a **pig-pen**, then the path is clearer.

There is a slight ascent, then slight descent on a scrubby slope covered in **huge boulders**. A short detour along a cairned path, off to the right, reveals the **Grotte des Anges** – a cave beneath enormous wedged boulders. Rejoin the **track** at another bend and follow it downhill. There is little shade as the trees alongside are too young. The track soon gives way to a tarmac road. ◀

Follow the road gently uphill beside mixed pines and chestnut trees to reach **Calasima** at 1095m (3593ft). There is a church, but no food, drink or other services.

The D318 leaves the village and crosses

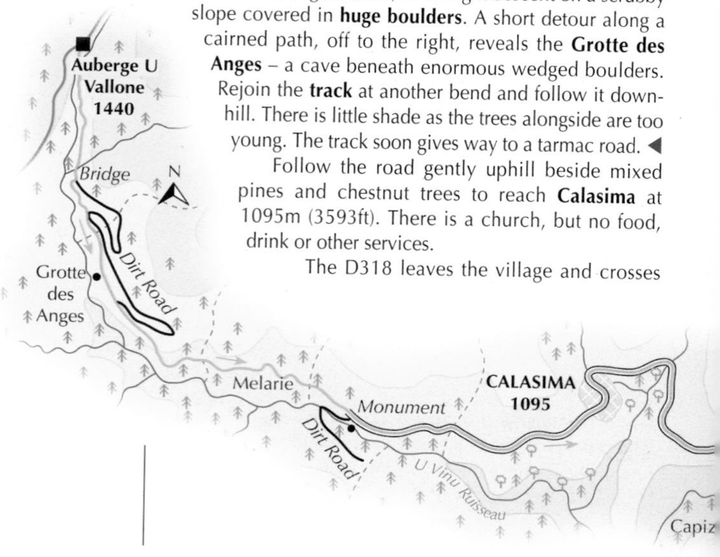

The rocky peak of Paglia Orba, seen from the Grotte des Anges, where there is a cave beneath huge boulders.

bridges over the **Ruisseau de Sambuchellu** and Ruisseau de Fiuminasca as it turns round a valley full of mixed woodland. Lose sight of the village while turning a **rocky corner**, then the road descends gently across a rocky, scrubby slope where there are very few trees. Pass a fenced **chestnut woodland** where there may be pigs, then there is a slight ascent into the village of **Pietra**. Follow the road through the village and turn sharp right at a **junction**. Walk down the road in broad loops, passing houses, family tombs and little vegetable plots. Either stay on the road all the way down to the main D84 in **Albertacce**, to reach the *gîte d'étape,* or shortcut straight downhill from the **church** to reach a couple of snack bars in the centre of the village.

ALBERTACCE

The little village of Albertacce straggles along the bendy main D84 around 860m (2820ft). It features a limited range of services, but offers enough to feed and accommodate walkers until they can catch a bus. The Musée Archéologique du Niolu is the main attraction for most visitors.

Accommodation The 24-bed Albertacce Gîte, tel 04 95 48 04 60, mobile 06 24 24 24 90, is the only place offering accommodation in the village.

Food and Drink The Auberge U Cintu and La Paglia Orba are restaurants serving good Corsican fare in Albertacce, though there are also a couple of snack bars in the village centre with more limited offerings. Blaring horns announce the arrival of visiting mobile shops.

Transport A bus service linking Albertacce with Corte and Porto is operated by Autocars Mordiconi, tel 04 95 48 00 04, from 1 July to 15 September, except Sundays. Taxi services in Albertacce are provided by Étienne Luciani, tel 06 11 05 69 49, or contact Jean-Charles Antolini in Pietra, tel 04 95 48 01 97, mobile 06 10 60 55 24.

The village of Albertacce offers a small choice of lodgings, restaurants and bars, as well as a summer bus service.

STAGE 5

Auberge U Vallone to Hôtel Castel di Vergio

The first four stages of the GR20 are really quite tough, and most walkers will agree that the traverse of the Cirque de la Solitude is the toughest part, but that is all behind you now. Ahead lies an easier day's walk, and one that could be broken into two parts by climbing to the Refuge de Ciottulu di I Mori and staying overnight. However, it is still possible to continue downhill from the refuge to the Hôtel Castel di Vergio and agree that the whole day's walk is not as tough as any of those earlier stages. There is a choice of accommodation options at the hotel, as well as abundant food and drink. On the other hand, those who decide to stay at the Refuge de Ciottulu di I Mori could also climb Paglia Orba, the third highest mountain in Corsica. (See the next section for an ascent route.)

Distance	15km (9½ miles)
Total Ascent	850m (2790 feet)
Total Descent	870m (2855 feet)
Time	6 hours
Map	IGN 4250 OT
Terrain	An easy walk through a forested valley gives way to a steep and rocky climb to Bocca di Foggiale and the Refuge de Ciottulu di I Mori. The descent through the valley of the Golo is steep, stony and rocky in places, but fairly easy to complete. An easy woodland walk ends the day.
Shelter	There is good shelter in the trees at the beginning and end of the day, and a break can be taken at the Refuge de Ciottulu di I Mori in the middle of the day. Even in poor weather, the valley of the Golo is more sheltered than the surrounding mountains.
Food and Drink	Water can be taken from streams on the flanks of Paglia Orba, or from the Refuge de Ciottulu di I Mori. Water from the River Golo should probably be treated before drinking. Both the refuge and the Hôtel Castel de Vergio offer opportunities to replenish food supplies.

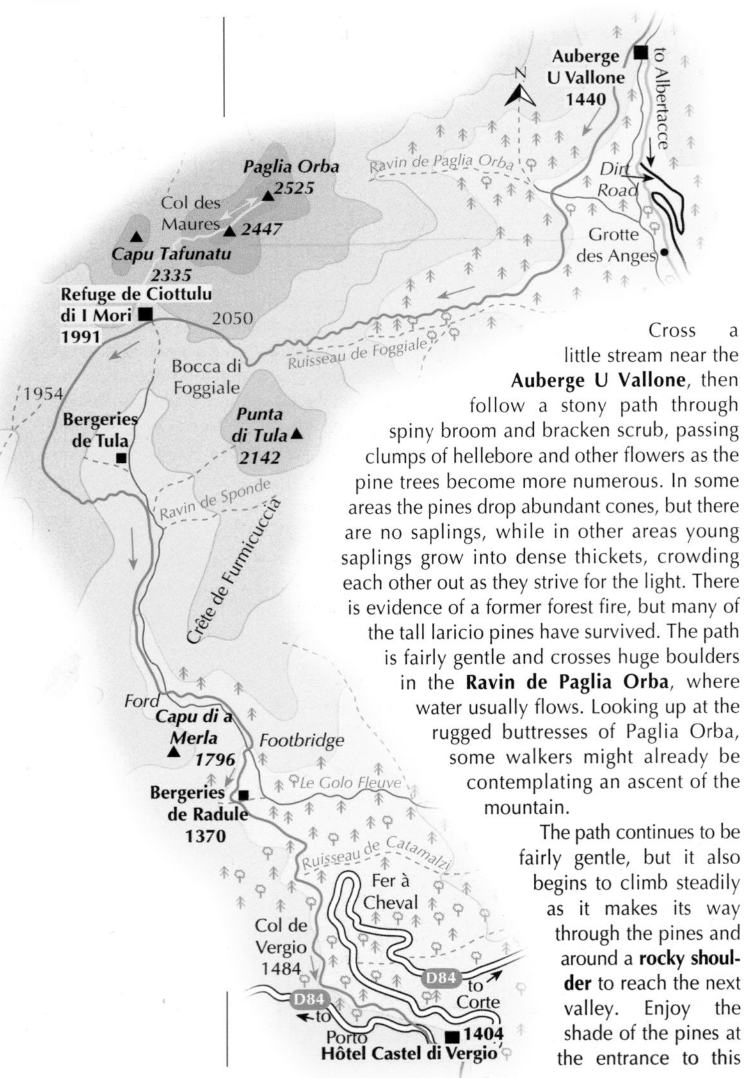

Cross a little stream near the **Auberge U Vallone**, then follow a stony path through spiny broom and bracken scrub, passing clumps of hellebore and other flowers as the pine trees become more numerous. In some areas the pines drop abundant cones, but there are no saplings, while in other areas young saplings grow into dense thickets, crowding each other out as they strive for the light. There is evidence of a former forest fire, but many of the tall laricio pines have survived. The path is fairly gentle and crosses huge boulders in the **Ravin de Paglia Orba**, where water usually flows. Looking up at the rugged buttresses of Paglia Orba, some walkers might already be contemplating an ascent of the mountain.

The path continues to be fairly gentle, but it also begins to climb steadily as it makes its way through the pines and around a **rocky shoulder** to reach the next valley. Enjoy the shade of the pines at the entrance to this

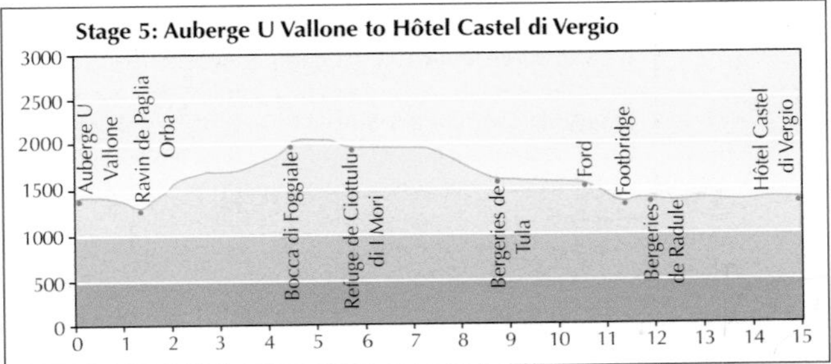

valley, as they quickly thin out and the path leads onto a more open slope of spiny broom and juniper scrub, where only a handful of laricio pines stand. The path becomes **steep and stony** as it climbs uphill, then it suddenly reaches a slope of **bare rock**. Watch carefully for paint flashes to follow the best line of ascent, and cross a **stream** at a series of cascades.

Looking up to the pinnacles and buttresses of Paglia Orba, you may spot *mouflon* grazing on what appears to be bare rock. Looking down the valley, the barrage and artificial lake at Calacuccia are visible. There is less rock and more of a **stony path** further uphill. One area is wet enough to support plenty of butterworts, and there is a tiny **water source**. The juniper, spiny broom and alder scrub is remarkably flowery in places. Keep climbing, grappling with rock where necessary or shuffling up the stony, **bouldery path** while following route markers. Cross an area of **bare rock** and swing to the right to rise above the **Bocca di Foggiale** at 1962m (6437ft).

A walker reaches the gap of the Bocca di Foggiale after a steep and rocky climb from the valley.

The path cuts through patches of spiny broom on a reddish **scree slope**. Pass a cairn at 2050m (6725ft), then descend through patches of alder scrub with a view of the **Refuge de Ciottulu di I Mori** ahead. A few camping spaces and a helipad are passed before reaching the refuge, and in early summer the grassy areas support plenty of Corsican crocuses. The refuge should be reached about 3¼ hours after leaving the Auberge U Vallone. Most walkers take at least a short break here, while others consider the possibility of staying overnight, or even contemplate climbing **Paglia Orba**.

REFUGE DE CIOTTULU DI I MORI

The PNRC Refuge de Ciottulu di I Mori is built in the *bergerie* style and situated at 1991m (6532ft), with a fine terrace overlooking the Golo valley and the mountains far beyond. There is a dormitory with 24 beds and a kitchen/dining room, while the *gardien*'s quarters are at one end of the building. Meals and supplies of food and drink can be purchased. A toilet and shower are located in a small building just below the refuge. A path leading towards Paglia Orba and Capu Tafunatu is signposted behind the refuge, where the source of the Golo, the longest river in Corsica, is located. (Those staying at the refuge to climb Paglia Orba should refer to the next section for details of the ascent.)

Continue along the path as signposted for the Refuge de Manganu, contouring along a **stony path** across a slope covered in spiny broom scrub, while the view down the valley stretches as far as distant Monte Alcudina. The path leads across a gentle gap and climbs a short way to a **rounded summit** at 1954m (6411ft), where the view westwards includes the sea around the Golfe de Porto. The path is a little more rugged as it begins to descend into the valley, passing through alder scrub and zigzagging down a slope covered in spiny broom. There are fine views back to Paglia Orba, Capu Tafunatu and the Refuge de Ciottulu di I Mori at the head of the valley, while the ruined **Bergeries de Tula** are visible at the foot of the slope.

Swing to the right and follow the path downstream, walking fairly close to the **Golo**. The path is stony, but relatively easy, passing areas of juniper, spiny broom and alder scrub. On hearing and seeing little **waterfalls** plunging into deep green pools, the thought of taking a dip and basking on the warm rocks may cross your mind. Reach a point where the valley bends to the left, and at this point cross the Golo on **bare rock**, just below a fine little **waterfall** and deep pool. Watch carefully for this crossing, which some walkers miss.

Those walking during wet weather, who think the river is too dangerous to ford, should proceed carefully, without crossing the river, to rejoin the GR20 further downstream. Avoid slippery slabs near the river if you take this option.

After crossing the river, views of Paglia Orba and Capu Tafunatu give way to the Monte Ritondu massif in the distance. Walk over **rock slabs** and cross bouldery slopes to continue downstream. Note the splendid laricio pines in this part of the valley. ▶ Some of the pines are over 300 years old and stand over 30m (100ft) tall.

The Reserve Biologique Dirigée de la Forét Domaniale de Valduniellu has been established in this area to study the longevity of the laricio pines.

An **old path** leads down through the valley, created by nudging boulders to one side and somehow making a route across the steep and rocky slopes. Follow the paint flashes,

The Golo has to be forded at a point where there are broad, bare slabs of granite.

which reveal a zigzag path, then cross over the Golo again using a wooden **footbridge**.

Blue paint flashes in this area indicate the Sentier de Radule, which runs concurrent with the GR20 for a while. A **bouldery path** leads across a steep slope covered in bracken and hellebore, and crosses rocky slabs to reach the **Bergeries de Radule**, perched on a rocky ledge at 1370m (4495ft). This point can be reached about 1½ hours after leaving the Refuge de Ciottulu di I Mori, and cheeses can be bought here. The GR20 runs just above the *bergeries* on a rocky slope, crossing a small dam that holds a water supply below a small **waterfall**. You may notice a path rising to the right, marked with yellow flashes of paint, offering a route to the Col de Vergio. This provides fine views, but would later entail a road walk down to the Hôtel Castel di Vergio.

The GR20 stays lower on the slope, passing through tangled **birch woods** dotted with stout laricio pines. Views are limited, but the path is mostly easy, though **fallen trees and boulders** are common, requiring short diversions at times. In some parts the ground has been dug over by pigs, and several plump specimens may be seen before ending the day's walk. Avoid a path dropping down to the left, which leads to the **Fer à Cheval** on a road bend. At another **path junction**, the Mare a Mare Nord crosses the GR20, so stay straight ahead and keep following the route markers to reach the main D184 at a bend. Turn left and the **Hôtel Castel di Vergio** will be reached in mere minutes, situated at 1404m (4606ft), some 1¼ hours after leaving the Bergeries de Radule.

HÔTEL CASTEL DI VERGIO

The Hôtel Castel di Vergio, tel 04 95 48 00 01, will win no prizes for prettiness, facing a ski tow across the road, but it provides a number of services for passing walkers. Free camping is permitted in a fenced enclosure near the hotel, with *gîte d'étape* accommodation available in the basement of the hotel, or a little more comfort in the 40 rooms upstairs. The bar and restaurant are open to everyone, and although the helpings of food could be more generous, it is good Corsican fare and enough to keep body and soul together for the duration of your stay. The bar also sells overpriced food supplies, and a smile clearly costs extra. A bus service, operated by Autocars Mordiconi, tel 04 95 48 00 04, links the hotel with Corte and Porto, from 1 July to 15 September, except Sundays.

Ascent of Paglia Orba from Refuge de Ciotullu di I Mori

Paglia Orba, at 2525m (8284ft), is the third highest mountain in Corsica, and its profile displays very steep, bare rock in most views. The ascent is a considerable challenge for the ordinary walker. Be warned at the outset that the scrambling required on this mountain, even by the easiest route, is a little more serious than that encountered on the toughest parts of the GR20. There are plenty of good holds for hands and feet, made possible because of the nature of the rock, which is a coarse puddingstone conglomerate, rather than the usual granite, but some moves are awkward and exposed. Don't try this ascent with a large pack, but take only the bare essentials, so as not to limit your movements. The effort involved in reaching the summit, or even getting part way, is rewarded by awesome rock scenery at close quarters and splendid views of distant ranges of mountains. There is no harm in climbing the mountain as far as you can, then beating an honourable retreat to the refuge, but ensure that you are able to reverse your steps for the descent. (See map on p.92.)

Distance 3.5km (2 miles) there and back
Total Ascent 600m (1970 feet)
Total Descent 600m (1970 feet.)
Time 3 hours there and back
Map IGN 4250 OT
Terrain Easy paths at the start and near the summit, but bouldery in other places, with some quite difficult scrambling on steep rock. This is the most difficult scrambling in the whole book.
Shelter Some shade in rock gullies, but the mountain is very exposed to wind and rain, in which conditions an ascent is not recommended.
Food and Drink Take water and a little food from the Refuge de Ciottulu di I Mori.

Start behind the **Refuge de Ciottulu di I Mori,** situated at 1991m (6532ft), where a path is signposted 'Paglia Orba' and 'Capu Tafunatu'. Even at the start, Paglia Orba looks

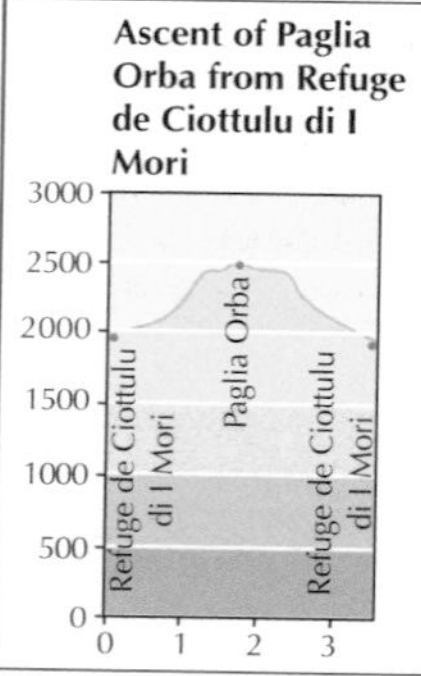

unassailable to ordinary walkers, and those who spot people already engaged in the ascent will realise that this is no ordinary walk. The path is initially quite easy, rising gently across a scree slope and crossing the **Source du Golo** – source of the longest river in Corsica. Walkers enter a wild and rocky hollow, couched between Paglia Orba and Capu Tafunatu, with the rocky **Col des Maures** directly ahead. Watch out for a path branching off to the right, marked by **small cairns**, leading towards the rocky flanks of Paglia Orba. The scree becomes more and more bouldery, and walkers are led into a **leaning gully full of boulders**, with a lumpy tower of rock watching over their progress.

There are two or three cairned routes leading off to the left – assess them in turn and choose one to your liking. Continue up a series of **slabs and rocky paths**, crossing more

The route towards the rocky dome of Paglia Orba is signposted behind the Refuge de Ciottulu di I Mori.

boulders and following the cairns as they lead ever upwards. As the path begins to swing to the right, you may think that the scrambling is pretty easy, but on entering a steep rocky gully above some **enormous jammed boulders**, flanked by leaning towers of rock, the ascent suddenly looks quite intimidating. Look around to see the famous hole pierced through the neighbouring summit of Capu Tafunatu, which sometimes looks like a baleful blue eye. This eye watches unblinking while walkers negotiate the hardest part of the ascent.

The **cairns** lead to the right-hand side of the gully. Scramble up some **steep rocksteps** that slant rather awkwardly downwards, making feet feel that they are not too securely planted. Stay well to the right where it isn't too exposed, but please ensure that you are capable of reversing all your moves later in the day. Approaching the top of the rocky gully, things become easier, and the cairns lead left to a **rocky notch** where there is an awesome view of the far side of the mountain. Walkers may also notice that the eye of Capu Tafunatu is no longer watching them – maybe because the next move is too awkward and exposed to watch!

Look carefully for the **cairns**, which lead above the rocky notch, along a **narrow and exposed ledge**, then up an exposed little scramble where you simply cannot afford to slip. Above this, easier slabs and bouldery slopes lead to a summit. This is not the main summit of Paglia Orba, but a subsidiary summit at 2447m (8028ft).

The **cairns** lead down a slope of **slabs and boulders**, **cutting well beneath a rocky gap**, then a rather circuitous course leads back onto the main crest of the mountain. An amazingly easy path, brightly speckled with the yellow flowers of Alpine avens, leads along the crest towards the summit. Climb to the summit cairn on **Paglia Orba** at 2525m (8284ft) and enjoy the view, marvelling at how steeply the slopes fall in every direction except that used for the final ascent. It takes about 2 hours to reach the summit from the refuge.

From there, look back towards Monte Cinto and the early stages of the GR20, and ahead to Monte Rotondu and the next stages of the route. Hopefully you will be able to retrace your steps to the refuge without too much difficulty. The descent can be accomplished in as little as an hour.

STAGE 6

Hôtel Castel di Vergio to Refuge de Manganu

Despite its length, this is a relatively easy day's walk. Indeed, considerable stretches are virtually level, such as the woodland walk at the start of the day and the walk past Lac du Ninu in the middle of the day. Even when there is an ascent to complete, up to the Bocca San Petru and on to the Bocca â Reta, the path features easy zigzags and gradients. For much of the day you can stride out and walk in a manner that simply isn't possible on the rough and stony slopes of the earlier stages of the GR20. The scenery may not always be dramatic, but it is nevertheless charming. This is a day to savour, where you shouldn't dash ahead and overtax yourself, but prepare for more hard walking over the next few days on the way to Vizzavona.

Distance	17km (10½ miles)
Total Ascent	670m (2200 feet)
Total Descent	475m (1560 feet)
Time	5¾ hours
Map	IGN 4251 OT
Terrain	A well-wooded walk around the head of a valley gives way to a relatively easy walk over the mountains and easy walking near Lac du Ninu. A more rugged path leads through a broad and bouldery valley, with some patchy woodlands. Generally easy walking throughout the day.
Shelter	The wooded slopes offer plenty of shade, but other parts of the route are more exposed. Patchy woodlands in the latter parts of the walk offer a little shade.
Food and Drink	There is a water source near Lac du Ninu. Basic food supplies are available from the Bergeries de Vaccaghja, while the Refuge de Manganu offers meals and keeps a stock of food and drink.

Walk a short way down the D184 from the **Hôtel Castel di Vergio**, and a sign on the right indicates the way to Lac du

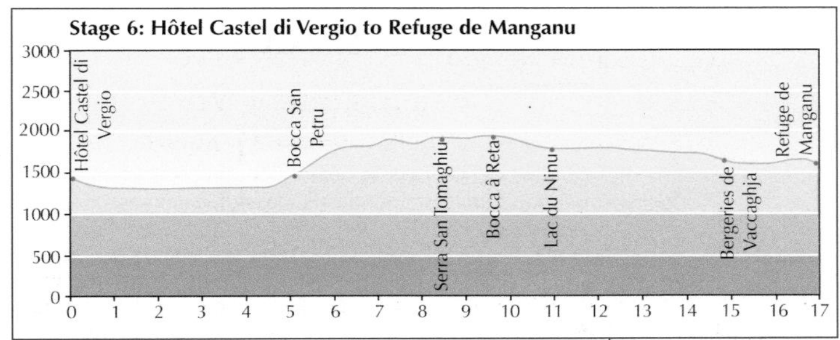

Ninu and the Refuge de Manganu. A **forest path** runs downhill, gradually levelling out as it swings to the right, contouring easily across the slopes. Tall laricio pines and young saplings share the slopes with slender birch and a few stout beech trees. The path is well engineered and a joy to walk. Walkers can stride out and strike a good rhythm after those earlier days watching every step on the rocky mountains. There are views back towards Paglia Orba and Monte Cinto, as well as down the

Map continues p.103

forested valley and ahead to the mountain called u Tritore. The path weaves in and out on the slopes as it crosses **streambeds**, some of which carry water early in the summer.

Watch carefully for a sudden right turn uphill. This turning is well marked and there is a **signpost** for San Petru. Another signpost points downhill for the Fontaine Caroline, but don't imagine that this is a useful water source, as it is actually a long way down the wooded slope beside the D184. The path initially looks as though it zigzags up a steep, stony slope exposed to the sun, but it quickly becomes a gently graded zigzag route in the shade of tall beech trees. ◀

Look out for pigs rooting for beech mast.

The **Bocca San Petru**, or Col St Pierre, is a grassy gap with fine views of the valleys on either side. You can also look back to Capu Tafunatu, Paglia Orba and Monte Cinto. There is a tiny **oratory** on the gap at 1452m (4764ft), and this point should be reached about 1½ hours into the day's walk.

Turn left up a **grassy ridge** featuring low outcrops of rock. A zigzag mule track leads up the open slope and passes an **electricity pylon**. ◀

Note how some isolated beech trees have been shaped by the westerly wind into grotesque shapes.

At a higher level, the path leaves the ridge and heads left across the slopes of **u Tritore**. The path is gently graded, passing beech trees and alder scrub. You may have to clamber over some fallen trees or detour round them.

Watch out for a sudden right turn, where the path zigzags up onto a more open slope, crossing areas of rock and alder scrub. Follow the path close to the crest of the **Serra San Tomaghiu**, and take a peep through a couple of gaps at the valley on the southern side. The path leads through a **rocky gap**, zigzagging downhill a short way, then uphill across the stony slopes of **Capu a u Tozzu**. It rises gently to the broad and grassy gap of **Bocca â Reta**, at 1883m (6178ft), where fine views of the mountains ahead can be enjoyed.

The path descends easily towards **Lac du Ninu**, which is a remarkably pleasant spot on a fine day. The blue lake is surrounded by short green turf grazed by cattle and horses, while the mountains in the distance lend grandeur to the scene, and may hold streaks of snow well into the summer. The lake is at an altitude of 1743m (5718ft), is 11m (36ft) deep, and is frozen for almost half the year. It is the source of one of Corsica's finest rivers, the **Tavignanu**.

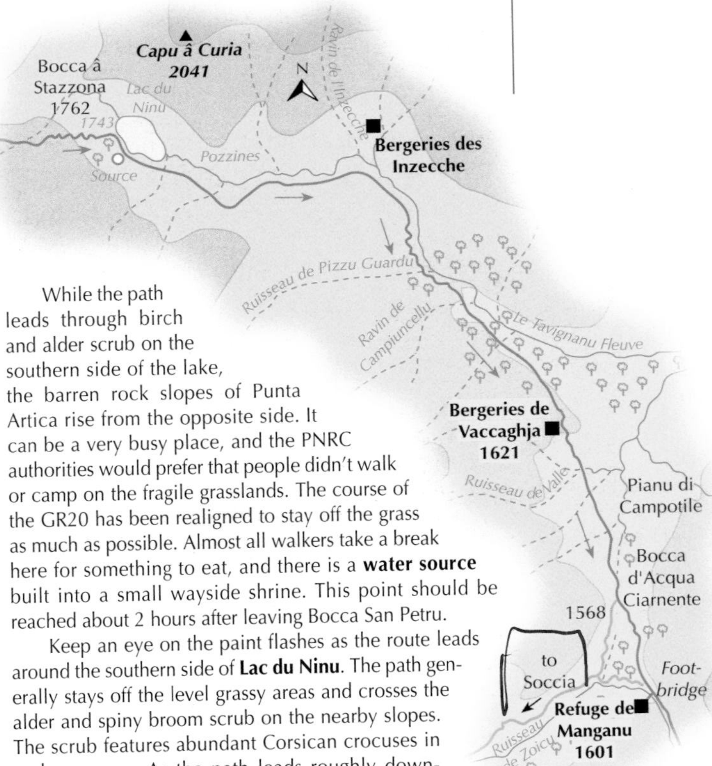

While the path leads through birch and alder scrub on the southern side of the lake, the barren rock slopes of Punta Artica rise from the opposite side. It can be a very busy place, and the PNRC authorities would prefer that people didn't walk or camp on the fragile grasslands. The course of the GR20 has been realigned to stay off the grass as much as possible. Almost all walkers take a break here for something to eat, and there is a **water source** built into a small wayside shrine. This point should be reached about 2 hours after leaving Bocca San Petru.

Keep an eye on the paint flashes as the route leads around the southern side of **Lac du Ninu**. The path generally stays off the level grassy areas and crosses the alder and spiny broom scrub on the nearby slopes. The scrub features abundant Corsican crocuses in early summer. As the path leads roughly downstream parallel to the **Tavignanu**, the Bergeries des Inzecche are visible, tucked into a heap of boulders on the lower slopes of Punta Artica. The path becomes quite bouldery too, while the river is filled with **rock pools** that look quite inviting on a hot day.

The slopes of boulders, spiny broom and juniper give way to a patchy area of beech trees and beech scrub. The trees and scrub become denser, and fallen trees can make it difficult to spot the continuation of the path, which is vague at times. Watch carefully for the markers, and the path will eventually lead across an **open slope** of juniper and spiny

The GR20 runs through an area sparsely wooded with beech trees on its way to the Bergeries de Vaccaghja.

broom scrub, scattered with boulders, to turn a rocky corner and suddenly come upon the **Bergeries de Vaccaghja,** at 1600m (5250ft). Walkers should reach the Bergeries de Vaccaghja about 1½ hours after leaving Lac du Ninu, and although not far from the Refuge de Manganu, it is a good place to take a break.

BERGERIES DE VACCAGHJA

The Bergeries de Vaccaghja overlook the flat grasslands of Pianu di Campotile, which are surrounded by mountains and used for grazing cattle and horses. The *bergeries* sell food and drink, including their own cheeses and meat products. Look round the place to find little storage spaces under overhanging rocks, where cheeses mature. There are small camping spaces, and fixed tents may be available for hire. The *bergeries* are popular with crosscountry horse-riding groups.

MARE A MARE NORD

The waymarked Mare a Mare Nord crosses Corsica from Moriani on the east coast to Cargèse on the west coast, passing the Bergeries de Vaccaghja. It runs concurrent with the GR20 between the *bergeries* and Lac du Ninu, and the routes cross just north of the Hôtel Castel di Vergio. The Mare a Mare Nord could be followed alongside the Tavignanu for a whole day to reach the ancient citadel town of Corte, and there is a variant route offering a link westwards from the GR20 with the village of Soccia. (The route to Soccia is described in the next section.)

On leaving the **Bergeries de Vaccaghja,** walk down a grassy, bouldery slope and cross the level, grassy **Pianu di Campotile**. The Refuge de Manganu is visible ahead, but there is a climb up a short, steep, rocky slope to reach it, crossing the **Bocca d'Acqua Ciarnente** at 1568m (5144ft). The mountain rising to the left is the Punta di a Femina Morta. Cross a stream on its slopes, then cross a wooden footbridge on the right to reach the **Refuge de Manganu**, at 1601m (5253ft), about ¾ hour after leaving the *bergeries*.

REFUGE DE MANGANU

The PNRC Refuge de Manganu is built in the *bergerie* style, featuring a dormitory with 31 beds and a kitchen/dining room. The *gardien*'s quarters are in the same building, while the showers and toilets are in a small building behind the refuge. Some walkers prefer to take a dip in one of the pools in the nearby river, rather than take a shower. Small camping spaces are located in the alder scrub behind the building. A hot meal can be ordered, or food supplies can be bought. Freshly baked bread from an outdoor oven is a speciality, but it sells out very quickly! The terrace in front of the refuge looks back along the route of the GR20, with the mountains of Cimatella and Punta Artica dominating the scene.

The broad, level, grassy Pianu di Camptile is crossed on the way to the Refuge de Manganu.

Link from Refuge de Manganu to Soccia

Soccia is a quiet and pleasant village, originally huddled around a 15th-century church. Its stone houses now rise up the hillside and around the valley sides. Walkers who are running out of time can leave the GR20 by walking from the Refuge de Manganu to Soccia. A day visit might also be considered, especially if a nasty weather forecast renders the higher parts of the GR20 unsafe to negotiate. A walk down to the village and back again takes all day, but there is a hotel if you wish to stay overnight, as well as a marvellous restaurant. It is also worth walking halfway down the valley just to visit Lavu a Crena in a pine forest, and return to the Refuge de Manganu.

Distance	10km (6 miles)
Total Ascent	60m (195 feet)
Total Descent	930m (3050 feet)
Time	3 hours
Map	IGN 4251 OT
Terrain	A rough and stony path leads down through a valley, becoming easier along the way, but ending quite steep and rugged.
Shelter	A pine forest offers some shade halfway through the walk, but the valley itself is very sheltered throughout.
Food and Drink	There are water sources near Lavu a Crena, a café above Soccia and two bars and a restaurant in Soccia.

Leave the **Refuge de Manganu** by crossing the footbridge and turning left, as signposted for Lac du Ninu along the GR20. However, turn left again at a **path junction** in an area of juniper scrub, as signposted for Soccia – a path which is flashed with **yellow paint**. The narrow, rough and stony path descends to cross a **streambed**, then climbs and swings left to begin its journey down the valley. Note how parts of the path have been buttressed, and later watch carefully to spot one short section that has been consolidated with concrete.

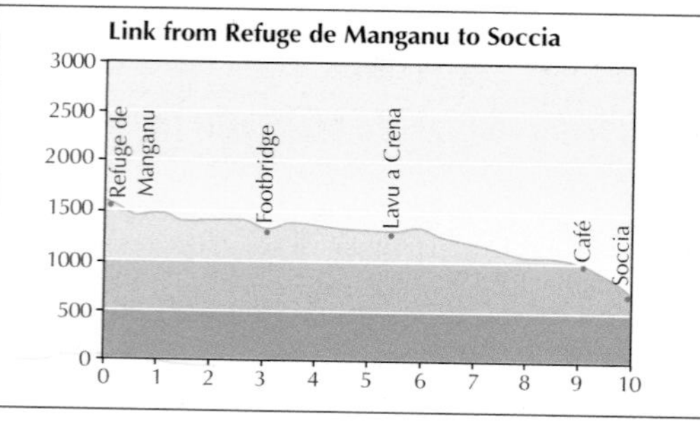

The path zigzags down to a fairly level area, then passes a bulbous mass of granite with a prominent **beech tree** growing alongside. Cross a rocky area and note the little spring, the **Source de Zoicu**. The course of the **Ruisseau de Zoicu** is fairly well wooded, but there are few trees growing alongside the path. Another rugged zigzag stretch leads down to a stout wooden **footbridge** spanning the river. Cross over and turn right to continue downstream, gradually pulling away from the course of the river. There is a view of the tiny **Bergeries de l'Izzola** across the valley before a forest of laricio pines is reached.

According to local lore, the lake was created by the devil, either from a blow of his hammer or a kick from his horse.

The path climbs gently among pines, where pigs may have dug over the ground. A slight descent leads to **Lavu a Crena**, at an altitude of 1310m (4298ft). The lake is 6.5m (21ft) deep, and is frozen for three or four months in the winter.

The charming grassy shore gives way to reed-fringed waters with lily-pad islets. Look out for coots on the water

A view along the length of the Zoicu valley, which runs down towards Lavu a Crena and the village of Soccia.

and Corsican nuthatches in the surrounding pines. It is worth walking round the shore, where the view from the outflow stretches across a deep valley to distant Monte d'Oru. There is a **water source** beside a small stone hut.

Look carefully for the continuation of the yellow-flashed path, which is not immediately obvious, though once it has climbed a little from the lake it is quite clear. It passes the **Funtana di a Veduvella,** where water spills onto the path, then later enjoys a view of the valley. Expect to see a lot of day walkers on this part of the path, which descends gradually through sparse pines and deep heather.

Keep right at a signposted **path junction** for Soccia – the other way goes to Ortu. The path runs almost level across the valley side, with chestnut trees being prominent, then later aligns itself to a gentle **rocky ridge** covered in deep heather and clumps of 'everlasting', where goats regularly graze. The path crosses a track, where there is an attractive view down to Soccia, but first walk past a prominent tubular **cross** and drop down to a road-end **car park**. There is a café at this point, as well as donkey and pony rides offered back along the path to Lavu a Crena.

Follow the road round a **bend**, then go through a **metal gate** on the right. A clear, but steep and rather gritty path descends among scrub and chestnut trees. Keep a close eye on its course to land on a road end beside some houses at the top end of **Soccia**. Walk down the road in lazy loops, unless you later spot **flights of steps** shortcutting some of the bends. What few services exist in Soccia are either obvious from the road or are clearly signposted, and all are located within a few minutes of the **church**.

SOCCIA

Soccia has expanded, from its promontory position around its 15th-century church, up the hillside and down the valley, with lush gardens hung with grapevines. The church is open at certain times to allow visitors to view a fine triptych. Facilities in the village are few, but there is accommodation, food, drink and a post office. Most people who pass through the village are on their way to or from Lavu a Crena.

Accommodation The Hôtel U Paese, tel 04 95 28 31 92, is the only place offering lodgings in the village.

Food and Drink The Restaurant A Merendella is a wonderful garden restaurant in the old part of the village, and is one of the best within reach of the GR20. The Bar Restaurant Chez Louis provides drinks, but rarely offers even snack food, despite its name. The Hôtel U Paese has a bar, but the only meal available is breakfast. There are no shops, beyond a house selling goats' cheese just above the hotel, but blaring horns announce the arrival of visiting mobile shops.

Transport There is no longer a bus service to and from Soccia. The local taxi service is provided by Luc Canale, tel 04 95 26 64 02 or mobile 06 07 49 71 09 or 06 07 25 90 19. The nearest place with a bus service is Vico, where Autocars Ceccaldi, tel 04 95 21 38 06 or 04 95 21 01 24, links with Ajaccio all year round, except Sundays.

The village of Soccia was originally huddled on a promontory close to its 15th-century church.

STAGE 7

Refuge de Manganu to Refuge de Petra Piana

After yesterday's easy stage, there is another tough day's walk along the GR20. The path climbs through a valley to reach the highest point on the main route, the Brèche de Capitellu, at 2225m (7300ft). Views beyond the gap are magnificent, taking in the twin lakes of Lac de Capitellu and Lac du Melo. There are some awkward slabs, boulders, gullies and short scrambles to deal with as you make your way along the high ridges to reach another high gap called the Bocca Muzzella, also known as the Col de la Haute Route. After crossing the gap, simply walk down a stony slope to the Refuge de Petra Piana. Be warned that all water for the day should be carried, as there is little along the way apart from seasonal streams. Also bear in mind that snow can lie late into the summer on the higher slopes.

Distance 10km (6 miles)
Total Ascent 980m (3220 feet)
Total Descent 740m (2430 feet)
Time 7 hours
Map IGN 4251 OT
Terrain Steep and rocky mountainsides, with some rocky stretches and gullies requiring scrambling. This is the highest part of the GR20 main route and some slopes can hold snow well into the summer.
Shelter There is hardly any tree cover on this section, and the mountain ridges are particularly exposed to sun, wind and rain.
Food and Drink Apart from the river above the Refuge de Manganu, there is no reliable supply of water on the route until the Refuge de Petra Piana.

Leave the **Refuge de Manganu** by crossing the footbridge and turning right. The path running upstream is not too steep at the start of the day, though it is **rough and stony**. The ground

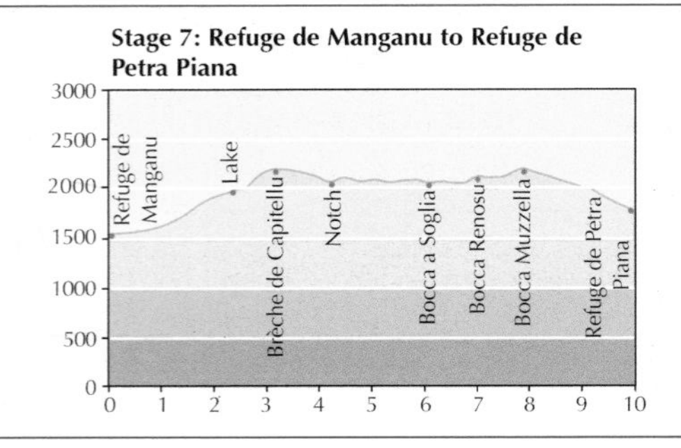

is often wet enough to support butterworts. The path climbs up a steep and bouldery slope to pass a fine **waterfall**. Climb over **bare rock** for a while to reach a fine, level, grassy patch. There is a good view around the head of the valley, displaying ominously spiky peaks of rock. There is another **waterfall** and more grassy areas with butterworts. Climb a little more to reach a wider area of grass at 1783m (5850ft).

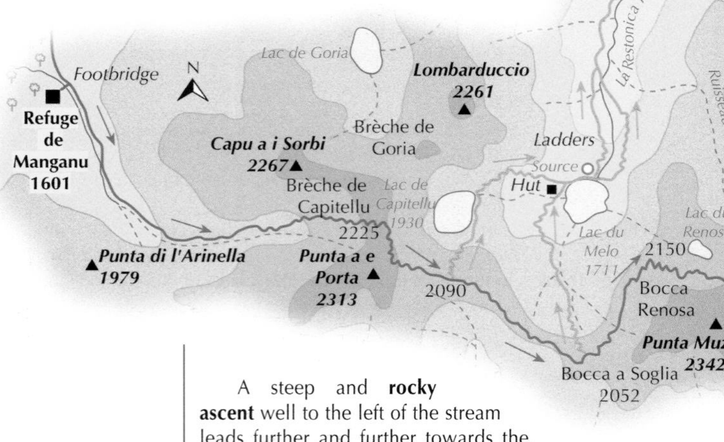

A steep and **rocky ascent** well to the left of the stream leads further and further towards the rugged head of the valley. From here look

Looking down on Lac de Capitellu and Lac du Melo from the rocky slopes below the Brèche de Capitellu.

down into narrow, **rocky gorges** containing small waterfalls and cascades, as well as at the jagged Crête de Rinella and the towering peaks and pinnacles of Capu a i Sorbi and Punta a e Porta. The path levels out for a while in a narrow grassy area flanked by alder scrub, and a **tiny lake** is visible off to the right at 1969m (6460ft).

As the path begins to steepen again, it becomes quite stony and bouldery, and walkers have to grapple with a heap of **huge boulders**, and pick their way across some slabs of rock to reach a narrow rocky gap called the **Brèche de Capitellu,** at an altitude of 2225m (7300ft). This is the highest point reached on the main route of the GR20, and it is possible for snow to lie well into the summer in gullies on both sides of the gap. The *brèche* should be reached about 3 hours after starting this day's walk. ▶

The view from the gap is one of the best, taking in steep and rocky slopes on both sides, with rocky pinnacles soaring skywards.

From here onwards, walkers' attention is often drawn to two deep blue lakes far below the rugged peaks. **Lac de Capitellu** and **Lac du Melo** lie in rocky hollows so steep

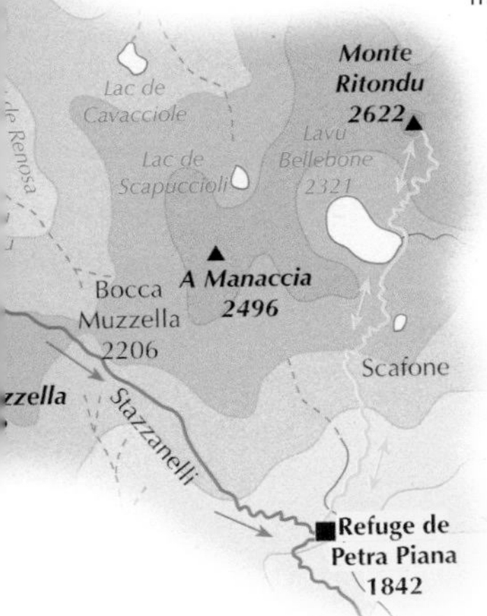

and rugged that they look like craters. Monte Ritondu rises beyond, with Monte d'Oru also prominent. Quite a few people may be milling about the lakes, having climbed from a car park at the head of the Restonica valley.

Leave the **Brèche de Capitellu** and turn right to cut across the steep and rocky slopes of **Punta a e Porta**. Be warned that the slope can hold a considerable amount of snow into the summer, either on the open slopes or tucked away in gullies. Walkers have to grapple with rocky slabs, boulders and awkward **steep gullies** as the route cuts across the mountainside. While scrambling down one gully you'll notice that the rock has been bolted, but there are no cables or chains to hang on to. A **rocky notch** is reached at around 2090m (6855ft), between towering pinnacles on the ridge, about ½ hour after leaving the Brèche de Capitellu. (Yellow paint marks indicate a way down to Corte, and a route down there is described in the next section.)

The GR20 cuts across to the southern side of the ridge, with views down into another deep and rugged valley. While traversing across the slope, walkers have to climb up and down, scrambling at times or following **rough and stony paths**. There is a stretch where it is possible to walk along the ridge for a while, enjoying a view of **Lac du Melo**, then the route cuts off to the right again, regaining the crest further along. The route follows a good stretch of the crest, then as it gets rockier, shifts to the flanks again.

Watch carefully as the route swings sharply round to the left, crossing the ridge, then follow the path down through alder scrub to reach the **Bocca a Soglia**, at 2052m (6732ft), about ¾ hour from the last major gap. There is a **junction of paths** just off the Bocca a Soglia. (A sign indicates another route flashed with yellow paint, leading down to Lac du Melo and the Bergeries de Grotelle, which is described in the next section.)

The GR20 climbs up a bouldery slope and is signposted for the Refuge de Petra Piana. The route involves clambering over **huge boulders** and pushing through dense alder scrub on the steep and rugged slopes of **Punta Muzzella**. The gradients are fairly gentle at first, but all of a sudden the path climbs steep and stony zigzags, verging on scrambling at times. This leads to the little gap of **Bocca Renosu,** at 2150m (7055ft), about 1¼ hours after leaving the Bocca a Soglia.

View of the little Lac du Renosu before crossing the Bocca Muzzella to descend to the Refuge de Petra Piana.

The path traverses a rocky, bouldery mountainside, but also passes through a delightful little grassy *pozzine* perched above the little **Lac du Renosu,** and within ½ hour crosses the **Bocca Muzzella**, which is more often called the Col de la Haute Route, at 2206m (7238ft). Take a break at this point and enjoy the view southwards, as most of the hard work is over and it's downhill all the way to the Refuge de Petra Piana. Looking northwards, Monte d'Oru and Monte Renosu are seen.

The path used for the descent slices across rough and stony slopes at **Stazzanelli**. Watch for the markers as they switch to the left across the mountain ridge. The path zigzags rough and stony down through alder scrub, where the ground is wet enough to support butterworts, and lands on a level area where the **Refuge de Petra Piana** has been built, at 1842m (6043ft). Walkers should reach the refuge an hour after leaving the Bocca Muzzella.

REFUGE DE PETRA PIANA

The PNRC Refuge de Petra Piana is a fairly small wooden structure, built in the chalet style, having a dormitory with 28 beds and a little kitchen/dining room. There is a bit of extra space in the roof, but not much. The building sits on quite a small base and it is held down with cables – be warned that it rocks a little bit in a strong wind! The *gardien* occupies a separate stone building nearby, where hot meals and supplies of food and drink can be bought. Another little building houses the toilet and shower. Water pours from the Funtana di Petra Piana, and there are some good level camping spaces around the refuge. The terrace looks along the length of the Manganellu valley to Monte d'Oru. Monte Ritondu is close to hand, though the summit cannot be seen. (If you are considering an ascent, see the last section before Stage 8 for details.)

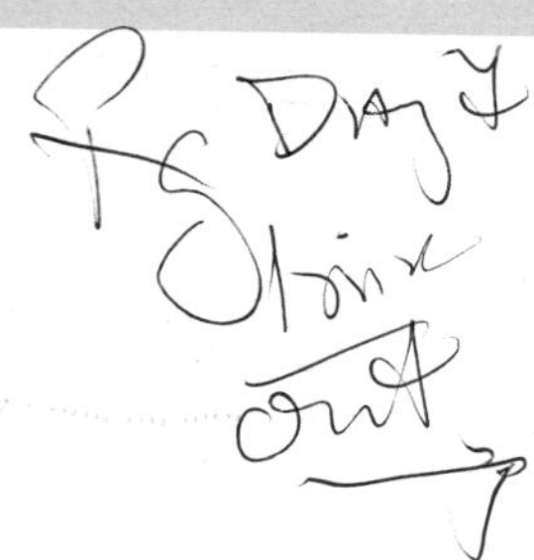

Link from Bocca a Soglia to Bergeries de Grotelle

Walkers who follow the GR20 above Lac de Capitellu and Lac du Melo will be aware of the deep, rock-walled cleft of the Restonica valley dropping steeply beyond. There are nearly always crowds of people in view around the lakes and this should alert walkers to the fact that there is a road nearby, even if it is hidden from sight. It is possible to leave the GR20, either to take a closer look at the lakes and enjoy food and drink at the Bergeries de Grotelle, or to catch a minibus down to the ancient mountain citadel of Corte. There are two roughly parallel routes available on this descent, with an option to switch from one to the other at the outflow from Lac du Melo. (See map on p.112.)

Distance	4km (2½ miles)
Total Ascent	20m (65 feet)
Total Descent	700m (2295 feet)
Time	2¼ hours
Map	IGN 4251 OT
Terrain	Steep and rocky slopes, with a choice between a rough and rocky series of paths, or a route involving a chain and metal ladders.
Shelter	The higher parts of the route are exposed to the sun, wind and rain, but there is more shelter in the valley and a little tree cover at the end.
Food and Drink	There is a water source near the outflow from Lac du Melo. A few of the Bergeries de Grotelle operate as small snack bars and restaurants.

There are two points at which walkers can leave the GR20 on this descent – one from a **rocky notch** at 2090m (6855ft) and the other from the **Bocca a Soglia** at 2052m (6732ft). The first route passes both Lac de Capitellu and Lac du Melo, while the second route passes only Lac du Melo. Continuing downhill, there are two more options to consider – one described as *plus sportif* and the other as *facile*. (Think of them as 'sporty' and 'easy'!) Walkers can switch from one route to the other at the outflow from Lac du Melo.

Descent from the Gap at 2090m

Leave the GR20 at a **rocky notch** between towering pinnacles, at around 2090m (6855ft). A route down a **gully** is clearly marked with the word 'Corte' painted on the rock, and abundant yellow flashes of paint. Scramble down **jammed boulders** to reach a gentle **grassy hollow**, then follow the paint flashes as they lead around a rocky lip holding **Lac de Capitellu** in place. Pause to admire the deep corrie lake, with its sheer granite headwall and rocky shore. The altitude is 1930m (6332ft), the water is 42m (138ft) deep, and it can be frozen for up to eight months in the year.

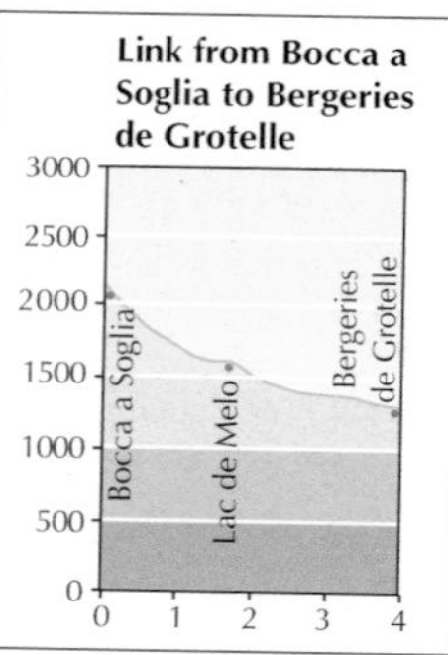

Continue steeply downhill, watching carefully for the yellow flashes that reveal easy scrambling routes down steep, **bare rock**, leading to stony, bouldery paths through alder scrub. The path passes close to a *PNRC gardien's* hut on the way to **Lac du Melo**. Keep to the left-hand side of the lake, following a path through alder scrub, to reach the **outflow**. The altitude is 1711m (5614ft), the water is 15.5m (51ft) deep, and it can be frozen for almost half the year.

Don't cross the outflow, but follow the yellow markers downstream, passing a small **water source**. When bare rock is reached, look for a **short chain** that helps on a steep part of the descent. (This is described as *plus sportif* on a sign later, but there is no indication of this given at the top of the route.) A zigzag path has been mortared in place, and this leads to a series of three short metal **ladders**, rather like fire escapes, that help on the next part of the descent.

Almost 30 steps are negotiated using the ladders, but there is still some walking down bare, unprotected **rock slabs**. Stony and bouldery paths are also followed through

The towering peak of Lombarduccio as seen from a level grassy space close to Lac du Melo.

alder scrub, then a clear path continues down through the valley. A small *bergerie* sells food and drink before the path reaches another *bergerie* operating as a snack bar at a car park at 1370m (4495ft).

Descent from Bocca a Soglia

The **Bocca a Soglia** lies at 2052m (6732ft) on the GR20 and there is a sign nearby indicating a route down to Lac du Melo and the Bergeries de Grotelle. The path is clearly marked with **yellow paint** flashes, and is initially steep and bouldery, passing through alder scrub to reach wide and gentle slopes of grass. A **small lake** will be noticed off to the right, though this is soon lost to view. Watch carefully for the markers, which indicate a path roughly aligned to a **small stream**.

The route crosses from side to side, but also crosses grassy areas and expanses of **bare granite**. Once there is a clear view of Lac du Melo, be sure to cross the stream before it flows down through a sheer, **rock-walled gorge**. The route later swings left to traverse **rock slabs**, then drops straight downhill onto level ground. Cross a grassy area near a PNRC *gardien*'s hut on the way to **Lac du Melo**. Keep to the left-hand side of the lake, following a path through alder scrub, to reach the **outflow**. The altitude is 1711m (5614ft), the water is 15.5m (51ft) deep, and it can be frozen for almost half the year.

Cross the **outflow** and follow yellow markers onwards, swinging left to continue the descent. (This is described as *facile* on a sign later, but there is no indication of this given at the top of the route.) A rough and **bouldery path** is hemmed in between sloping slabs and alder scrub. It needs care all the way down to the floor of the valley, where a **stream** is crossed. Keep right to follow a clear path down through the valley. A small *bergerie* sells food and drink before the path reaches another *bergerie* operating as a snack bar at a car park at 1370m (4495ft).

BERGERIES DE GROTELLE

The Bergeries de Grotelle is like a small, secret mountain village, where most of the buildings are tucked away behind boulders and outcrops of rock. A couple of them offer snacks and drinks, but one of them operates a small restaurant and offers very basic *gîte d'étape* accommodation, with a few camping spaces nearby. The D623 through the spectacular Gorges de la Restonica runs 15km (9½ miles) down to the ancient citadel of Corte. There is a *navette* service along the road in the summer, operated by Autocars Cortenais, tel 04 95 46 02 12. When this is not running, there are three taxis based in Corte: Michel Salviani, tel 04 95 46 04 88, mobile 06 03 49 15 24, Thérèse Feracci, mobile 06 12 10 60 60, or Corsica Taxi, tel 04 95 48 06 29, mobile 08 26 80 46 46. It is often possible to get a lift down to Corte simply by asking around the car park.

Ascent of Monte Ritondu from Refuge de Petra Piana

Monte Ritondu is the second highest mountain in Corsica, topped only by the mighty Monte Cinto. An ascent and descent is possible in a mere half-day from the Refuge de Petra Piana, and this is an option some walkers might want to consider, especially as the next stage of the GR20 is one of the easier stretches. Small cairns mark the usual line of ascent and paths can be rather vague in places. Be aware that there are other cairned routes that could lead to confusion on the slopes. Make the ascent in clear weather and leave the mountain well alone in rain, mist or wind. The latter parts of the climb to the summit involve scrambling on steep slabs and boulders, and the higher slopes can hold snow well into the summer. (See map on p.113.)

Distance	6km (3¾ miles) there and back
Total Ascent	850m (2790 feet)
Total Descent	850m (2790 feet)
Time	4½ hours there and back
Map	IGN 4251 OT
Terrain	Rough and rocky slopes, quite steep in many places, requiring some scrambling. It is important to look carefully for small cairns marking the route. The ascent is not recommended in poor visibility.
Shelter	The mountain slopes are very exposed to sun, wind and rain. There is a very basic hut on the summit.
Food and Drink	Take water and a little food from the Refuge de Petra Piana.

The **Refuge de Petra Piana** stands at 1842m (6043ft), which gives a fair leg-up onto Monte Ritondu. There is a **stream** just to the east of the refuge. Start this walk by fording it, then climb uphill through alder scrub and ford another **stream**. Look carefully, parallel to the stream, to spot a line of **small cairns** leading roughly northeast up a steep and **rocky slope**.

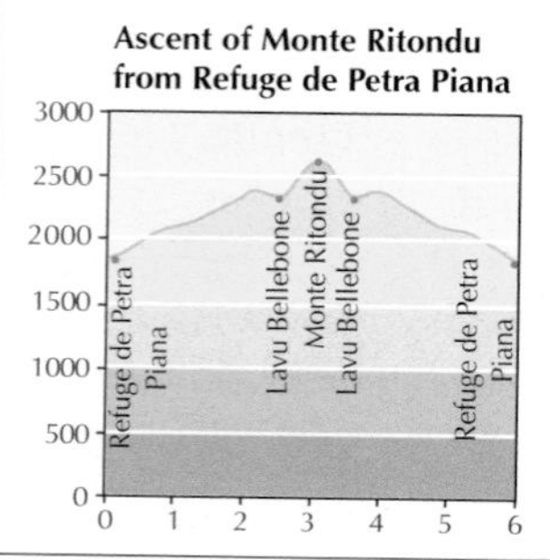

Climb uphill a short way, and look to the left higher up the slope to see a **grassy hollow** in the mountainside containing a level area of short grass, around 1950m (6400ft). This is a sheltered *pozzine* where animals may be grazing.

Keep an eye open for more **cairns** as the path crosses over some boulders, then climb steeply up a **blunt ridge** on the mountainside. Height is gained in a combination of stony zigzags and very short rocky scrambles. There are fine views of Monte d'Oru, its close neighbour Punta Migliarello, and the high-level route of the GR20 along the *crêtes,* for walkers interested in following that route. The Refuge de Petra Piana also looks quite interesting from this height – quite definitely a bird's-eye view.

The path slices across the mountainside to avoid rocky buttresses, then swings to the right to start climbing more steeply again. Scramble up a **gully** full of broken rock and boulders to reach a **narrow gap** at the top, around 2280m (7480ft). Walkers should reach this point an hour after leaving the refuge.

The view from the gap is startling, as Monte Ritondu is visible in all its glory, maybe streaked with snow as the high cirque can hold snow well into the summer. There are a couple of **tiny lakes** in the boulder-fields below, with attractive grassy areas nearby, but follow a cairned route off to the left, across and up a **bouldery slope**, to reach the larger **Lavu Bellebone**. This lake is frozen for most of the year, and is at an altitude of 2321m (7615ft). Spend a while admiring the lake and the rugged peaks and pinnacles clustered around the cirque, then focus your attention on Monte Ritondu.

Walk round the shore of **Lavu Bellebone**, crossing the outflowing stream, and study the steep and rugged slope rising above. There is a lot of **scree and boulders**, but look for cairns and pick a way up this slope to reach the gap called

Walking high above the Refuge de Petra Piana on the way to climb the mighty Monte Ritondu.

Seen at the beginning of June, ice covers Lavu Bellebone and Monte Ritondu holds considerable amounts of snow.

the **Col du Fer de Lance**, around 2490m (8170ft). The *lance* is the pinnacle of rock standing tall in the middle of the gap. Keep left of the *lance*, then start the final steep climb to the summit of Monte Ritondu. The slope is steep, bouldery and rocky, but can be climbed in a series of **easy scrambles**. Keep an eye peeled for the little cairns that steer walkers along the best line up the slope. The summit of **Monte Ritondu**, at an altitude of 2622m (8602ft), should be reached about 2¾ hours after leaving the refuge. A basic **hut** is available for shelter, wedged into a gap just below the summit.

The reward on reaching the summit is a wonderful view, taking in most of the major mountains running through the centre of Corsica. Spend a while trying to figure out the course of the GR20 around the prominent peaks of Monte Cinto and Paglia Orba, as well as ahead beyond Monte d'Oru and Monte Renosu. When ready to leave the summit, simply retrace your steps carefully to return to the Refuge de Petra Piana. Those who made the ascent early in the morning, and still feel fit, could continue along the GR20 to reach the Refuge de l'Onda. Others might prefer to have a relaxing afternoon rest.

STAGE 8

Refuge de Petra Piana to Refuge de l'Onda (low-level)

Here is a stage where walkers can relax and take things easy for a change. This low-level route is actually the main GR20 route, and the high-level route over the *crêtes* is the variant. There is a steep descent from the Refuge de Petra Piana, but this is followed by a gentle walk through a valley clothed in laricio pines, where walkers can enjoy the shade and maybe even take a dip in the river. At the Bergeries de Tolla there is an opportunity to indulge in basic Corsican food and drink, and stock up on supplies when you leave. An ascent through a valley full of beech trees demands a bit more effort on the way to the Refuge de l'Onda, especially for those who have eaten and drunk rather more than they should have at the Bergeries de Tolla!

Distance	11km (6¾ miles)
Total Ascent	500m (1640 feet)
Total Descent	910m (2985 feet)
Time	5 hours
Map	IGN 4251 OT
Terrain	Steep and rugged slopes at the start and finish, but relatively easy forest and woodland paths for most of the way.
Shelter	Shade is available in the forest and woodland along the way. This stretch is particularly well sheltered.
Food and Drink	The Bergeries de Gialgo offer cheese near the start. The Bergeries de Tolla provide food and drink low in the valley. Water can be drawn from rivers that flow all year, or from either of the *bergeries*. Food and drink can be bought from the Bergeries de l'Onda.

Leave the **Refuge de Petra Piana** by walking beyond the Funtana de Petra Piana, where a sign points the way to the Refuge de l'Onda. In fact, walkers have a choice of routes, indicated as 'Par la vallée' or 'Par les crêtes'. At a path junction, the main route is down to the left into the valley, while the high-level variant is off to the right, cutting across a rugged slope. (See the next section for details of the high-level route.)

The steep and rugged descent into the valley is along a **stony path** flanked by alder scrub. On reaching the **Bergeries de Gialgo**, turn left as marked. Walkers may stop here to buy cheese or fill up with water. The path continues its descent into the valley, but also cuts across the slope and crosses a couple of streambeds. After crossing the **Ravin de Monte Ritondu**, walk downstream to reach a more gently graded path running parallel to the **Ruisseau de Manganellu**. This is a bouldery river full of cascades and rock pools, where many walkers are tempted to take a dip. The route passes small, ruined **drystone buildings**, and the path is

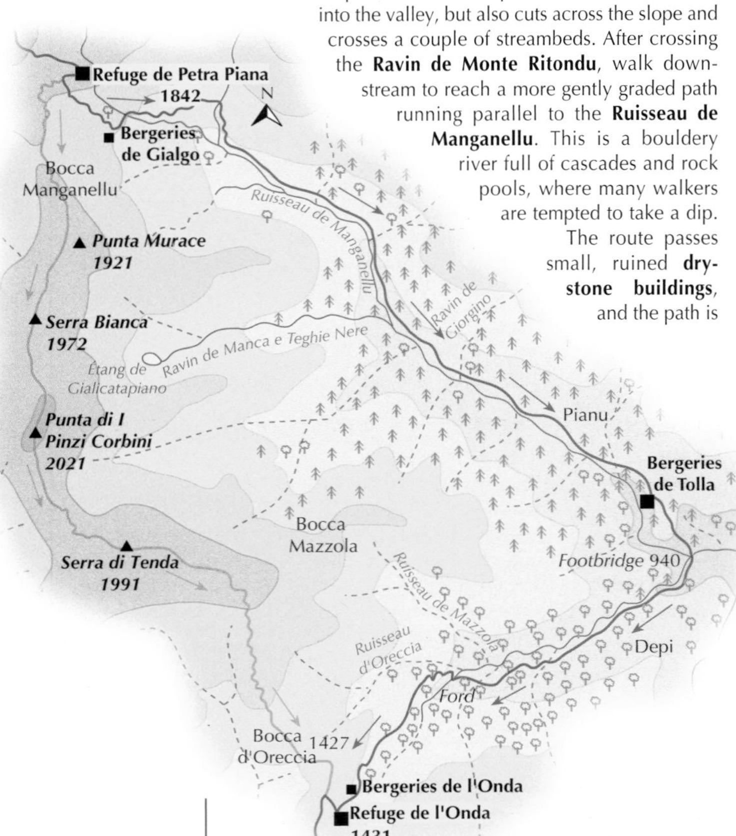

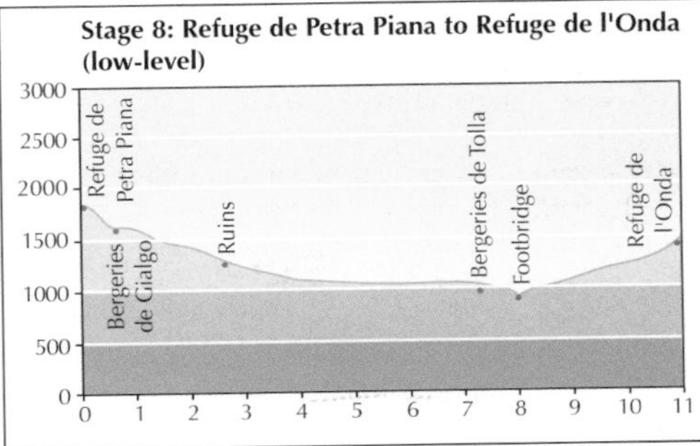

built up with stone on one side and quite clear to follow. Small pine trees give way to large laricio pines further down the valley. Although the path is **broad and stony** for most of the way through the forest, there are a couple of rugged breaks in its course and some parts are narrow. On hot days there is plenty of shade in the forest and several cool pools of water in the river. The path drifts away from the river from time to time, then does so rather more significantly to reach the **Bergeries de Tolla**. Walkers should reach the *bergeries*, situated around 1000m (3280ft), within three hours of leaving the Refuge de Petra Piana.

BERGERIES DE TOLLA

The Bergeries de Tolla are a huddle of low stone huts in a clearing surrounded by fences, with distant rocky peaks leading the eye towards Monte d'Oru. When the *bergeries* are occupied in the summer, food and drink are offered to passing walkers – either snacks with soft drinks or beer, or complete meals with wine, and there is an opportunity to stock up on food supplies in your pack. You may feel like dropping your pack and staying for the night, but there is no accommodation, nor is camping allowed. Make the most of the opportunity to eat and drink at the *bergeries*. (Walkers who need to leave the GR20 should refer to the section describing a link to the village of Tattone, found after Stage 8 (high-level).)

Walk past the lowest of the fenced enclosures on leaving the **Bergeries de Tolla**, and continue through sparsely planted pines and tall heather. A **stony path**, braided in

The Bergeries de Tolla provide wholesome, simple meals in a clearing in the forested Manganellu valley.

places, leads in just ¼ hour down to a footbridge called the **Passerelle de Tolla**, at 940m (3085ft). It spans the Ruisseau de Manganellu close to its confluence with the Ruisseau de Grottaccia. After heavy rain the water thunders though a rocky gorge, crashing over boulders. Climb a short way up a bouldery slope and reach a choice of signposted tracks.

The GR20 is marked off to the right above the Passerelle de Tolla. Don't be tempted to cross the footbridge over the **Ruisseau de Grottaccia**, but simply follow a stony track uphill roughly parallel to the river. Avoid the dirt road off to the left, which is the **Route Forestière de Manganellu**. ◀

Although there are still laricio pines present, beech trees dominate this valley. As a result, the path and the ground alongside are often pitted where pigs have been rooting for beechmast.

The **track** drifts away from the river as it climbs, then it becomes narrower and quite rugged in places. Fallen branches and leaf mould, as well as the activity of the pigs, conspire to obscure the way in places, so keep an eye peeled for the **paint flashes**.

The path drops down to ford the **Ruisseau de Grottaccia**, then zigzags up the other side and continues to trace the river roughly upstream. There is one tall stand of laricio pines in the beech wood, then a **clearing** where the Refuge de l'Onda can briefly be glimpsed at the head of the valley. The path wanders past more beech trees, then emerges on a rugged slope of bracken, juniper and spiny broom before reaching the **Bergeries de l'Onda**. Those who are camping should pitch their tent here, while those intending to stay at the **Refuge de l'Onda** should check first with the *gardien* at the *bergeries*, before following the path further uphill. A short, steep, rugged path leads up to the refuge, at 1431m (4695ft), which is reached about 1¾ hours after leaving the Passerelle de Tolla.

REFUGE DE L'ONDA

The PNRC Refuge de l'Onda is built in the *bergerie* style and surrounded by rocky mountains, with a view back down through the valley from its terrace. Its position is really only appreciated by those following the high-level variant over the *crêtes*. It is one of the smaller refuges, so the little 15-bed dormitory is quickly filled to capacity, and there can be a lot of pressure on the little kitchen/dining room. A shower and toilet are located alongside in a small building. The campsite is below the refuge, in a fenced enclosure next to the Bergeries de l'Onda, secure from the pigs and cattle that graze in the area. The campsite has its own toilet and shower block. The refuge *gardien* lives at the *bergeries*, where hot meals, as well as food and drink can be bought.

Looking down on the Refuge de l'Onda, where campers must stay down near the Bergeries de l'Onda.

STAGE 8

Refuge de Petra Piana to Refuge de l'Onda (high-level)

This high-level route is actually an alternative to the main route of the GR20. The main route stays low in the valleys between the Refuge de Petra Piana and the Refuge de l'Onda. Walkers who prefer to stay high will find that the route involves slightly less climbing and less distance, and can be completed in less time than the main route. Views are much more extensive, with Monte Ritondu and Monte d'Oru seen in all their glory. The drawback is that there is no opportunity to visit the Bergeries de Tolla deep in the valley, or to enjoy the food and drink offered there, nor is there a chance to enjoy a cool dip in the river. For those who enjoy the mountains and strive for the high places, however, this is the route to follow, which is fairly faithful to the crest of the mountains between the two refuges. (See map on p.126.)

Distance	8km (5 miles)
Total Ascent	390m (1280 feet)
Total Descent	800m (2625 feet)
Time	4¼ hours
Map	IGN 4251 OT
Terrain	Although the route is aligned to the mountain ridges between the two refuges, gradients are mostly gentle and the mountain slopes are easy to negotiate. There are some steep, rocky slopes requiring a bit of scrambling near the start and on the way to the Serra di Tenda.
Shelter	The route along the mountain ridges is exposed to sun, wind and rain, and is not recommended in misty or wet conditions.
Food and Drink	None available on this route. Take food and water from the Refuge de Petra Piana. Food and drink can be bought from the Bergeries de l'Onda.

Leave the **Refuge de Petra Piana** by walking beyond the Funtana de Petra Piana, where a sign points the way to the

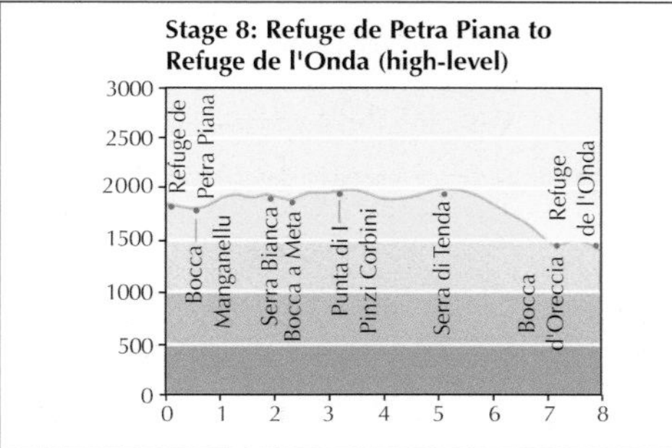

Refuge de l'Onda. In fact, walkers have a choice of routes, indicated as 'Par la vallée' or 'Par les crêtes'. At a path junction, the main route is down to the left into the valley, while the high-level variant is off to the right, cutting across a rugged slope. (See the previous section for details of the low-level route.)

The high-level route is flashed with **yellow paint** and includes a bit of scrambling as it cuts across a steep and rocky slope covered in alder scrub. A gentler path continues to a gap called the **Bocca Manganellu**, and a sign is passed indicating a path off-route to the village of Guagno. Follow the path marked in yellow as it climbs uphill, and turn round from time to time to enjoy the mountain scenery behind. The Refuge de Petra Piana is in view, perched on its rocky ledge on the mountainside. **Rocky stairways** and sharp arêtes are negotiated, then the path becomes quite easy as it slices across the higher, grassy slopes. Skirt the summit of **Punta Murace** at 1921m (6302ft) and reach a rounded summit on **Serra Bianca**, where there is a crude drystone windbreak shelter around 1970m (6465ft).

Look ahead along the crest to see other gentle summits. The one closest to hand is avoided as the path skirts around its eastern slopes. After climbing steadily up a **stony ridge** towards the two summits of **Punta di I Pinzi Corbini**, the path crosses only the first summit. As the route continues along a ridge of broken rock, the yellow markers shift to the left and narrowly miss the 2021m (6631ft) summit. A rather battered and broken path leads down a rocky slope to reach the **Bocca a Meta** at 1890m (6200ft).

Looking back along the stony ridge path that traverses the crêtes on the slopes of Punta Murace.

Watch carefully for the yellow flashes as the path drifts left from the gap and starts cutting across steep and rocky slopes on the Serra di Tenda. The route includes **short scrambles**, and walkers may have to grapple with the alder scrub where it presses in on the path. Swing gradually to the right and climb steeply uphill to reach a **rocky notch** on the crest of the Serra di Tenda. While crossing this notch, turn left and scramble only a short way to reach an **easy path**.

Follow the path parallel to the crest, narrowly missing the 1991m (6532ft) summit of **Serra di Tenda**. The high slopes are grassy, but also feature spiny broom and juniper. As the path starts to descend it becomes more and more rugged, passing boulders and low outcrops of rock. There is a fine view of Monte d'Oru, and the tiny shape of the Refuge de l'Onda is visible, tucked into a wooded hollow on its slopes. By the time the path leads down to the **Bocca d'Oreccia**, at an altitude of 1427m (4682ft), the refuge is out of sight and Monte d'Oru's slopes look lumpy and less interesting.

Follow a narrow path uphill from the gap to reach a minor **ridge**, then turn right to climb a short way along the crest. A **narrow path** on the left is signposted for the refuge, and a gentle descent across a rugged slope leads quickly to the **Refuge de l'Onda** at 1431m (4695ft). Those who are camping need to continue downhill to reach a fenced enclosure near the **Bergeries de l'Onda**.

REFUGE DE L'ONDA

The PNRC Refuge de l'Onda is built in the *bergerie* style and surrounded by rocky mountains, with a view back down through the valley from its terrace. Its position is really only appreciated by those following the high-level variant over the *crêtes*. It is one of the smaller refuges, so the little 15-bed dormitory is quickly filled to capacity, and there can be a lot of pressure on the little kitchen/dining room. A shower and toilet are located alongside in a small building. The campsite is below the refuge, in a fenced enclosure next to the Bergeries de l'Onda, secure from the pigs and cattle that graze in the area. The campsite has its own toilet and shower block. The refuge *gardien* lives at the *bergeries*, where hot meals, as well as food and drink can be bought.

Walkers drop steeply downhill from the crêtes to the Bocca d'Oreccia on their way to the Refuge de l'Onda.

Link from Bergeries de Tolla to Tattone

This is a simple link from the GR20 main route, near the Bergeries de Tolla, to the little village of Tattone. Walkers who find themselves running out of time, or lack the energy needed to cross over the mountains to Vizzavona, can bail out by completing a simple valley walk. The footbridge, the Passerelle de Tolla, is one of the lowest points on the GR20, and from there a riverside path and forest track lead to the hamlet of Canaglia. A simple road walk continues onwards, either to the little village of Tattone, or to Savaggio. This link offers the chance to find a couple of campsites and a basic *gîte d'étape*, as well as food and drink, bus and train services.

Distance	9km (5½ miles)
Total Ascent	110m (360 feet)
Total Descent	310m (1015 feet)
Time	3 hours
Map	IGN 4251 OT
Terrain	The forested riverside path can be easy or rugged in places, though a dirt road running parallel could be used instead. A tarmac road leads from Canaglia to Tattone.
Shelter	There is good shelter in the valley among the trees.
Food and Drink	There is a small restaurant and a water source at Canaglia.

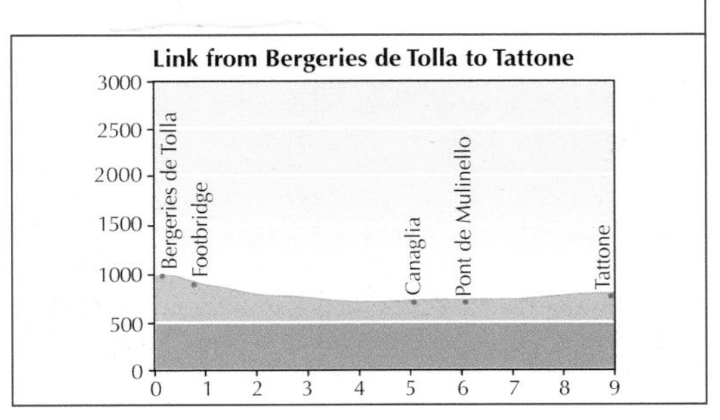

Leave the **Bergeries de Tolla** by walking past the lowest of its fenced enclosures and continue down through sparsely planted pines and tall heather. A **stony path**, braided in places, leads in just ¼ hour down to a footbridge called the **Passerelle de Tolla**, at 940m (3085ft). It spans the **Ruisseau de Manganellu** close to its confluence with the Ruisseau de Grottaccia. After heavy rain, the water thunders though a rocky gorge, crashing over boulders.

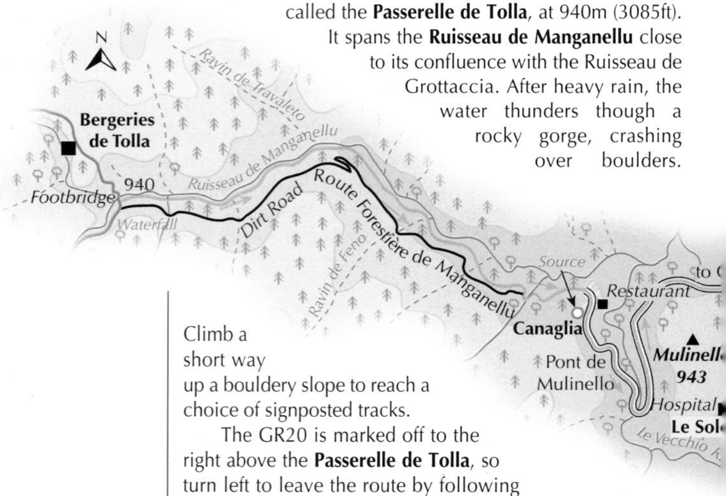

Climb a short way up a bouldery slope to reach a choice of signposted tracks.

The GR20 is marked off to the right above the **Passerelle de Tolla**, so turn left to leave the route by following the riverside path downstream. (**Note** that there is a dirt road running through the forest, just a short way uphill, called the Route Forestière de Manganellu. If you need the easiest exit, then follow the dirt road.) The riverside path is flashed with **orange paint** and is a variant route of the Mare a Mare Nord. Walk among tall laricio pines and cross a concrete bridge over a stream featuring a slender waterfall called the **Cascade du Meli**.

The broad but rough and rocky path descends alongside the rushing **Ruisseau de Manganellu**, where there are tall maritime and laricio pines, as well as an understorey of tall heather. On hot summer days almost every pool in the river will be full of bathers. The rugged path eventually leads onto **bare rock** close to the river, then links with an easier **track**. Follow this gently uphill past sapling pines, tall heather and even a solitary fig tree! The track joins the broader **Route Forestière de Manganellu**, then crosses a concrete bridge over a bouldery stream. Follow the track into **Canaglia**, to link with a tarmac road.

CANAGLIA

The little hamlet of Canaglia boasts a fine little bar–restaurant, the Osteria U Capitan Moru. There is a water source across the road. The nearest taxi is in Vivario, so if you want to avoid the onward road walk call Taxi Alain, tel 04 95 47 23 17. However, if you intend staying overnight at Tattone, then check if a *navette* service is available from your accommodation provider, as some of them will collect walkers from Canaglia.

Follow the D23 away from **Canaglia**, overlooking a well-wooded valley. Cross the **Pont de Mulinello** over a bouldery river and continue along the road, which later climbs gently uphill. Watch out for signs on the left, where you have a choice of two destinations – Savaggio or Tattone.

To reach Savaggio, turn left down a **track**, passing chestnut trees and tall pines. Cross a **footbridge** over a stream, then walk up a path flanked by bracken and stone walls. Turn right along the railway line to reach the tiny station/halt at **Savaggio**.

SAVAGGIO

Camping Savaggio, tel 04 95 47 22 14, offers a choice of accommodation, from a campsite to basic *gîte d'étape*. Food and drink are also available. As the site is next to the railway and timetables are posted, it is easy to catch a train, but give a clear signal to the driver as this is a request stop.

Stay on the D23 if you wish to reach Tattone. The road is flanked by trees, then watch out for a sign on the right which points along a **track**. Cross over the railway line at the little station at **Tattone** to reach the campsite.

A mouth-watering menu is posted outside the Bergeries de Tolla during the summer months.

TATTONE

Bar Camping Le Soleil, tel 04 95 47 21 16, is a camping and caravan site with a snack bar and pizzeria. It is close to the railway station in Tattone, but if catching a train, give a clear signal to the driver as this is often treated as a request stop. Timetables can be studied at the station, or checked with CFC/SNCF, tel 04 95 46 00 97, 04 95 23 11 03, 04 95 32 80 61 or 04 95 65 00 61. Anyone heading into the village of Tattone, which is on the nearby N193, can stay at the Refuge Chez Pierrot, which has 18 beds, tel 04 95 47 20 65, 04 95 47 22 28, or mobile 06 14 66 42 20. The main road is served by Eurocorse Voyages bus services, running daily except Sundays, between Bastia and Ajaccio, tel 04 95 21 06 30 14, 04 95 31 73 76 or 04 95 70 13 83.

STAGE 9

Refuge de l'Onda to Vizzavona (low-level)

This stage of the GR20 looks relatively straightforward on the map, climbing uphill along a ridge after leaving the Refuge de l'Onda, then wandering down through a valley to reach the village of Vizzavona. It is a bit more difficult in practice, as the ascent is unremitting, and the descent through the valley is likely to take longer than imagined. However, take things at a steady pace, enjoying the views and relishing the prospects of abundant food and drink around Vizzavona, and it is a wonderful stage. Some walkers might be interested to add a bit of height to the day's walk by climbing to the summit of Monte d'Oru. (See the next section for details of the high-level route.)

Distance	11km (6¾ miles)
Total Ascent	670m (2200 feet)
Total Descent	1180m (3870 feet)
Time	6 hours
Map	IGN 4251 OT
Terrain	A steep and stony ascent to a gap is followed by a long and gradual descent through a valley. Although steep and rocky at first, the gradients ease throughout the descent. The lower slopes of the valley are forested, and a series of easier paths and tracks lead to Vizzavona.
Shelter	There is little shelter at first on this stage. The mountain slopes are quite open and there is little shade from the sun, wind or rain, though there is good forest cover towards the end.
Food and Drink	Water is generally available from streams on the descent through the valley. There is a snack bar at the Cascade des Anglais. Vizzavona has restaurants and bars and offers the chance to stock up on all kinds of food supplies.

Leave the **Refuge de l'Onda** by following the path signposted for Vizzavona, rising gently across a rugged slope to reach a **blunt ridge**. A boulder on the ridge also carries a sign for Vizzavona – turn left here to start climbing uphill. The **stony**

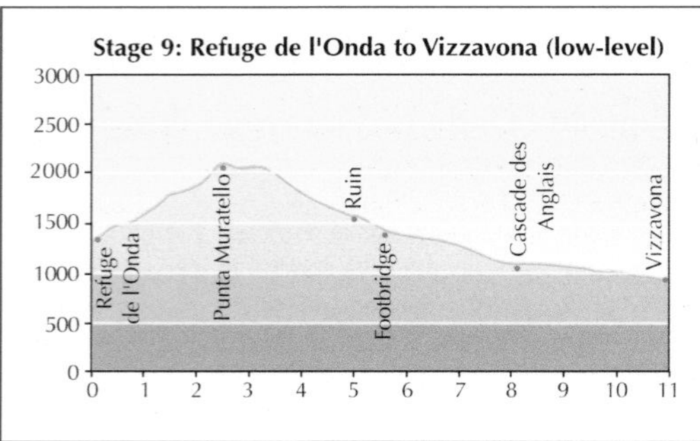

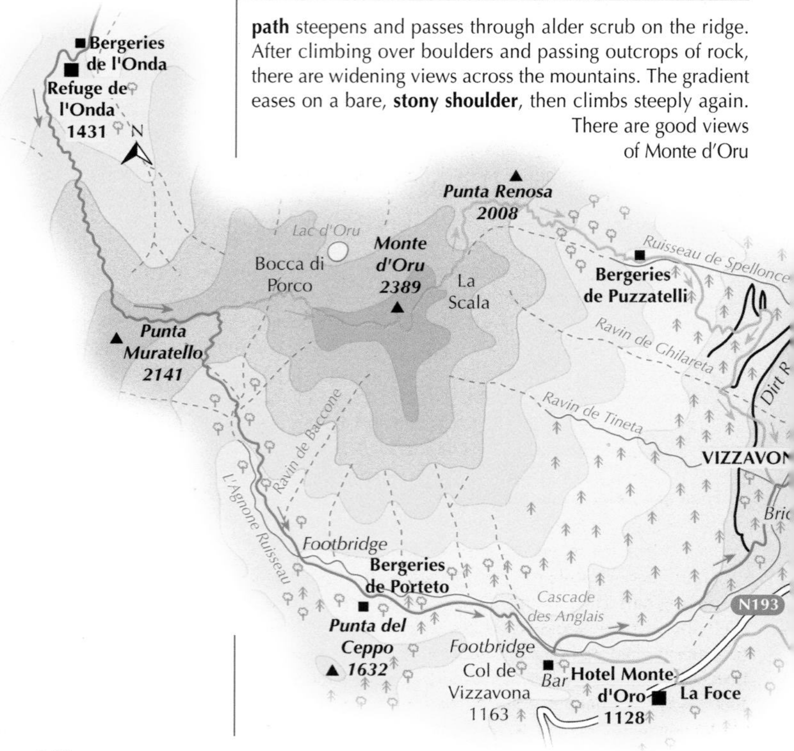

path steepens and passes through alder scrub on the ridge. After climbing over boulders and passing outcrops of rock, there are widening views across the mountains. The gradient eases on a bare, **stony shoulder**, then climbs steeply again. There are good views of Monte d'Oru and Punta Migliarello ahead. The path is generally on the ridge, but later it swings off to the right and goes through a **rocky notch**. Walk over boulders and bare rock and swing back onto the ridge, and almost immediately the path crosses the main crest near **Punta Muratello**, at an altitude of around 2100m (6890ft). This point should be reached 2½ hours after leaving the Refuge de l'Onda.

Continue following the red and white flashes of the GR20 down a rough and stony path zigzagging down from the crest. The route cuts across a couple of **bare slabs**, then the markers suddenly swing round to the right. At this point there is the option of following yellow paint marks and small cairns off to the left to climb Monte d'Oru (see the next section for details).

Staying on the main route, however, the path zigzags downhill and is quite rocky in places, but any **bare rock** encountered is usually gently sloping, and there is no real scrambling to do. Between areas of bare rock there are patches of alder scrub to squeeze through. After crossing over a couple of seasonal **streams**, follow a bouldery path down past slender sycamore and mountain ash. The trail drifts to the left across more bare rock and crosses a **larger stream**.

The sycamore trees offer shade as the rugged path continues downhill. After crossing another stretch of bare rock to reach a tumbled **ruined building**, walkers might like to detour a little to the right to look at a slender **waterfall** plunging into a deep and rocky gorge. Back on the trail, a **bouldery path** leads into denser woodlands dominated by beech trees. There is an open area where walkers cross a small footbridge, called the **Passerelle de Porteto**, spanning a narrow gorge full of fine waterfalls.

Leaving the footbridge, the route seems to be a fairly easy **woodland path**, descending across gently sloping **bare rock** in little clearings. The river off to the left, the **l'Agnone Ruisseau**, is full of waterfalls and lovely rock pools. The woods are a mixture of laricio pines and beeches, and there may be pigs rooting around for food. It all seems very easy, and you may think it is going to be like this all the way to Vizzavona. In fact, there are some **steep and**

Tiny walkers cross rock slabs on the way down towards l'Agnone Ruisseau, with Monte d'Oru towering above.

bouldery sections to negotiate, but they are quite limited, and an easy path continues alongside the **Cascade des Anglais**. Walk onto convenient rocky stances to admire the falls, and maybe enjoy a dip in one of the pools.

The path squeezes between some enormous boulders and a sign announces **La Cascade Bar** ahead. The wooden bar is tucked away behind a boulder almost as big as it, and so is not visible until the last possible moment. Walkers can take a break here for a snack and drink, at an altitude of 1092m (3582ft). It will probably take 2½ hours to descend through the valley from the Punta Muratello to the bar. There is a choice at this point, depending on where you want to stay for the night. Either follow the main route onwards to reach **Vizzavona**, which is what most walkers do, or take a shortcut to the **Hôtel Monte d'Oro**.

Shortcut to the Hôtel Monte d'Oro

The shortcut simply involves following a **clear track** away from La Cascade Bar, keeping to the right among tall laricio pines and beech trees, to reach the main **N193**. A right turn leads quickly to the **Hôtel Monte d'Oro**, only ¼ hour after leaving the bar. The hotel stands at an altitude of 1150m (3770ft), and so has a distinct height advantage over nearby Vizzavona. (If you take this route, refer to the section at the end of Stage 10 describing the link from the Hôtel Monte d'Oro to the Bocca Palmento to rejoin the main course of the GR20.)

The main GR20 route to Vizzavona leaves **La Cascade Bar** and crosses a **footbridge** over the river. A broad forest path becomes narrower, then broadens again when it reaches a couple of **wooden benches**. Follow the track gently downhill, and at a **junction of tracks** walk straight onwards to continue gently downhill in easy loops. The forest is very mixed in this area.

At a point where tracks cross each other, a **signpost** points left for Vizzavona. Follow the track down towards a **bridge**, but don't cross over it. Instead, turn right and follow a **path** downhill, as signposted again for Vizzavona. Cross a **footbridge** over a bouldery river. After the path makes a loop around a spur in beech woods, turn left to cross another footbridge over the **Ruisseau de Fulminato**. A woodland track leads to **Vizzavona**, becoming surfaced with tarmac as it reaches the village. Turn left to walk down into the village to avail of all its facilities. The altitude of Vizzavona is 920m (3020ft).

STAGE 9

Refuge de l'Onda to Vizzavona (high-level)

Monte d'Oru dominates the course of the GR20 for quite a few days, and walkers have a good view of the mountain as they cross the gap between the Refuge de l'Onda and Vizzavona. The ridge leading to the summit looks fairly straightforward, but there are some very steep and rocky parts that involve scrambling. Beyond the rocky parts of the ridge is more scrambling to the summit. The descent from the mountain is quite long, steep, rough and rocky in places, though there are easier forest paths and tracks on the lower slopes. For walkers who wish to follow the GR20 only as far as Vizzavona, the ascent of Monte d'Oru is a splendid climax, with magnificent views on a clear day. (See map p.140.)

Distance 13km (8 miles)
Total Ascent 990m (3250 feet)
Total Descent 1500m (4920 feet)
Time 7½ hours
Map IGN 4251 OT
Terrain A steep and stony ascent to a gap is followed by a traverse across a rugged mountainside. There are rocky stretches that need to be scrambled across on the way to and from the summit of Monte d'Oru. The descent is long, often following a zigzag path that can be steep and rocky in places. The lower slopes of the mountain are forested, and a series of easier paths and tracks leads to Vizzavona. The ascent is not recommended in misty, wet or windy conditions.
Shelter There is very little shelter on this stage. The mountain slopes are quite open, and there is little shade from the sun or shelter from wind and rain, though there is good forest cover towards the end.
Food and Drink Water is generally available only on the descent from Monte d'Oru, down in the forest. Vizzavona has a couple of restaurants and bars, and offers the opportunity to stock up on all kinds of food supplies.

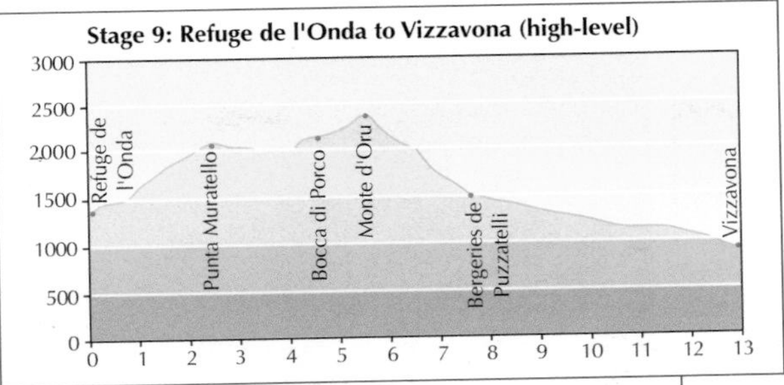

Leave the **Refuge de l'Onda** by following the path signposted for Vizzavona, rising gently across a rugged slope to reach a **blunt ridge**. A boulder on the ridge also carries a sign for Vizzavona – turn left here to start climbing uphill. The **stony path** steepens and passes through alder scrub on the ridge. After climbing over boulders and passing outcrops of rock, walkers gain widening views across the mountains.

The gradient eases on a bare, **stony shoulder**, then climbs steeply again. There are good views of Monte d'Oru and Punta Migliarello ahead. The path is generally on the ridge, but later it swings off to the right and goes through a **rocky notch**. Walk over boulders and bare rock and swing back onto the ridge, and almost immediately the path crosses the main crest near **Punta Muratello**, at an altitude of around 2100m (6890ft). This point should be reached 2½ hours after leaving the Refuge de l'Onda.

Continue following the red and white flashes of the GR20 down a rough and **stony path** zigzagging down from the crest. The path cuts across a couple of **bare slabs**, then the markers suddenly swing round to the right. At this point, head off to the left, following **yellow paint marks** and small cairns marking the way to Monte d'Oru.

The path contours across the mountainside, heading roughly eastwards. A short scramble and a **stony path** lead up to the crest near the **Bocca di Porco**, around 2160m (7085ft). Follow the stony path as it zigzags close to the crest, then **scramble** over a rocky part of the crest, watching carefully for the small cairns and yellow marks. The rocky summit of Monte d'Oru towers above, while the little **Lac d'Oru** is visible far below. The route clings to the ridge, then

The final rocky peak of Monte d'Oru is accessed by a series of steep and rocky little scrambles.

yellow markers reveal that it cuts beneath an awesome rocky face, before leading up a **shallow gully** of upended rocks. A **boulder** painted with the words 'Muratello' and 'Oro' is reached. You could leave excess baggage here while making a summit bid.

Climb up a **steep and bouldery slope**, with the rocky peak of the mountain above. The markers and cairns lead to the left of the peak, where a final series of **short scrambles** leads to the rocky summit of **Monte d'Oru** at 2389m (7838ft). It takes around 1½ hours to reach the summit from the crest near Punta Muratello. The view stretches back along the GR20 to Monte Ritondu and Monte Cinto, as well as ahead to Monte Renosu and Monte Alcudina.

Double back along the last series of short scrambles to return down the bouldery slope to the **painted boulder**, then watch carefully for the yellow marks leading off to the left across stony and **bouldery slopes** on the eastern side of the mountain. The path zigzags a little, then reaches gentler **grassy slopes** dominated by a towering mass of rock. The path is funnelled into a bouldery, north-facing gully called **La Scala**. This can become a rather awkward trap if it is filled with snow, which can lie late into the summer. Unfortunately, there is no way to see if this is the case in advance.

On the descent of **La Scala**, it is generally best to keep to the right, near the foot of a cliff. Take care not to dislodge boulders on the way down. At the bottom, exit to the left, crossing boulders and walking through flowery alder scrub, where parsley fern is also common. Amazing pinnacles of rock tower high above and **huge boulders** litter the slopes below. The path zigzags down through alder scrub, crossing rocky areas where thrift grows, and a couple of seasonal streams, before entering an area of slender sycamore woodland. There are a couple of clearings in the trees, reached near the ruined **Bergeries de Puzzatelli**. Walkers should reach this point, around 1500m (4920ft), about 1½ hours after leaving the summit of Monte d'Oru.

The path leads down a series of **steep zigzags** into denser forest dominated at first by laricio pines. Juniper and tall heather scrub grows in the clearings. Keep an eye peeled for the yellow markers, which lead across a bouldery stream called the **Ruisseau de Spelloncellu**. There are beech trees in this area, though as the path leads away from the stream they give way to laricio and maritime pines. The path is quite broad, steep and stony in places, though it narrows and becomes a zigzag path leading down to a **forest track**.

Cross over this track and descend along another path to cut out a sweeping bend. Turn round a **hairpin bend** to rejoin the track, then walk down another path to join the **track** at a lower level. A signpost points back to Monte d'Oru. Turn right and follow the forest track gently downhill. Walkers get a glimpse of Vizzavona just before leaving the track at a **hairpin bend**, where there is another signpost pointing back to Monte d'Oru.

Cross bouldery **stepping stones** near a seasonal waterfall and follow a forest path, turning left as signposted for Vizzavona. The path leads downhill and crosses another **forest track**. The woodlands are quite mixed and the ground cover is a rampant tangle of shrubs and flowers. At the next forest track, turn right to cross a **bridge**, then turn immediately left down another **path** signposted for Vizzavona. Once again walkers find themselves following a path marked by the red and white flashes of the GR20. Cross a **footbridge** over a bouldery river. After the path makes a loop around a spur in beech woods, turn left to cross another footbridge over the **Ruisseau de Fulminato**. A woodland track leads to **Vizzavona**, becoming surfaced with tarmac as it reaches the village. Turn left to walk down into the village and avail of its facilities. The altitude of Vizzavona is 920m (3020ft).

A patch of snow lingers through the middle of July, near La Scala, while flowers seem to burst from a barren scree slope.

Vizzavona and the Midpoint of the GR20

There are all sorts of ways of looking at Vizzavona. For anyone walking all the way along the GR20, it is roughly the middle of the route, and a fine place for a break to take stock of progress so far. For those walking only the northern half of the route, this is the finishing point. Alternatively, some walkers choose to walk the southern half of the route from Conca to finish at Vizzavona, or again simply reach the village at the halfway stage and continue to Calenzana.

As the village is on bus and rail routes, it is possible to join at this point and simply start walking either north or south. It is a place of comings and goings, or simply a place to halt and rest, maybe stocking up on food, enjoying a hearty meal, or morosely licking wounds and wondering what to do next. It can be a very busy place when full of GR20 walkers

It is interesting to bear in mind that Vizzavona owes its origin to early 19th-century English aristocrats, who came in such numbers that the Grand Hôtel de la Forêt (now in ruins) had to be built to accommodate them in style. The idea for the provision of a railway dates from 1870, although it wasn't developed until 1878. The construction of the railway was a daunting project, needing 43 important tunnels, 76 bridges and viaducts, as well as carefully engineered gradients, embankments and cuttings. Not only had natural obstacles to be overcome, but also the objections of landowners.

The line from Bastia to Corte opened in 1888. The link from Ponte Leccia to Calvi was opened in 1893. The line was extended from Corte to Vizzavona in 1894, and finally taken from Vizzavona through a 4km (2½ miles) tunnel to Ajaccio by 1898. It was at this station that one of the most famous of Corsican bandits, Antoine Bellacoscia, finally surrendered to the *gendarmerie*.

Those intending to take a break at Vizzavona might find themselves getting a bit restless after a few hours. If a short stroll appeals, then there are a couple of waymarked options. The Sentier des Cascades leads in an easy loop through the forest between Vizzavona and the Cascade des Anglais. Part of this loop is also followed by the GR20. The *cascades* were named after the English aristocrats who made them popular, seeking more adventurous tours away from the Côte d'Azur.

In the other direction the Sentier Archaéologique leads to an interesting cave structure formed beneath immense wedged boulders. With a bit of imagination, coupled with a perusal of the notes on an information board, you can envisage Neolithic hunter-gatherers residing at the very heart of Corsica 7000 years ago. In the summer they would have lived here and sought game in the forests, then walked down to the coasts for the winter months. The site was excavated by an Englishman called Charles Forsyth Major, and named l'Abri Southwell after a friend who used to accompany him on his tours around Corsica.

The mountain citadel town of Corte was once the capital of Corsica, and it remains a place of Corsican culture.

Walkers who want a bit of a break from the GR20 altogether, and a chance to take on board a good slice of Corsican culture, should get a train to Corte for the day. This ancient citadel town was once the capital of Corsica, and remains as a place of faded grandeur and power at the very heart of the island. Corte has a full range of services and is a stronghold of Corsican language and culture.

Accommodation Although there is only a small range of accommodation in Vizzavona, there are plenty of beds to suit all pockets. There is a free basic campsite available, along the railway line and off to the right, but ask first at the Restaurant du Chef de Gare. Showers are in the station building. Just across the road from the station, the Bar Restaurant de la Gare, tel. 04 95 47 22 20, operates a refuge with 32 beds. Just uphill from the station is the Hôtel Restaurant I Laricci, tel. 04 95 47 21 12, offering 12 rooms in the hotel or 14 beds in a separate *dortoir*. There is a full meal service and a laundry. Just above Vizzavona, off the main road in the direction of Corte, is the Casa Alta Chambres d'Hôte, tel. 04 95 47 21 09, which has 5 rooms. Further along the main road in the direction of Ajaccio is the Hôtel Monte d'Oro, tel. 04 95 47 21 06, a splendid old building with 45 rooms full of antique furniture and wooden panels. Here you can enjoy a high level of comfort, full meal service and laundry away from the bustle of the village. A 28-bed *gîte d'étape* and refuge accommodation is also offered. The hotel operates a *navette* service and will transport walkers to and from Vizzavona.

Food and Drink Places to eat and drink in Vizzavona include the Hôtel I Laricci, the Restaurant du Chef de Gare beside the station and Bar Restaurant de la Gare opposite the station. Outside the village at La Foce, the Hôtel Monte d'Oro and a restaurant called A Muntagnera are available. All these places offer extensive Corsican menus, and between them provide the widest choice of food and drinks since leaving Calenzana. If you simply wish to do your own thing and stock up with food, then the little *alimentation* in the station building is crammed full of provisions. If starting at Vizzavona, it shouldn't be necessary to carry much food away, as there are many places that provide basic foodstuffs north and south along the GR20.

Transport To get to or from Vizzavona, there are two options: Eurocorse Voyages operate bus services between Ajaccio and Bastia, passing Vizzavona all year round except Sundays. For timetable details, tel. 04 95 21 06 30 14, 04 95 31 73 76 or 04 95 70 13 83. Bear in mind that buses do not come down into the village, so you must stop them on the main road. The CFC/SNCF railway has immense appeal simply for its own sake, and links Vizzavona with Ajaccio, Bastia and Calvi. Timetables can be obtained from the little station, or tel. 04 95 46 00 97, 04 95 23 11 03, 04 95 32 80 61 or 04 95 65 00 61.

The Hôtel I Laricci is one of the few hotels on the GR20, and it also operates a more basic dortoir.

STAGE 10

Vizzavona to Bergeries d' E Capanelle

After the rigours of the northern part of the GR20, the southern stretch looks and feels somewhat gentler. Make no mistake, it is still a tough walk, but anyone who has come this far should have no problem finishing. You can leave Vizzavona with plenty of food inside you and a good selection of provisions in your pack. There is a long climb up a forested slope above the village, but gradients are fairly easy. Stony paths cut across rugged slopes, and there are some wonderful views ahead of Monte Renosu and its neighbouring peaks. There is a bit of a sting in the tail of the day's walk, when the path climbs up a steep and rugged woodland slope to cross over to the Bergeries d' E Capanelle, but then you can relax and enjoy good food and drink in the evening. Those who stay at the Hôtel Monte d'Oro can use an alternative variant route to rejoin the main course of the GR20 at Bocca Palmento. (See the next section for details.)

Distance	16km (10 miles)
Total Ascent	1000m (3280 feet)
Total Descent	335m (1100 feet)
Time	5½ hours
Map	IGN 4252 OT
Terrain	A forested ascent from Vizzavona is accomplished on well-graded paths. Other paths rise or fall gently, or simply contour across rugged forested slopes, though paths are more rugged towards the end.
Shelter	There is fairly good tree cover for most of the day, but some parts cross open slopes.
Food and Drink	There is a water source near Bocca Palmento and there are a couple of streams along the way. Meals and supplies of food and drink are available at the Bergeries d' E Capanelle.

On leaving **Vizzavona** follow the minor road uphill from the Hotel I Laricci. Turn left as signposted for the GR20 Sud and pass a little chapel dedicated to **Notre Dame de la Forêt**.

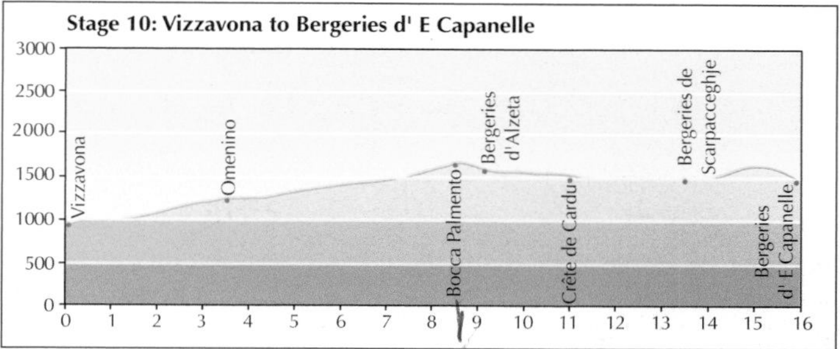

Follow the road across a **bridge**, then turn right to leave the road, again signposted for the GR20 Sud. A clear **rugged path** leads up a slope of beech trees and pines. Cross the main **N193** with care, as there is a bad bend and some cars travel too fast. Once across the road, turn left up a **track** signposted for the Refuge d' E Capanelle.

Follow the stony track uphill through the forest. There are tall laricio pines and beech trees, with a holly understorey. Turn left along a broader **forest road**, which is surfaced with concrete in a couple of places. The forest is predominantly pine, and there are glimpses through the trees to Monte d'Oru. Turn right as signposted for Capanelle, still following a broad and clear **forest track**. Later, a GR20 Sud signpost points left up a narrower, **stony path**.

The path zigzags up the slope of pines and is flanked by bracken and tall heather. It becomes narrower and passes a couple of **large boulders**. A clearing is reached, where the trees have been cut away to accommodate an overhead pylon line at 1200m (3935ft) at **Omenino**, then the route crosses a forest track where signs indicate the GR20 Nord and GR20 Sud. There is another good view of Monte d'Oru at this point.

As the path continues further uphill though the forest, the pines give way to beech trees, and the way rises gently or contours around a slope, leading almost to a **stream**. The path is evenly graded and can be covered quite quickly. Zigzags lead back towards the stream a couple more times, then the path leaves the woods and continues up a more **open slope**, passing patches of alder scrub. There is another fine view of Monte d'Oru. Watch out for the path crossing

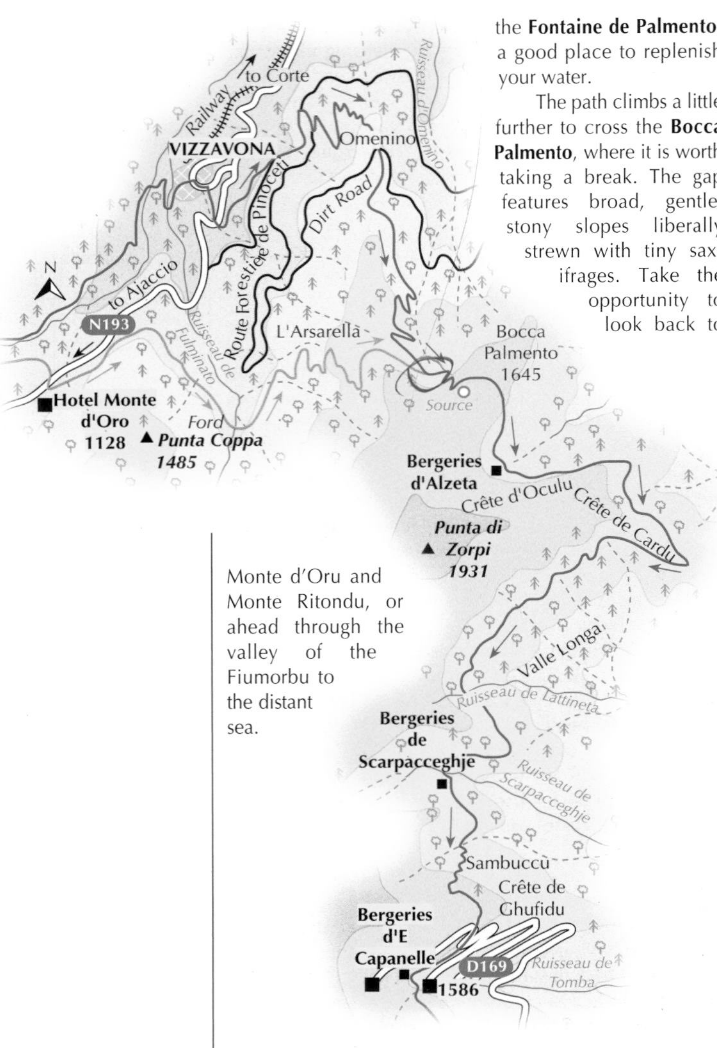

the **Fontaine de Palmento**, a good place to replenish your water.

The path climbs a little further to cross the **Bocca Palmento**, where it is worth taking a break. The gap features broad, gentle, stony slopes liberally strewn with tiny saxifrages. Take the opportunity to look back to Monte d'Oru and Monte Ritondu, or ahead through the valley of the Fiumorbu to the distant sea.

Walkers should reach the Bocca Palmento, at an altitude of 1645m (5400ft), about 2¾ hours after leaving Vizzavona.

The path swings to the right as it descends from the **Bocca Palmento**, and is quite rough and stony as it cuts across a slope of juniper to reach a patchy woodland of beech and alder. It then passes the picturesque **Bergeries d'Alzeta**, where there are often plenty of pigs foraging for food. Cross a **stream** just beyond the *bergeries* and continue following the path, roughly contouring across a slope covered in patchy beech woods. There is an open area sparsely clad with pines as the path turns around the ridge of the **Crête d'Oculu**.

The attractive Bergeries d'Alzeta crouch at the foot of an immensely tall beech tree below the Bocca Palmento.

Much of the GR20 is forested around Valle Longa, but there are glimpses of the mountains through the trees.

Continue walking through beech woods again, then, on reaching another area sparsely clad in pines on the **Crête de Cardu**, stop and admire the view. All of a sudden, Monte Renosu and neighbouring peaks are well displayed across the forested **Valle Longa**. Walkers should reach this point, at 1515m (4970ft), about an hour after leaving Bocca Palmento. There is a signpost pointing a way off-route to the village of Ghisoni.

Although the path continues to contour around the forested slopes, it is quite rough and stony underfoot. There are some blasted laricio pines at first, but later more beech trees appear where the path crosses a **stream**. Water is drawn off through a black plastic pipe, but even if the streambed is dry, there is water available at a bouldery cascade further along the path at the **Ruisseau de Lattineta**. This is a good place to enjoy the shade among bigger beech trees.

As the path continues around another **crest**, it again passes pines on the rugged slope where the ground is drier. Notice that the beeches re-establish themselves towards the next stream, where the route crosses the **Ruisseau de Scarpacceghje**. The path passes the **Bergeries de Scarpacceghje**, where a variety of interesting plants grow alongside.

Pass more laricio pines while swinging round into the next valley, and cross the **Ruisseau de Giargalozeo**. A signpost for the GR20 Sud points uphill to the right. Climb up a **bouldery slope** covered in beech trees, which is fairly short, but can be difficult underfoot. There is good shade, and in fact it is so shady that hardly anything grows on the ground, which is littered with leaf mould, fallen branches, toppled trees and stones.

Zigzags ease the gradient a little, then the path becomes easier and drifts more to the left. After it swings to the right on the shoulder of the **Crête de Ghufidu**, it hits a hairpin bend on a road at 1630m (5350ft). Walk gently uphill a short way along the road, then head off to the left as signposted for the Bergeries d' E Capanelle (unless you want to stay on the road for a few minutes to reach the Gîte d'Étape U Renosu).

Follow a **rugged path** gently downhill on a slope sparsely covered in beech trees. By following the markers exactly, you will be led to the **Refuge d' E Capanelle** before swinging left down to the **Gîte d'Étape U Fugone**. The temptation, of course, is to shortcut straight down to U Fugone, at 1586m (5303ft). Walkers should reach it 1¾ hours after leaving the Crête de Cardu.

BERGERIES D' E CAPANELLE

The Bergeries d' E Capanelle have been transformed over the years. Originally there was nothing more than a huddle of stone huts, and a few of these remain, but the area was developed as a ski-station with access provided by a lengthy zigzag extension of the D169. There is a choice of accommodation options, as well as the chance to enjoy an ascent of nearby Monte Renosu, but some walkers decide to make the most of the good paths in the area, and press onwards to reach Bocca di Verdi.

Accommodation The PNRC Refuge d' E Capanelle is very small and basic, built in the *bergerie* style with a 15-bed dormitory, a little kitchen and a cold shower, but walkers can stay for half the normal refuge price. Free camping is available beside the refuge, near the *gîte d'étape* and at the foot of the ski slope. Most walkers are happy to stay at the Gîte d'Étape U Fugone, tel 04 95 57 01 81 or 04 95 56 39 34, which is a large building with 62 beds in a variety of dormitories. Those who are staying in the refuge or camping can pay for a hot shower here. The Gîte d'Étape U Renosu, mobile 06 33 35 25 02, is located at the end of the road crossed by the GR20. It has 20 beds and, a rarity on the GR20, a broad and level grassy space for tents!

Food and Drink The busy U Fugone and the quieter U Renosu both have bar–restaurants offering good Corsican food and drink. A tiny *epicerie* is available at U Fugone for those who wish to cook their own food, but the choice tends to be rather limited.

Link from Hôtel Monte d'Oro to Bocca Palmento

Walkers who choose to stay at La Foce, near the Col de Vizzavona, can rejoin the GR20 without having to descend to the village of Vizzavona. They can avoid the hustle and bustle, and keep something of a sense of remoteness about the route, without losing the chance to obtain food, drink and accommodation. A signposted and waymarked variant is available from La Foce to a point where it rejoins the GR20 below Bocca Palmento. The variant uses forest tracks and a zigzag path up a slope covered in beech trees, and represents a saving of 2km (1¼ miles) and 270m (885ft) of ascent over the main route. (See map on p.154.)

Distance	5km (3 miles)
Total Ascent	460m (1510 feet)
Total Descent	60m (195 feet)
Time	1½ hours
Map	IGN 4252 OT
Terrain	Gentle woodland paths and forest tracks are followed by a steep zigzag path climbing from the woods onto open scrubby slopes.
Shelter	The woodlands offer good shade and shelter.
Food and Drink	There is a water source near Bocca Palmento.

Leave the **Hôtel Monte d'Oro** at La Foce by walking down the main N193 in the direction of Vizzavona, turning right beside a small **truck depot** as signposted for the GR20. Turn left to follow a clear track signposted 'Sentier Femme Perdue', which leads into beech woods behind a restaurant called **A Muntagnera**. The track rises and falls very gently, then narrows as it rises to a path junction. Left is signposted for Vizzavona, so keep right to zigzag up to a **forest track**. Walk along the track, which is later signposted 'GR20', and avoid the path signposted 'Sentier'. The track is flashed with

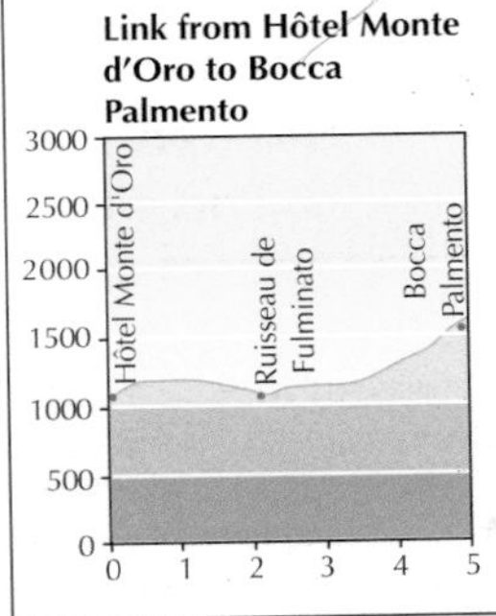

both blue and yellow paint at intervals, and it drops gently past tall pines to ford the cobbly bed of the **Ruisseau de Fulminato**.

Continue along the track, but watch for a sharp turn to the right up a more rugged **stony track**. Follow this, taking note of the blue and yellow paint flashes at any junctions along the way. The woods are mostly pine, but when they become mostly beech, a GR20 **signpost** indicates a sharp right turn. Follow the rough and stony path up to a bouldery **junction of paths**. Turn left, as signposted for the Bocca Palmento.

There is only one obvious zigzag path climbing uphill, sometimes easy underfoot, but sometimes **rough and stony**. Mixed beech and pines give way at a higher level to pines, then to beech. Eventually, emerge from the trees to cross a small **rocky outcrop** and enjoy a splendid view of Monte d'Oru across the valley. The path leads back into the beech woods and almost immediately joins the main course of the GR20 on a **hairpin bend**.

Keep right to follow the GR20 uphill, out of the woods, zigzagging up a more **open slope**, passing patches of alder scrub. There is another fine view of Monte d'Oru. Watch out for the path crossing the **Fontaine de Palmento**, a good place to replenish your water supply. The path climbs a little further to cross the **Bocca Palmento**, at an altitude of 1645m (5400ft), about 1½ hours after leaving La Foce. It is worth taking a break. The gap features broad, gentle, stony slopes liberally strewn with tiny saxifrages. Take the opportunity to look back to Monte d'Oru and Monte Ritondu, or ahead through the valley of the Fiumorbu to the distant sea.

Continue walking to the Bergeries d' E Capanelle as described in the previous section.

STAGE 11

Bergeries d' E Capanelle to Bocca di Verdi (low-level)

This is one of the easier stages of the GR20, and although the first part is actually quite rugged, it is quickly completed. For the most part the route rises and falls gently, and basically contours across forested mountainsides. There is good shade, as well as water in a number of streams, and food and drink on offer at the end of the day. An alternative high-level route is also available, crossing Monte Renosu (see the next section for details). It is also possible, after reaching Bocca di Verdi, to continue along the GR20 and endure a stiff climb to reach the Refuge de Prati. It is up to you to decide whether to stop at Bocca di Verdi or climb to the Refuge de Prati, and either way it is likely that your next stop will almost certainly be the Refuge d'Usciolu. You can ponder over the alternatives while walking during the day.

Distance	14km (8¾ miles)
Total Ascent	320m (1050 feet)
Total Descent	620m (2035 feet)
Time	4½ hours
Map	IGN 4252 OT
Terrain	The route traverses forested slopes for most of the day. Although there are some steep and rugged ascents and descents, these are quite short, and most of the time the gradients are gentle, and the paths and tracks followed are fairly easy.
Shelter	The trees provide good shade and shelter throughout the day.
Food and Drink	There is plenty of food and drink available at the Bergeries d' E Capanelle. Water can be obtained from streams along the way. Food and drink is available at the Relais San Petru di Verdi at the end of the day.

Leave the **Gîte d'Étape U Fugone** and turn left after passing the first two ski-lift pylons. A sign points left at a small *bergerie* building, indicating the course of the GR20. Climb up a

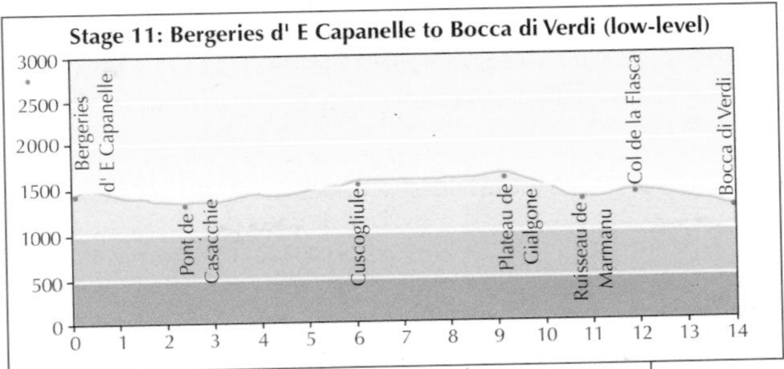

short, **rocky slope** and turn round a corner, noting that beech and alder scrub gives way to laricio pines and juniper. There are glimpses of high mountains on the way down a rugged path, then there are much better mountain views near the **Bergeries d' E Traghjete**.

View of the mountains from the Bergeries d' E Traghjete, shortly after leaving the Bergeries d' E Capanelle.

There is a view between the trees across to the mountains, taking in the Punta Kyrie Eleison.

Swing left and follow the path as it zigzags down stony slopes between the pines. It is quite bouldery in places, with a **water source** just to the left and cascades down to the right. Clumps of hellebore grow in profusion among lush undergrowth. After landing on the D169 at the bottom, turn right and cross a bridge over the river. This bridge, the **Pont de Casacchie** at 1344m (4409ft), is reached about ½ hour after leaving the Bergeries d' E Capanelle.

Head off to the right, away from the road, as signposted for Bocca di Verdi. A broad **track** narrows as beech trees give way to pines on a steep and rugged slope. ◀

The path climbs up a rocky slope for a short way, below the **Rocher d'Accella**, then crosses a slope covered in pines to reach a cut filled with beech trees.

Keep climbing gradually, turning sharply to the right around a ridge at **Serconaccie** where pine trees grow. As the stony path continues onwards, the pines give way more and more to beech as it

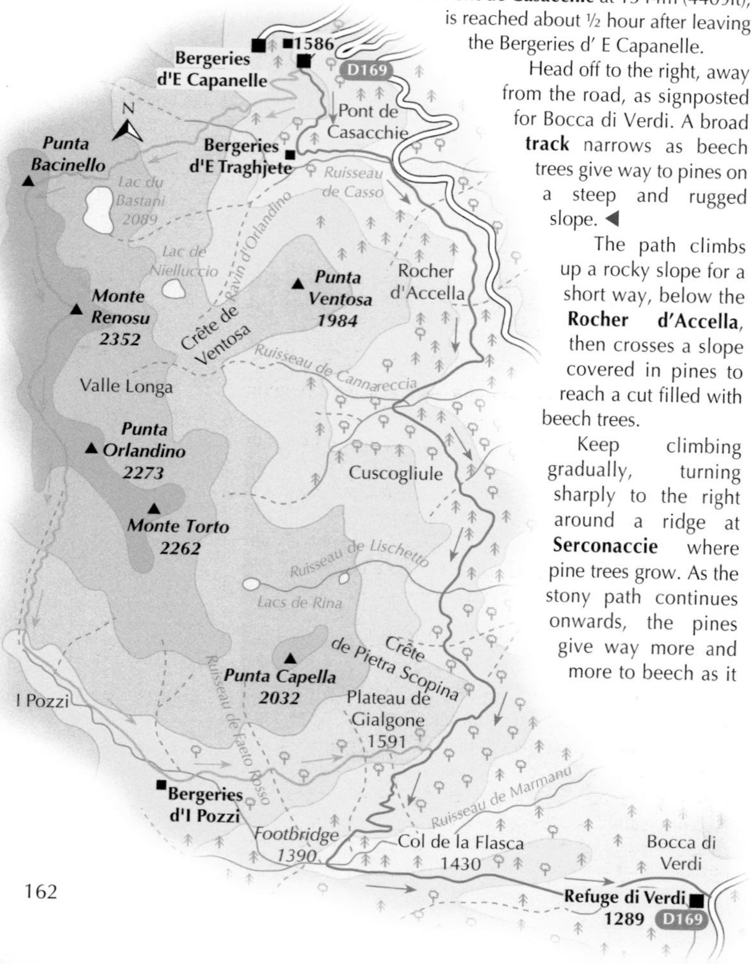

The GR20 cuts straight across an open slope on its way to the Plateau de Gialgone.

approaches the **Ruisseau de Cannareccia**. There are good views of the mountains in more open areas, then there is more forest cover as the route crosses a couple of bouldery streams at **Cuscogliule**.

The path continues rising gently on a rough and **bouldery slope** covered in beech trees, though in a couple of places pines grow on more arid ridges. Take a sharp right turn around one of these ridges, then cross a couple of open slopes covered in scrub and young pines. There is a denser cover of beech trees as the route crosses the **Ruisseau de Lischetto**. After the path contours across a slope of spiny broom and crosses the foot of some rock slabs, there is a mixture of dense beech woods with some more open spaces. (You might notice pigs rooting for food.)

Turn right around the **Crête de Pietra Scopina**. Cross another broad area of spiny broom to reach a point where signboards announce the **Plateau de Gialgone**. This is a bouldery area of scrub with a few tall beech trees, reached some 2½ hours from the Pont de Casacchie at an altitude of 1591m (5220ft).

Keep to the left, and the path zigzags down an open slope then passes a mixture of beech and pine trees, becoming rather more rugged by the time it reaches the **Ruisseau de Marmanu**. Cross the river using a footbridge, at 1390m (4560ft), then turn left to follow a rugged path through flowing water, passing a number of **giant fir trees**. One of these trees has a rather battered sign attached, pointing out that it stands 53.2m (174½ft) high. Walkers stepping back to take a picture, however, will realise that the top is missing. Maybe there is another contender for 'the tallest tree in Corsica', and maybe one day someone will highlight the fact!

Follow the route onwards and gradually rise through beech woods until the path levels out on the broad **Col de la Flasca**, around 1430m (4690ft). As the path begins to descend, watch carefully for the red and white flashes indicating another path heading off down to the right. Very tall laricio pines give way to a mixture of beech and maritime pines, and the path can be rather vague in places.

Later, the path broadens to a **stony track** and passes a big boulder, continuing rough and stony down through a plantation of young pines. There is a **river** running roughly parallel, and although a couple of spur tracks head off to the right, don't follow them and don't cross the river. On reaching a **car park** and picnic site, follow a broad, firm track gently uphill. This reaches the **Relais San Petru di Verdi**, more generally known as the Refuge di Verdi, situated on the **Bocca di Verdi** at 1289m (4229ft). It takes about 1½ hours to walk from the Plateau de Gialgone to the refuge.

RELAIS SAN PETRU DI VERDI

The Relais San Petru di Verdi, tel 04 95 24 46 82, is a bar–restaurant serving meals, snacks and drinks, which can be enjoyed out on a terrace. Basic food supplies can be bought to take away. Walkers who start to feel comfortable can stay at a refuge alongside – a small wooden chalet with 26 beds, showers and toilets. There are camping spaces, as well as ready-pitched tents for hire. Water is available from a fountain near the road. The D69 crosses Bocca di Verdi, but there are no bus services. Walkers who need to leave the route could ask around a nearby car park to try to secure a lift down to Cozzano or Zicavo. Those with plenty of energy can continue through the afternoon to reach the Refuge de Prati high in the mountains.

STAGE 11

Bergeries d' E Capanelle to Bocca di Verdi (high-level)

The GR20 main route from the Bergeries d' E Capanelle to Bocca di Verdi is fairly easy, so some walkers might prefer more of a challenge. A path marked by cairns allows an ascent of Monte Renosu, and this is offered as a high-level route. One option is to climb the mountain simply for its own sake, walking with a lightweight pack from the Bergeries d' E Capanelle to the summit and back. Alternatively, take all your gear, climb the mountain and descend the far side to I Pozzi, then walk to the Plateau de Gialgone to continue along the GR20 to Bocca di Verdi. This is a surprisingly easy ascent, when compared to other mountain climbs on or near the route, but the descent is quite rugged and needs more care. There are delightful *pozzines,* or waterholes, to study at I Pozzi. (See map on p.162.)

Distance	16km (10 miles)
Total Ascent	815m (2675 feet)
Total Descent	1110m (3640 feet)
Time	7¼ hours
Map	IGN 4252 OT
Terrain	The ascent of Monte Renosu is relatively easy in clear, calm weather, though the ridge beyond is rough and rocky. There is a long, steep, stony descent to level grasslands at I Pozzi. Remaining paths are well graded, and cross open slopes or run through woods to reach Bocca di Verdi.
Shelter	There is very little shelter on the mountain, but there is good tree cover towards the end of the day's walk.
Food and Drink	Water is absent on the mountain, but can be obtained from streams in the valleys. Food and drink is available at the Relais San Petru di Verdi at the end of the day.

Leave the **Gîte d'Étape U Fugone** and follow a zigzag path uphill, weaving between the pylons of the **ski tow**. The GR20 main route heads off to the left at a small *bergerie* building,

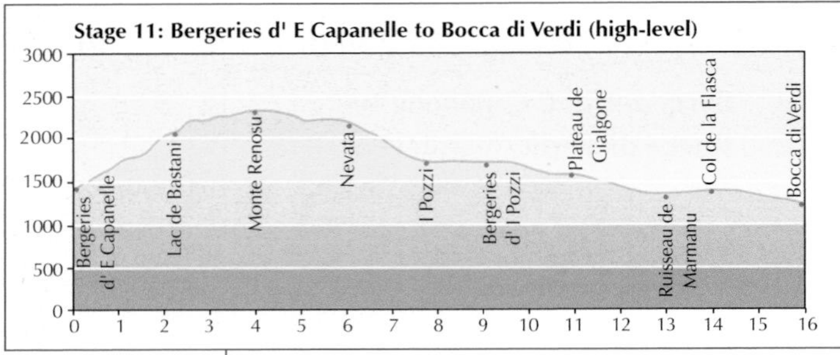

while the path climbing uphill is signposted for Lac de Bastani and Monte Renosu. Follow the zigzag path all the way to the **top pylon** of the ski tow. After enjoying a view of Monte Renosu from this point, continue along a clear, **cairned path** up a blunt ridge. The route passes boulders and continues through alder scrub, and there is a big **protuberance of rock** off to the right. This rock is prominent even from the start of the walk.

Masses of Corsican crocuses grow around the lake early in the summer as the snow melts. The lake is green with algae, 24m (79ft) deep, and frozen for seven months of the year.

Continue up the ridge, then cross a little **stream** near a level grassy area before climbing again. The path is rather vague as it climbs up a gently sloping, grassy, bouldery valley, but follow it faithfully and suddenly reach a point overlooking **Lac de Bastani**, at 2089m (6854ft), where Monte Renosu is seen rising beyond the water. ◀

The path runs up a short, steep, **bouldery slope** to reach the main crest of the mountain, around 2240m (7350ft), near **Punta Bacinello**. Follow the line of cairns to swing to the left along the crest, then continue along a surprisingly easy, level, gritty path. The crest is broad and boulder-strewn, with only little clumps of moss and tiny flowers growing. The path climbs directly to the bouldery summit of **Monte Renosu** at 2352m (7716ft). Walkers should reach the summit about 2¾ hours from the start. Look back towards Monte d'Oru, Monte Ritondu and distant Monte Cinto, as well as ahead to Monte Alcudina, and try to trace the course of the GR20 through the mountains.

Walkers climbing the mountain only for its own sake can retrace their steps back to the Bergeries d' E Capanelle. The rest of this route description leads to Bocca di Verdi.

Continue along the cairned path to leave the summit of **Monte Renosu**, walking down a slope of boulders and gritty

Monte Renosu reflects in the Lac du Bastani and holds snow well into the summer.

There is a fine view off to the right down to the little Lac de Vitalaca.

inclines to reach a narrow, rocky, complex gap near the **Punta di Valle Longa**. Follow the cairned route carefully, bypassing rocky obstacles and completing simple scrambles. ◀

The rocky ridge ends quite suddenly on a **gap** at 2244m (7362ft). The cairned path leads up a broad and stony slope, littered with boulders, in the direction of **Punta Orlandino**. Don't climb to the summit, but drift off to the right instead, then swing right again to walk down into a grassy, stony hollow on the mountainside at **Nevata**. A seasonal stream flows down to I Pozzi, and walkers need to step over the **streambed** to continue downhill.

Look very carefully for a sparse line of **small cairns** while walking down a steep and rugged slope. There are patches of juniper and spiny broom, broken rock and alder scrub, all to be negotiated with care. Keep looking ahead for those elusive little cairns and don't venture onto precarious rocky edges. Even when the path reaches the lower ground, walkers have to pick their way carefully through the alder scrub, where the **narrow path** is almost totally obscured. On emerging, swing left to follow the path down through the valley.

Things become much easier while walking beside the closely cropped grasslands of **I Pozzi**, just below the 1800m (5900ft) contour. The valley floor is level and the bongling bells of grazing cattle break the silence as your feet make hardly any sound on the velvet underfoot. Complex waterholes, or *pozzines*, drain the valley floor, and little streams sometimes rush along or flow more sluggishly. Leave the grasslands to continue through more rugged scrub further down the valley, and cross a **stream** using a boulder as a stepping stone. Paint marks and cairns on boulders indicate the path to follow through the spiny broom to reach the **Bergeries d' I Pozzi**.

Note the blasted beech trees on the slope of boulders, spiny broom and juniper scrub.

Beyond the *bergeries*, the paint-marked route heads off to the right, but walkers should follow another **cairned path** off to the left. Watch carefully for the line of the path, which is vague in places, and cross a wooded **stream** further along. Follow the path across the rugged slopes to cross another stream, the **Ruisseau de Faeto Rosso**, and continue across the slopes beyond. ◀ The stony path leads down to signboards on the **Plateau de Gialgone** at 1591m (5220ft). It will probably take about 3 hours to reach this point after leaving the

summit of Monte Renosu. Rejoin the main GR20 route and turn right to follow it as signposted for Bocca di Verdi.

The path zigzags down an **open slope** then passes a mixture of beech and pine trees, becoming rather more rugged by the time it reaches the **Ruisseau de Marmanu**.

Distant walkers explore the delightfully lush and grassy pozzines *around I Pozzi.*

Cross the river using a footbridge, at 1390m (4560ft), then turn left to follow a rugged path through flowing water, passing a number of **giant fir trees**. One of these trees has a rather battered sign attached, pointing out that it stands 53.2m (174½ft) high. Walkers stepping back to take a picture, however, will realise that the top is missing. Maybe there is another contender for 'the tallest tree in Corsica', and maybe one day someone will highlight the fact!

Follow the route onwards, and gradually rise through beech woods until the path levels out on the broad **Col de la Flasca** around 1430m (4690ft). As the path begins to descend, watch carefully for the red and white flashes indicating another path heading off down to the right. Very tall laricio pines give way to a mixture of beech and maritime pines, and the path can be rather vague in places.

Later, the path broadens to a **stony track** and passes a big boulder, continuing rough and stony down through a plantation of young pines. There is a **river** running roughly parallel, and although a couple of spur tracks head off to the right, don't follow them and don't cross the river. On reaching a **car park** and picnic site, follow a broad, firm track gently uphill. This reaches the **Relais San Petru di Verdi**, more generally known as the Refuge di Verdi, situated on the **Bocca di Verdi** at 1289m (4229ft). It takes about 1½ hours to walk from the Plateau de Gialgone to the refuge.

RELAIS SAN PETRU DI VERDI

The Relais San Petru di Verdi, tel 04 95 24 46 82, is a bar–restaurant serving meals, snacks and drinks, which can be enjoyed out on a terrace. Basic food supplies can be bought to take away. Walkers who start to feel comfortable can stay at a refuge alongside – a small wooden chalet with 26 beds, showers and toilets. There are camping spaces, as well as ready-pitched tents for hire. Water is available from a fountain near the road. The D69 crosses Bocca di Verdi, but there are no bus services. Walkers who need to leave the route could ask around a nearby car park to try to secure a lift down to Cozzano or Zicavo. Those with plenty of energy can continue through the afternoon to reach the Refuge de Prati high in the mountains.

STAGE 12

Bocca di Verdi to Refuge d'Usciolu

This stage starts with a climb from Bocca di Verdi to Bocca d'Oru, except for those who took the option to walk to the Refuge de Prati on the previous day, for whom almost half of the climbing is done. What follows is essentially a ridge walk – not exactly along the ridge, but along a path to one side or the other. The ridge is rocky in some places and progress can be slow, but in other places there is a good path and easy gradients, and progress is much faster. Water is absent along the ridge, so remember to fill up at the Refuge de Prati and Bocca di Laparo. In hot weather plenty of water is necessary, as there is little shade from the sun, apart from a couple of wooded areas. Views are excellent, overlooking forested valleys and taking in distant ranges of mountains. The proximity of the sea is a reminder that the GR20 is in its closing stages, but there is plenty of exciting terrain to cross before reaching Conca.

Distance	16km (10 miles)
Total Ascent	1290m (4230 feet)
Total Descent	830m (2725 feet)
Time	7¼ hours
Map	IGN 4252 OT
Terrain	A forested climb gives way to steep, open mountainside. The route drifts to one side or the other of a long ridge, and can be steep and rocky in some places but quite easy in others. There is forest cover around the Bocca di Laparo, followed by a climb onto open mountainsides again.
Shelter	Apart from forest cover at the start and around Bocca di Laparo, there is very little shade or shelter from sun, wind or rain. The Refuge de Prati is available shortly after crossing the ridge, and there is a basic refuge off-route near Bocca di Laparo.
Food and Drink	Water is available at the Refuge de Prati and Bocca di Laparo. Food and drink can be obtained at the Refuge de Prati and at the Refuge d'Usciolu.

Cross the D69 to leave **Bocca di Verdi**, as signposted for the Refuge de Prati. Swing right and follow a **stony track** uphill.

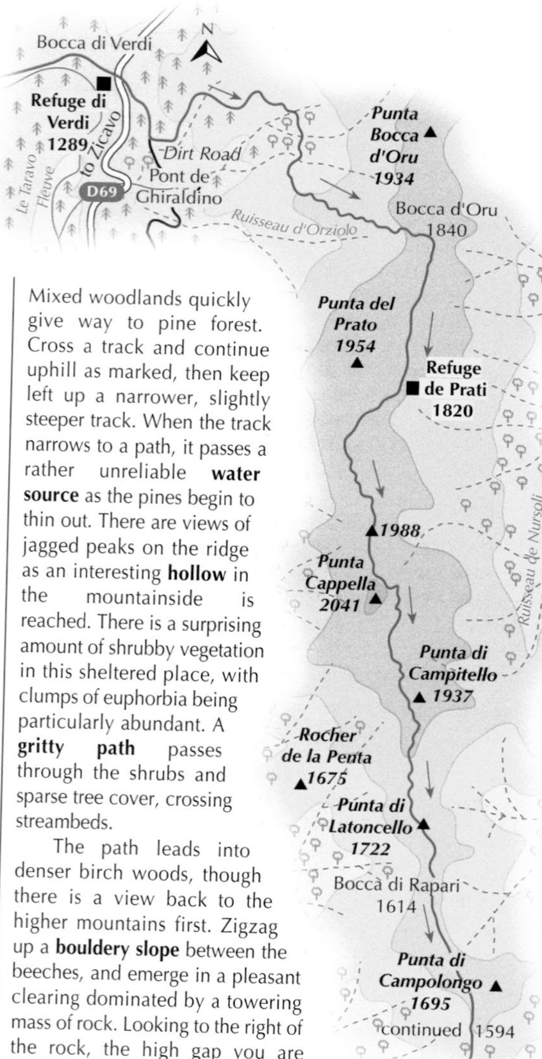

Mixed woodlands quickly give way to pine forest. Cross a track and continue uphill as marked, then keep left up a narrower, slightly steeper track. When the track narrows to a path, it passes a rather unreliable **water source** as the pines begin to thin out. There are views of jagged peaks on the ridge as an interesting **hollow** in the mountainside is reached. There is a surprising amount of shrubby vegetation in this sheltered place, with clumps of euphorbia being particularly abundant. A **gritty path** passes through the shrubs and sparse tree cover, crossing streambeds.

The path leads into denser birch woods, though there is a view back to the higher mountains first. Zigzag up a **bouldery slope** between the beeches, and emerge in a pleasant clearing dominated by a towering mass of rock. Looking to the right of the rock, the high gap you are

Map continues p.175

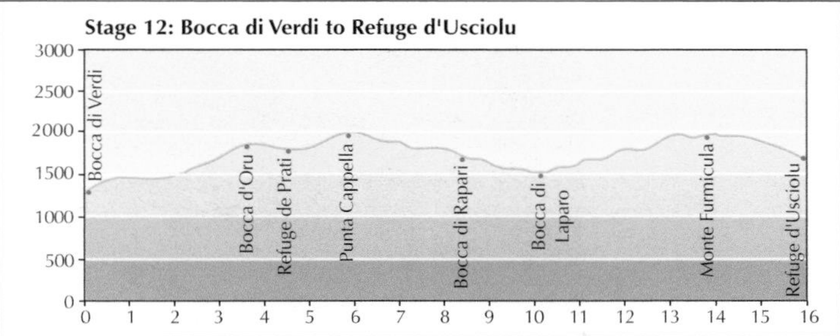

aiming for is visible on the ridge. Keep following the path uphill, zigzagging up a bouldery slope covered in juniper, spiny broom and a wealth of colourful flowers.

The path finally levels out as it crosses the broad and stony gap called the **Bocca d'Oru**, where there are only a few low clumps of vegetation. A **cairn** and a sign stand at this point, around 1840m (6035ft), which should be reached around 1¾ hours after leaving Bocca di Verdi. ▶

There is a view of the fertile coastal plain and the sea near Ghisonaccia on the far side of the ridge, looking surprisingly close. Looking back, Monte Renosu, Monte d'Oru and Monte Ritondu are also visible.

Follow a path that climbs very gently through spiny broom, passing patches of short grass favoured by grazing cattle. The main crest of the ridge is off to the right, but to the left are **granite tors**. A short descent on a stony path through alder scrub leads to the **Refuge de Prati**. It is only a ¼ hour walk from the Bocca d'Oru, and stands at an altitude of 1820m (5970ft), being only 85m (280ft) below the summit of Punta del Prato.

REFUGE DE PRATI

Following a lightning strike in 1997, the PNRC Refuge de Prati was rebuilt in its original *bergerie* style and appears quite modern inside. There is one large dormitory with 28 beds, a large kitchen/dining room and the *gardien's* quarters. A terrace looks out towards the sea and along the rest of the high ridge. Water is available to one side of the building, and there is a toilet and shower in a little building just downhill. A grassy slope is used for camping. Meals and supplies of food and drink can be obtained. Walkers might notice a plaque fixed to a nearby rock. This records the landing of arms by parachute during World War II, enabling Corsicans to fight Nazi and fascist occupation forces.

Horses are frequently used to re-supply the Refuge de Prati from the road crossing Bocca di Verdi.

Leave the **Refuge de Prati** as signposted for Bocca di Laparo and Usciolu. The path is narrow and easy, crossing **grassy areas** at first, with alder scrub taking over as it climbs steep and **bouldery slopes** to gain a point on the ridge at 1988m (6522ft). ◄

There are fine views back to the refuge, as well as beyond to Monte Renosu, Monte d'Oru and Monte Ritondu.

Watch carefully as the marked route drops off to the left of the crest, crossing **sloping slabs** of rock that need special care when wet. Follow the line indicated by the markers, which lead first across the slabs, then reveal a zigzag **rocky climb** back onto the crest. Turn left to continue along the crest, then drift left of the crest, skirting close to the summit of **Punta Cappella** around 2000m (6560ft). The slope is littered with huge boulders and alder scrub. It takes about an hour to reach this point from the Refuge de Prati, as the terrain is so awkward.

When the path descends from Punta Cappella it is much easier underfoot. There are grassy patches and juniper scrub, then a **gap** where there are some large outcrops of rock. Slip to the right, across the crest, then walk down across **bare rock** and follow a rather worn and **stony path** further downhill. There are good views down the forested valley to the villages of Palneca and Cozzano, but walkers are more likely to be watching where they plant their feet.

Pick a way across the rugged slopes of **Punta di Campitello** and cross a notch in a spur ridge. Continue down another worn and stony path as marked, taking care when crossing a slope of **big boulders**, then cross another **rocky notch** and aim to regain the main crest of the ridge. This involves following rough and **bouldery paths**, then passing jagged outcrops on a gap. An easier path crosses a **gap** on the crest, drifting to the left side of the ridge and aiming for a beech wood beyond the **Bocca di Rapari** at 1614m (5295ft). If it is a hot day, enjoy the shade in the wood.

Follow the path uphill through the beech wood, crossing a **gap** and slicing down across the slopes of **Punta di Campolongo**. The path leads into another beech wood to reach a junction of paths on the **Bocca di Laparo**. There are abundant signposts for destinations such as Usciolu, Prati, Catastaghju and Cozzano, as well as for paths including the Sentiers du Taravo and Sentiers d' u Fiumorbu.

Bocca di Laparo is at an altitude of 1525m (5003ft), and it should be reached about 1½ hours after starting the descent from Punta Capella. Walkers who reach this point in a state of desperation should note that there is a basic, unstaffed **refuge** downhill and off-route

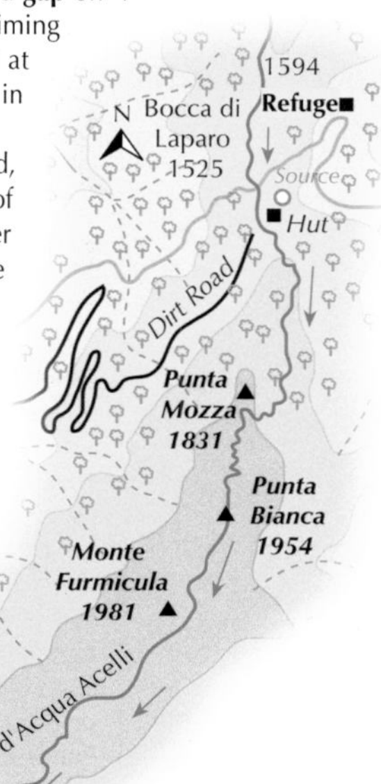

Cloud drifts across the gap of Bocca di Laparo, with Punta Cappella seen far beyond.

to the left that could be reached in ¼ hour, otherwise keep following the course of the GR20.

There is a painted instruction stating that there is a water source 10 minutes further along the trail. Follow a path covered in leaf mould, with beech trees to the left and mossy **rock walls** to the right. The path rises and falls, sometimes crossing bare rock, but mostly confined to the woods.

Follow the red and white flashes for the GR20, but also note the arrows and the word 'Source' if water is needed at this point. The arrows point off-route to the left, down to a **wooden building** where water runs from a pipe into a sink further downhill. The building is not a refuge, but a sign formerly forbidding camping has been replaced by a sign allowing it! After obtaining water here, follow the path signposted for the Refuge d'Usciolu to rejoin the GR20.

The path zigzags uphill, crossing **rocky slopes** in the shade of beech trees. It is a well-engineered route, and there is a stretch that is more or less level, then another climb leads to a **bouldery hollow** where the trees thin out a bit. The higher slopes of **Punta Mozza** look like cliffs, but follow the markers and another series of stony zigzags climb even further up the steep slopes. Walk into and out of a patch of beech, then zigzag up the path to cross **rocky slopes** covered in juniper and spiny broom. Walk through a patch of alder and gain the crest of the ridge again. Keep following the **stony path** uphill, enjoying the views while negotiating areas of boulders and patches of alder.

The path levels out at the top, then dips gently as it crosses a slope and rises ruggedly to the crest of the ridge not far from the summit of **Monte Furmicula**. The crest is crossed at an altitude of 1950m (6400ft) and is reached about 2 hours after leaving the Bocca di Laparo. The summit of Monte Furmicula is all bare rock, but it is quite close to hand and rises only another 30m (100ft), so some walkers might like to make a summit bid. Others may be happy simply to look back to Monte Renosu and ahead to Monte Alcudina.

Follow the path gently downhill across the slopes of **Monte Furmicula**, but watch carefully for markers, as there are a couple of places where other paths drop down too far to the left, leading into awkward terrain. The course of theGR20 swings around a **hollow** in the mountainside, and even climbs a little before finally descending. The descent crosses bare, **sloping rock**, then gradually steepens until a final series of awkward, eroded, **stony paths** lead down to the **Refuge d'Usciolu**, at an altitude of 1750m (5740ft). It takes about ¾ hour to reach the refuge from the gap near Monte Furmicula

REFUGE D'USCIOLU

The PNRC Refuge d'Usciolu is built in the bergerie style and can often be heard before it is seen, if the gardien is playing loud 'mood music' to the walkers! The refuge has 29 beds in two dormitories, a kitchen/dining room and the gardien's quarters. A terrace looks out across a steep-sided valley towards Monte Alcudina. A nearby hut is filled with an abundance of food and drink, if your stocks need replenishing, and meals are available. Tables and chairs spreading from the refuge, complete with parasols, give the place the air of a street bar! A toilet and shower are located below the refuge, as well as spaces for camping. The gardien is in the habit of riding his horses to Cozzano every morning for fresh supplies, and he also takes postcards, offering a unique 'pony express' service!

Link from Refuge d'Usciolu to Cozzano

There can be compelling reasons to descend from the Refuge d'Usciolu to Cozzano. Severe weather or thunderstorms could make any continuation along exposed ridges unwise. Walkers who run out of energy may wish to avoid the long stretch leading over Monte Alcudina to the Refuge d'Asinau. Others may simply feel that they are running out of time, and a descent to Cozzano links with a bus service to Ajaccio, for onward connections around Corsica. A pity to have to descend when the end is so close, but in any case some walkers believe that a visit to Cozzano is well worth the detour. (See map on p.175.)

Distance	5km (3 miles)
Total Ascent	55m (180 feet)
Total Descent	1075m (3525 feet)
Time	3 hours
Maps	IGN 4253 ET and IGN 4253 OT
Terrain	A steep and stony path for the most part, needing care at times. The path is mostly confined to woodland but has some open stretches.
Shelter	Woodlands offer good shade and shelter throughout the descent.
Food and Drink	Water is available from the Fontaine du Pantanellu on the descent. Cozzano has a couple of snack bars and restaurants and local produce can also be bought.

Leave the **Refuge d'Usciolu** as signposted for Bocca di l'Agnonu and Refuge d'Asinau. A rough and **stony path** slices up a steep slope to reach a ridge, where there is a signpost indicating a way down to the village of Cozzano. The path is flashed with **yellow paint**, and the upper parts are rather badly eroded stony zigzags, which have taken a pounding by the horses used to supply the refuge. Walk down past a **rocky pinnacle** and follow the path into beech woods.

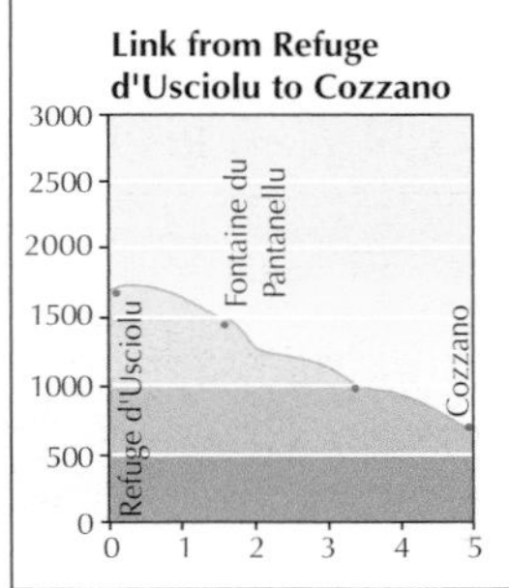

A more open stretch of path runs gently across a slope, then passes through a **notch** between two towers of rock. Continue down through the beech woods, gradually losing height. The path actually runs parallel to the main GR20, which is on the rocky ridge above, but the ridge is only glimpsed from time to time. Later, swing right and drop more steeply, winding between huge, **smooth outcrops** of granite.

Descend further and cross a streambed above a water source at the **Fontaine du Pantanellu**. The path pulls away from the stream and descends among tall beeches. If fallen leaves and broken branches obscure the path, keep an eye open for **yellow paint** marks. Emerge in a clearing where there is a stone-walled enclosure on the **Crête du Miratoju**. A yellow arrow points right, but after a few paces turn left to follow a **narrow path** down a slope of spiny broom.

Head back into beech woods further downhill, and follow the paint marks to land on a broad turning space at the end of a **forest track**, at the foot of a prominent granite dome with fluted sides. There may be pigs in a nearby pen, often turned loose to forage in the woods.

Turn left down an awkward slope of bracken, broom and boulders, heading back into beech woods as marked. Cross the **Ruisseau de Carpa** and walk roughly downstream, crossing it again as marked. Walk out of the woods to cross a tangled slope of **thorny scrub**, then back into the woods again. Drop down a steep and rugged slope dotted with boulders, and watch for the markers while passing some **giant chestnut trees**. After briefly contouring across the slope, head further downhill, then contour roughly alongside a tumbled wall and wire fence. Arbutus and heather begin to feature among the trees, and the path suddenly lands on a **forest track** where a signpost points back uphill for Usciolu.

Cross the track and look out for short, steep, gritty paths marked with **orange paint**. These cut out sweeping bends

The village of Cozzano is seen huddled on a rounded hilltop, apparently surrounded by woodlands.

from the track, and there is a brief glimpse of Cozzano perched on a rounded hilltop. The path runs close to the **Ruisseau de Mezzanu**, passing a gateway, to land on the D69 at a bridge. Either turn right to reach the **Gîte d'Étape Bella Vista**, or left to pass the **U Mezzanu** restaurant and walk into **Cozzano**.

COZZANO

The first glimpse of Cozzano reveals the village as a huddle of stone houses on a rounded hill, dominated by its church tower. On closer acquaintance, the village spreads out along the main D69, and this is where you will find two *gîtes d'étape*, one on either side of the village. Services are sparse, but are nevertheless adequate for an overnight stop, and there is a year-round bus service linking with Zicavo and Ajaccio.

Accommodation The Gîte d'Étape Bella Vista, tel 04 95 24 41 59, has 36 beds and spaces for tents, and is on the D69 just northeast of Cozzano. The Auberge la Filetta, tel 04 95 24 44 57, has 30 beds and is on the D69 just southwest of Cozzano.

Food and Drink The U Mezzanu restaurant is beside the bridge on the D69 outside Cozzano. The Gîte d'Étape Bella Vista and the Auberge la Filetta have bar–restaurants. The Snack Bar Terminus is at a crossroads in the middle of Cozzano. All these places offer good Corsican food and drink.

Transport There is a bus service to Zicavo and Ajaccio, which runs all year round except Sundays, operated by Autocars Santoni, tel 04 95 21 29 56.

STAGE 13

Refuge d'Usciolu to Refuge d'Asinau

This looks like a very long stage on the map, but most of it is relatively easy. The only difficult sections are at the beginning and end, when the route leaves the Refuge d'Usciolu along a rocky ridge, and when it descends from Monte Alcudina to the Refuge d'Asinau. So far, it has been possible to walk the GR20 without having to climb any mountains. Walkers only pass between them or cut across their slopes, unless they sampled some of the high-level alternatives and included summits bids. Today, however, Monte Alcudina has to be climbed, and it is a big mountain. If you find that your energy levels aren't equal to the task, or if the weather is deteriorating, then it might be better not to climb it. Hold back for a day or so at the Refuge d'Usciolu, or take the option of visiting the village of Zicavo by following an alternative waymarked loop. (See the next two sections for descriptions of links to Zicavo and the Bergerie de Basseta.)

Distance	17km (10½ miles)
Total Ascent	1010m (3315 feet)
Total Descent	1225m (4020 feet)
Time	7¼ hours
Map	IGN 4253 ET
Terrain	There is a long, rocky ridge at the start of this stage, and walkers need to scramble along some parts. There are patchy woodlands and the open spaces of the Plateau du Cuscione later, where progress is much quicker. The ascent of Monte Alcudina is easy in good weather, but the descent is steep and rocky.
Shelter	Apart from patchy beech woods on either side of the Plateau du Cuscione, there is very little shade. The mountains are very exposed to sun, wind and rain. There are two basic refuges off-route in case of foul weather.
Food and Drink	Water is available from a source near Monte Occhiatu, from streams on the Plateau du Cuscione, and from a source above I Pedinieddi. Food and drink are available at the Refuge d'Asinau and Bergeries d'Asinau.

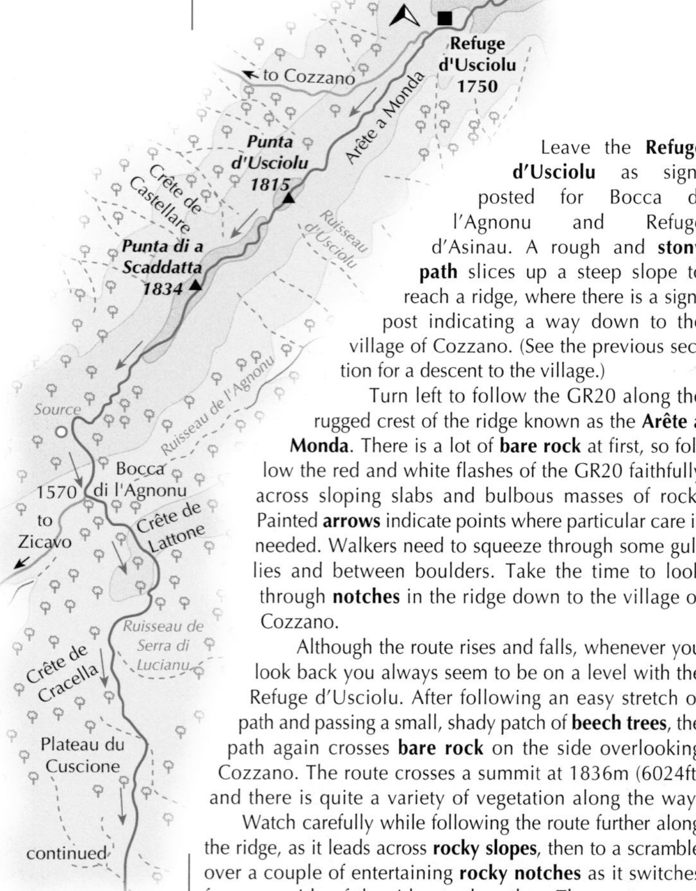

Map continues p.184

Leave the **Refuge d'Usciolu** as signposted for Bocca di l'Agnonu and Refuge d'Asinau. A rough and **stony path** slices up a steep slope to reach a ridge, where there is a signpost indicating a way down to the village of Cozzano. (See the previous section for a descent to the village.)

Turn left to follow the GR20 along the rugged crest of the ridge known as the **Arête a Monda**. There is a lot of **bare rock** at first, so follow the red and white flashes of the GR20 faithfully across sloping slabs and bulbous masses of rock. Painted **arrows** indicate points where particular care is needed. Walkers need to squeeze through some gullies and between boulders. Take the time to look through **notches** in the ridge down to the village of Cozzano.

Although the route rises and falls, whenever you look back you always seem to be on a level with the Refuge d'Usciolu. After following an easy stretch of path and passing a small, shady patch of **beech trees**, the path again crosses **bare rock** on the side overlooking Cozzano. The route crosses a summit at 1836m (6024ft) and there is quite a variety of vegetation along the way.

Watch carefully while following the route further along the ridge, as it leads across **rocky slopes**, then to a scramble over a couple of entertaining **rocky notches** as it switches from one side of the ridge to the other. The route passes **Punta di a Scaddatta**, and walkers might notice plants such as thrift and campion, more commonly associated with low-lying coasts than high mountains. The path becomes easier for a while, then suddenly ascends to cross a very prominent

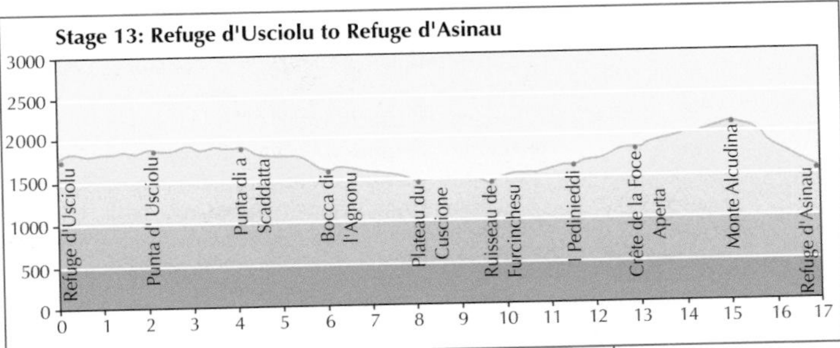

rocky gap. A bouldery path leads down through beech scrub, then continues across an **open slope** to enter taller beech woods. ▶

Pigs and cattle are to be found in grassy areas in the woods, as well as a signpost for a water source just up to the right.

Follow the path steeply downhill through the woods, then more gently to an open gap covered in boulders and spiny broom. This is the **Bocca di l'Agnonu**, reached 2½ hours after leaving the Refuge d'Usciolu, at an altitude of 1570m (5150ft). There are signposts indicating the way back to Usciolu, ahead to Asinau, or off-route down to the village of Zicavo.

Walkers wishing to visit Zicavo or the Bergerie de Basseta should refer to the route described in the next two sections.

After following the Arête a Monda away from the Refuge d'Usciolu, the GR20 passes Punta di a Scaddatta.

The course of the GR20 undulates through the beech woods, often following a **track**, but sometimes departing from it for short stretches. Later, a **path** heads left from the track, leaving the beech woods to descend gently onto the **Plateau du Cuscione**. The plateau is generally between 1450 and 1500m (4760 and 4920ft), with Monte Alcudina rising beyond. The **narrow path** is flanked by spiny broom, and the surface is stony or sandy. A couple of **streams** are to be crossed and there is a bit of shade in an area of beech trees.

Follow the path over a slope of juniper and spiny broom, noting the large, **rounded boulders** of granite dotted around and the array of flowers among the scrub. Cross a wide expanse of spiny broom, then cross a couple more streams, the latter being the **Ruisseau d'Allucia**, before climbing up a slope of ancient beech trees. Some of the trees have toppled and are rotting on the ground.

Walk over another broad rise of spiny broom, passing more rounded boulders, then walk down into a wildly vegetated area to cross the **Ruisseau de Cavallare**. Climb up a

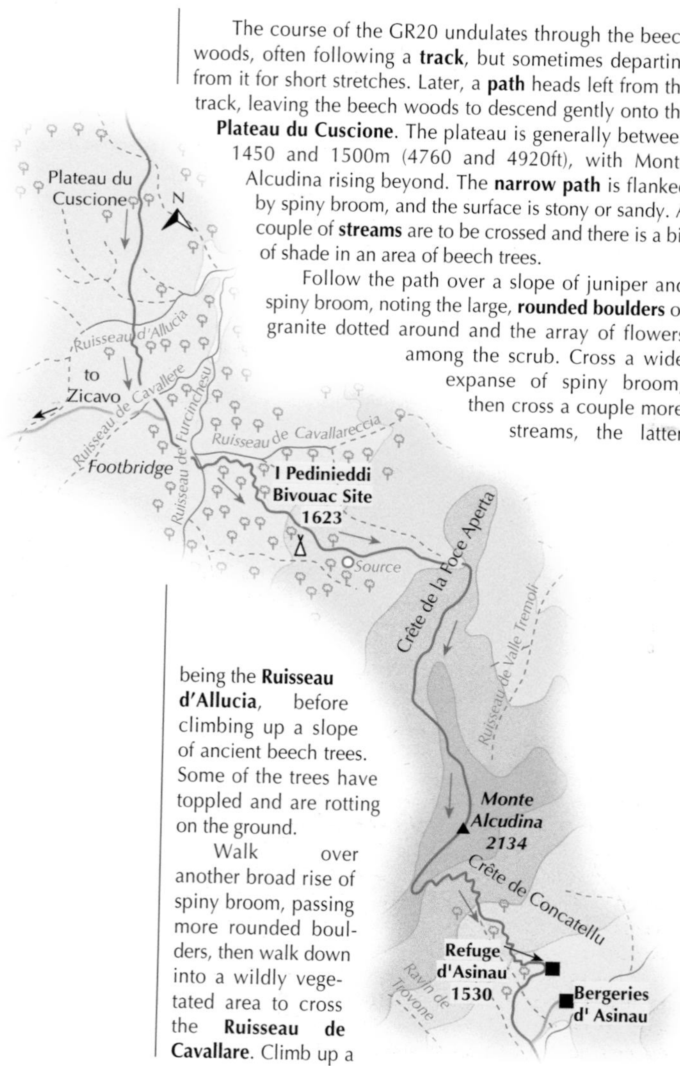

slope bearing a few beech trees to reach a clear **track**. There are signposts for Usciolu, Asinau and Zicavo, as well as for Monte Alcudina. The track should be reached about an hour after leaving the Bocca di l'Agnonu, and the altitude is 1480m (4855ft). ▶

Bear in mind that a route flashed with yellow paint leads off this track, and could be used to reach basic refuges at Matalza and San Petru, or the comfortable Bergerie de Basseta.

Cross over the track, just to cut a loop out of it, then turn right and follow it as marked. Turn left after a short while and walk down to a river, the **Ruisseau de Furcinchesu**, which is well wooded with beech. Walk upstream to reach a wobbly suspension **footbridge** and cross it. The path doubles back downstream a little, then rises up a **bouldery slope** covered in beech trees. There are some open areas, then the path reaches a much wider expanse of spiny broom and juniper scrub. There are signs for **I Pedinieddi Aire de Bivouac** off to the right.

I PEDINIEDDI AIRE DE BIVOUAC

The PNRC Refuge d' I Pedinieddi was destroyed by a lightning strike in 1981 and never rebuilt. Bear this in mind if storms are forecast, as the summit of Monte Alcudina is more than 500m (1640ft) higher than this site! Masonry from the ruins has been used to mark out a number of camping spaces, and this is the only place along the whole of the GR20 where you can legally pitch a tent for the night away from a refuge or *gîte*. A water source is signposted and this is the only facility available, so if planning to use the bivouac area, remember to carry all other food and drink supplies with you.

Continue following the course of the GR20, which rises from the bivouac area of scrub onto another slope of beech trees. A **water source** is located just to the left of the path. As it climbs higher on the slope and crosses a flowery scrub, the path is either on **bare rock** or has a stony surface. There is plenty of juniper scrub on the way to a broad, gently sloping gap on the **Crête de la Foce Aperta**, at an altitude of 1805m (5920ft). This gap should be reached 1¼ hours after leaving the track on the Plateau du Cuscione.

Look up to the summit of Monte Alcudina from the gap and follow the path steadily as it rises along the **crest**. The ascent poses no problems, though the path drifts away from the crest to cross a **rugged slope** to the right, then after

A path climbs gently along the Crête de la Foce Aperta towards the sprawling summit of Monte Alcudina.

turning a corner the summit is much closer to hand. The path keeps away from the **rocky crest**, yet still crosses plenty of bare rock and weaves between boulders and alder scrub. When the summit of **Monte Alcudina** is gained, pass the monumental **cross** that stands on a bare dome of granite at 2134m (7001ft). Walkers should reach the summit within an hour of leaving the Crête de la Foce Aperta, and can spend a while enjoying the view, looking back along the course of the GR20 and ahead to the exciting rocky spires and towers of the Aiguilles de Bavella.

A signboard gives directions for Usciolu and Asinau. Follow the **rocky ridge** southwest for the descent to the Refuge d'Asinau. Walk across **bare rock** and scramble around immense boulders to reach a **gap** at 2025m (6645ft), where there is a signpost pointing left for Asinau. Walk downhill and swing to the left, then pick a way across the **rocky face** of the mountain. Watch carefully for markers, as the route zigzags down more **rocky slopes** and weaves in and out of patches of alder scrub. Although the refuge is often plainly in view below, and looks quite close, getting down to it is slow and difficult. Take your time and tread carefully, especially if the rock underfoot is wet.

A few slender sycamore trees rise above the alder scrub, and the path continues zigzagging downhill on rock, boulders or loose stones. Eventually, and with some relief, walkers reach the **Refuge d'Asinau**, at an altitude of 1530m (5020ft), about 1½ hours after leaving the summit of Monte Alcudina.

REFUGE D'ASINAU

The PNRC Refuge d'Asinau is a simple stone *bergerie*-style building clinging to a steep and rugged slope below Monte Alcudina. It has a dormitory with 30 beds, a kitchen/dining room and the *gardien's* quarters. A fine terrace looks across the valley to the spiky crest of the Aiguilles de Bavella. A shower and toilets are located in a small building near the refuge, along with a water supply. There are small camping spaces located downhill from the refuge and in the direction of the shower block. Meals, basic foodstuffs and drinks are on sale. The Bergeries d'Asinau, plainly in view below the refuge, operates a very basic *gîte d'étape* with 20 beds, meals, toilet and a primitive shower.

Link from Refuge d'Usciolu to Zicavo

The walk along the GR20 is coming to an end, and you may feel that you haven't had very much contact with Corsican people or stayed in a truly Corsican village. Now you have a chance to put that right by visiting Zicavo. Two links between the GR20 and Zicavo form a wide loop, so you can spend a night in the village, then return to the GR20 the next day. Even then another break between Zicavo and Monte Alcudina may be needed. It is a big mountain, but it may be approached in more confident mood after sampling the fleshpots of Zicavo. After leaving the Refuge d'Usciolu, scramble along the Arête a Monda to reach the Bocca di l'Agnonu. Bear in mind that the path leaving the GR20 at this point can be vague, and the yellow paint markers are sparse in places. Once safely across the rugged crest at Tignosellu, paths and tracks leading down through the forest to Zicavo are much clearer. (There is also a link with the Auberge Gîte Bergerie de Basseta, described in the short section following this one.)

Distance	12km (7½ miles)
Total Ascent	250m (820 feet)
Total Descent	1300m (4265 feet)
Time	5 hours
Maps	IGN 4253 ET and 4253 OT
Terrain	There is a long, rocky ridge at the start of this stage, and walkers need to scramble along some parts. The descent is initially on vague paths through a wooded valley, leading onto better paths and tracks across largely wooded slopes.
Shelter	There is little shade on the rocky ridge, or shelter from sun, wind and rain, but shade is available in woodlands once the descent commences.
Food and Drink	Water is available from a source near Monte Occhiatu and from a couple of streams on the descent. Zicavo has a couple of restaurants, bars and shops.

Leave the **Refuge d'Usciolu** as signposted for Bocca di l'Agnonu and Refuge d'Asinau. A rough and **stony path** slices up a steep slope to reach a ridge, where there is a signpost indicating a way down to the village of Cozzano. (See the previous section for a descent to the village.)

Turn left to follow the GR20 along the rugged crest of the ridge known as the **Arête a Monda**. There is a lot of **bare rock** at first, so follow the red and white flashes of the GR20 faithfully across sloping slabs and bulbous masses of rock. Painted **arrows** indicate points where particular care is needed. Walkers need to squeeze through some gullies and between boulders. Take the time to look through **notches** in the ridge down to the village of Cozzano. Although the route rises and falls, whenever you look back you always seem to be on a level with the Refuge d'Usciolu.

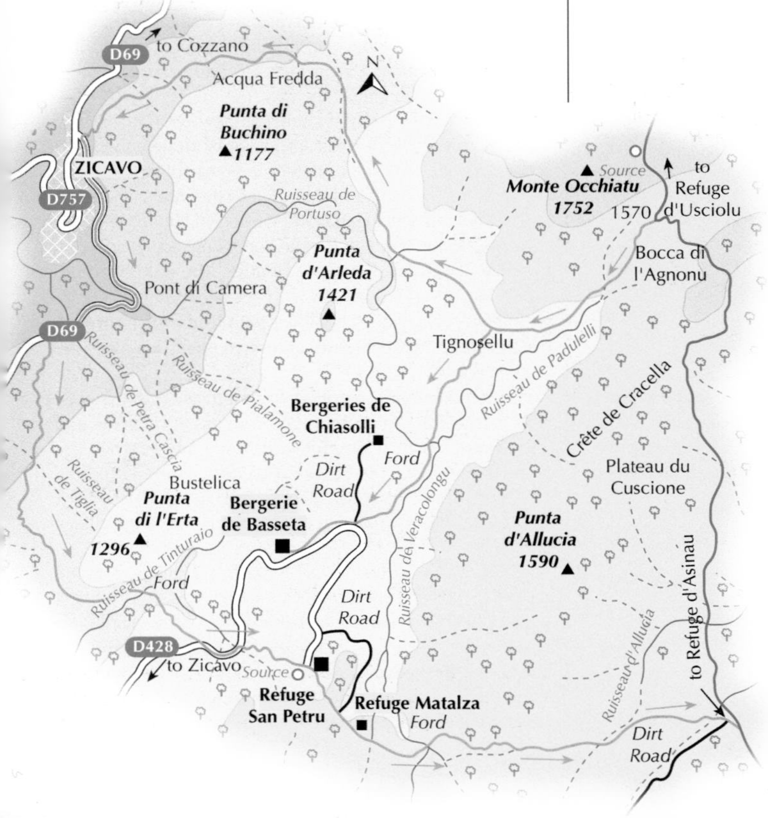

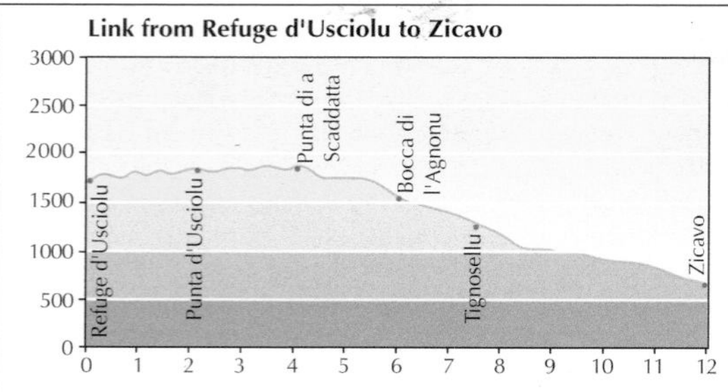

After following an easy stretch of path and passing a small, shady patch of **beech trees**, the path again crosses **bare rock** on the side overlooking Cozzano. The route crosses a **summit** at 1836m (6024ft) and there is quite a variety of vegetation along the way.

Watch carefully while following the route further along the rocky ridge, as it leads across **rocky slopes**, then to a scramble over a couple of entertaining **rocky notches** as it switches from one side of the ridge to the other. The route passes **Punta di a Scaddatta**, and walkers might notice plants such as thrift and campion, more commonly associated with low-lying coasts than high mountains. The path becomes easier for a while, then suddenly ascends to cross a very prominent **rocky gap**. **A bouldery path leads down through beech scrub, then continues across an open slope** to enter taller beech woods. ◀

Pigs and cattle are to be found in grassy areas in the woods, as well as a signpost for a **water source** just up to the right.

Follow the path steeply downhill through the woods, then more gently to an open gap covered in boulders and spiny broom. This is the **Bocca di l'Agnonu**, reached 2½ hours after leaving the Refuge d'Usciolu, at an altitude of 1570m (5150ft). There are signposts indicating the way back to Usciolu, ahead to Asinau, or off-route down to the village of Zicavo.

Turn right and walk roughly southwest away from the signposts, but look carefully as the route starts descending a slope of beech trees to spot a **cairn** and a **yellow paint** flash on a boulder. Keep your eyes peeled for more cairns and yellow flashes on the way downhill, as these indicate the rather vague path to be followed down through this first valley. Cross the **Ruisseau de Padulelli** just below a point where its

A winter view of Monte Occhiatu on the way down from the Plateau du Cuscione towards Zicavo.

bed is choked with boulders. This stream may be dry, but there may be water further downhill.

A **steep slope** is covered in beech trees and boulders, and walkers need to keep looking for markers to follow the path further downhill. As it drifts away from the stream, watch very carefully to spot the route rising across a slope of spiny broom, juniper scrub and boulders to cross a rugged crest at **Tignosellu**. Small cairns mark the rather sketchy line of the path, rising to 1380m (4530ft). (Note the short variant route marked in blue, for the Auberge Gîte Bergerie de Basseta, described in the next short section.)

Continue walking down into another valley and back into **beech woods**. The path wanders down through the woods, zigzagging quite steeply at times. Cross over a rocky lip in the stream called the **Ruisseau de Monte Occhiatu**, then follow the path across an **open slope**. There are fine views of mountains far across the Taravo valley beyond Zicavo, but no sight of the village itself. The path leads past more beech trees, then cuts across another open slope of broom and brambles, thistles and thorns. Notice a **drystone wall** to your left, and the route then quickly reaches a junction with another drystone wall on a little **gap** on the mountainside, at 1190m (3905ft).

Turn right to descend from the gap, following the path as it zigzags down past some mighty gnarled oak trees, later passing three giant **chestnut trees**. On reaching a **junction** with another path here, turn left to follow it further downhill. The path is flashed with **orange paint** and becomes a broad **track** that is often enclosed by drystone walls or fences, descending gently in some places and more steeply in others as it cuts across slopes covered in chestnut trees. Accumulations of dead leaves can conceal uneven surfaces beneath, so tread with care. When there are fallen boughs and tree trunks it can be like an obstacle course, but the way ahead is always clear.

The track runs through an eroded **groove** and narrows later, running down **bare granite** to a signboard beside a road at **Zicavo**. It is possible to reach this point, at 721m (2365ft), about 2½ hours after leaving Bocca di l'Agnonu.

ZICAVO

The road at the top of the village is the D69, or Promenade Jacques-Pierre Fiamma. This road is virtually level and has most of the facilities in Zicavo. However, by walking downhill, the steep zigzag D757 passes a *boulangerie,* post office and bar. Make the most of a break in Zicavo, where blocky three- and four-storey granite houses bear faded names and dates, and fine Corsican food and drink can be enjoyed in bars and restaurants.

Accommodation The Hôtel du Tourisme, tel 04 95 24 40 06, has 15 rooms and is directly below the point where the path reaches the road in Zicavo. The Gîte d'Étape le Paradis, tel 04 94 24 41 20, is off to the right along the D69, offering 20 beds and a space for tents. The Hôtel le Florida, tel 04 95 24 43 11, has 12 rooms and is further along the D69.

Food and Drink Both hotels and the *gîte d'étape* in Zicavo offer meals. There is also the Prestige Club bar–restaurant and the Pacific Sud bar–restaurant, both of which serve pizzas. A small but exceptionally well-stocked *alimentation* is located between both bars on the D69. Anyone walking down through the village will find another bar and a *boulangerie*.

Transport There is a bus service to Ajaccio, all year round except Sundays, operated by Autocars Santoni, tel 04 95 21 29 56. It passes both hotels and the *gîte d'étape* in Zicavo, and also serves Cozzano.

Link from Bocca di l'Agnonu to Bergerie de Basseta

The Bergerie de Basseta might appear too far off-route to interest walkers on the GR20. However, consider the alternatives if there is little chance of crossing Monte Alcudina – a long descent and subsequent re-ascent from Zicavo, the very basic refuge huts at Matalza and the Chapelle San Petru, or the even more basic bivouac area at I Pedinieddi. The Bergerie de Basseta has a good reputation for accommodating stray GR20 walkers, and it offers a bar and restaurant in an area with only sparse facilities. Walkers who leave the GR20 at the Bocca di l'Agnonu to descend to Zicavo can change their plans and follow a narrow, waymarked, easy and scenic path to Basseta instead. (See map on p.189.)

Distance	5km (3 miles)
Total Ascent	100m (330 feet)
Total Descent	320m (1050 feet)
Time	1½ hours
Map	IGN 4253 OT
Terrain	Fairly gentle wooded and scrubby slopes, with a river crossing in the middle that might be awkward after heavy rain.
Shelter	Woodlands offer some shade and shelter.
Food and Drink	Food and drink are available at the Bergerie de Basseta.

Leave the **Bocca di l'Agnonu** some 2½ hours after leaving the Refuge d'Usciolu, at an altitude of 1570m (5150ft). There are **signposts** indicating the way back to Usciolu, ahead to Asinau, or off-route down to the village of Zicavo. Turn right and walk roughly southwest away from the signposts, but look carefully as the route starts descending a slope of beech trees to spot a **cairn** and a **yellow paint** flash on a boulder. Keep your eyes peeled for more cairns and yellow flashes on the way downhill, as these indicate the rather vague path to be followed down through this first valley.

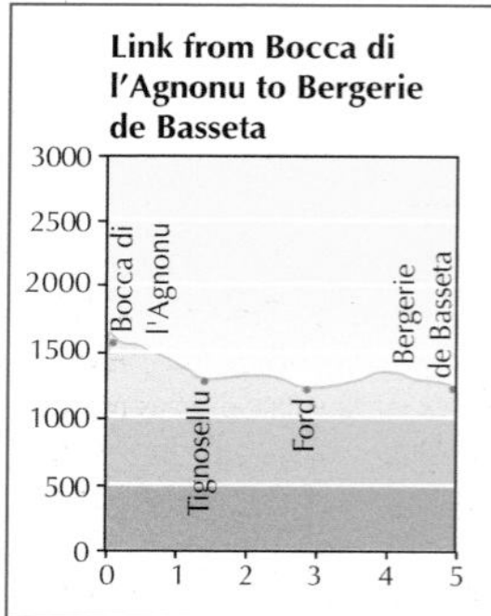

Cross the **Ruisseau de Padulelli** just below a point where its bed is choked with boulders. This stream may be dry, but there may be water further downhill. A **steep slope** is covered in beech trees and boulders, and walkers need to keep looking for markers to follow the path further downhill. As it drifts away from the stream, watch very carefully to spot the route rising across a slope of spiny broom, juniper scrub and boulders to cross a rugged crest at **Tignosellu**. Small cairns mark the rather sketchy line of the path, rising to 1380m (4530ft).

A **sign** and a boulder are marked with the name 'Basseta'. Turn left and follow a narrow path marked with small **cairns** and **blue paint** flashes. The path runs at gentle gradients, undulating across a slope of spiny broom. It runs roughly southwest, then swings more to the south to drop towards the **Ruisseau de Partuso**. Cross this at a point where the channel is narrow and rocky, but bear in mind that this charming spot could be a dangerous place after heavy rain, where the river flows vigorously through rock pools and over **waterfalls**.

Climb gently and follow the blue-flashed path, passing fallen beech trees to enter a beech wood. Walk upstream beside the **Ruisseau de Veracolongu**. Later, the path climbs from the river and reaches a **track** on top of a scrubby slope. Either cross the track to continue towards Basseta as marked, or follow the track up to a nearby **minor road** and turn right to walk gently downhill. Either way, this variant soon leads to the **Bergerie de Basseta**.

On the following day, simply walk up the road for ½ hour to reach the **Chapelle San Petru**, where the link rising from Zicavo can be joined.

AUBERGE GÎTE BERGERIE DE BASSETA

The Auberge Gîte Bergerie de Basseta, tel 04 95 25 74 20, offers a range of accommodation from a handful of small wooden chalets to a large dormitory, offering 45 beds in total. Camping is available and there are toilets and showers. The main building features a bar–restaurant where good Corsican food and drink are available.

Link from Zicavo to Refuge d'Asinau

Most walkers who head down from the Bocca di l'Agnonu to Zicavo will be happy to follow another route back onto the GR20, even though it means omitting 5km (3 miles) of the main route on the Plateau de Cuscione. It may be expecting too much to walk from Zicavo, over Monte Alcudina and down to the Refuge d'Asinau, so take note of a *gîte* and two refuges on the Plateau du Cuscione if you would prefer to break this long day into two easier days. After leaving Zicavo by road, a rugged path rises up a wooded slope, then there are more open areas. Walkers will find a chapel and two basic refuges before the Plateau du Cuscione is reached. Anyone set on the ascent of Monte Alcudina will need to keep moving to ensure a successful traverse. (See map on p.189.)

Distance	18km (11 miles)
Total Ascent	1525m (5000 feet)
Total Descent	710m (2330 feet)
Time	6½ hours
Maps	IGN 4253 OT and 4253 ET
Terrain	Easy paths and tracks lead up to and across the Plateau du Cuscione through a series of wooded and open areas. The ascent of Monte Alcudina is easy in good weather, but the descent is steep and rocky.
Shelter	Shade is available in woodlands on the ascent. There are very basic refuges offering shelter on the Plateau du Cuscione. The higher parts of the route are open and have little shade or shelter from sun, wind and rain.
Food and Drink	The Bergerie de Bassetta is off-route and offers food and drink. There are water sources near the Chapelle San Petru and above I Pedinieddi. Food and drink are available at the Refuge d'Asinau and Bergeries d'Asinau.

Leave **Zicavo** by walking along the D69, as signposted 'Aullene/Audde'. The road passes an *alimentation* and the Prestige Club bar. Blocky three- and four-storey granite

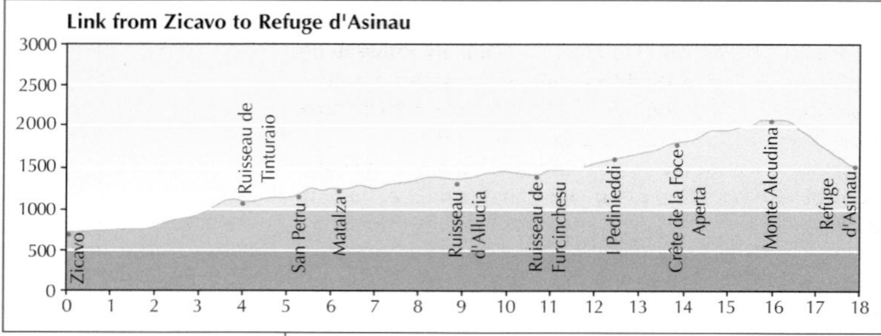

houses bear faded names and dates. There are views down to the church and the Taravo valley, as well as of the surrounding mountains. After passing the Pacific Sud bar, the road is called the **Cours Abbaticci**. The road rises gently, passing a small family burial plot beside a pig-pen.

As the road curves around the head of a steep-sided wooded valley, cross a bridge called the **Pont di Camera** and enjoy a view of a fine waterfall in a granite chute. The woods are holm oak and chestnut, with a rampant, tangled understorey. Cross a smaller bridge and look back to see the village of Zicavo spilling down its steep hillside. Watch out on the left for a path marked with **yellow paint** flashes rising from the road.

Pig-pens are tucked away in the woods, explaining any grunting and squealing that might be heard.

The path climbs uphill through a **groove** in the granite bedrock on a wooded slope. At a higher level the path is flanked by **drystone walls** and has plenty of shade. When the path levels out for a while, notice the huge charred chestnut trunks, whose roots continue to sprout new boughs. ◀

When the wire and wooden fencing alongside runs out, the path zigzags up a sort of **rugged stairway, and holm oaks give way to beech trees. At a higher level, the path runs through a rocky, stony groove** and the tree cover thins out, giving good views of distant mountain ranges. There are tufts of broom and thorny scrub, then the path emerges quite suddenly into more open terrain, though there are **drystone walls** to one side or the other.

Keep an eye on the yellow flashes, which lead over an **outcrop** of granite at 1163m (3816ft), where there are walls on both sides. There is a short descent, then a left turn along a path following an **old terrace**. Bracken, brambles and other scrub cover former cultivated slopes. Another short descent leads into a beech wood to cross the bouldery **Ruisseau de Tinturaio**. Follow a **bouldery path** zigzagging up onto a slope covered in broom, then follow a fence into an area sparsely covered in beech trees to reach a **track**.

Turn left along the track, then when it loops to the right, turn left again and continue uphill as marked by yellow flashes to reach a **road** close to a **monument**. ▶ Turn left to follow the road gently uphill as it makes a loop to cross a small bridge and a larger **bridge**. Walkers intending to visit the Auberge Gîte Bergerie de Basseta should follow the road onwards, otherwise turn right uphill on a **bouldery slope** covered in tall beech trees to reach a **signpost**. To the right is the Sentier de l'Aconit, but turn left here and follow a grooved path marked by yellow flashes.

The monument was raised to Pierre Kemp, who died while employed on the construction of the road.

After crossing an **open slope** covered in spiny broom, walkers reach picnic benches and an information board. There are notes about the Forêt du Cuscione and the Plateau du Cuscione. The Sentier de l'Aconit is a short walking trail, and there are notes about the Corsican aconite, which grows only on the Plateau du Cuscione alongside the streams and *pozzines,* or waterholes. Although poisonous to grazing animals, it is also a protected species. There is a **water source** beneath the road end. Walk to the little **Chapelle San Petru** – a lovely little granite chapel in a wooded bower at 1370m (4495ft). This should be reached 2¼ hours after leaving Zicavo.

CHAPELLE SAN PETRU

The lintel stone of the Chapelle San Petru carries a date of 1891. At the beginning of August it is customary for livestock to be blessed as part of a shepherds' festival. For centuries livestock has grazed the grasslands of the plateau each summer. There is a very basic refuge beside the chapel, consisting only of two rooms and no facilities apart from the nearby source of water. (Walkers could follow the road away from the chapel, keeping straight ahead at a junction, to reach the Auberge Gîte Bergerie de Basseta, only half an hour's walk away, where accommodation, food and drink are offered.)

To continue from the **Chapelle San Petru**, walk up a short, bouldery slope covered in tall beech trees. At the top is a **signpost** pointing the way ahead to Alcudina and the GR20. Step down onto a **stony track** and follow it gently uphill from a bend. A large rounded boulder confirms that walkers are on course for the GR20, then there is a signboard announcing the **Plateau du Cuscione**. Pass a barrier gate and follow the track over a rise, noting the presence of the **Refuge de Matalza** off to the left. This is a very basic two-roomed refuge with no facilities, apart from water available from nearby streams. The **Ruisseau d'Orticacciu** is crossed by means of a granite slab ford, then the track rises up another gentle slope.

When the track bends suddenly to the right, leave it and walk down to the **Ruisseau de Veracolongu**. The stream can be forded at a point where a boulder bears a yellow paint flash. A path on the far side rises across a slope of short grass and juniper, passing close to some **beech trees**, many of them dead or fallen. Above the tall trees is a slope of spiny broom and juniper scrub. Look out for little **cairns** on

The link from Zicavo to the GR20, seen here in winter, is flashed with yellow paint onto the Plateau du Cuscione.

boulders that mark the path over a rise at 1505m (4938ft) and down into a broad depression. Walk across a lovely carpet of short grass, crossing deeply cut streams and passing isolated pools. This is one of many *pozzines* that occur on the **Plateau du Cuscione**.

Cross the *pozzine* and also cross the **Ruisseau d'Allucia**, following its course onwards a short way. Watch for the little cairns and yellow flashes, which lead gradually to the right as the path rises across a broad slope and into a **gentle valley**. **Climb up a slope bearing a few beech trees to reach a clear track**, where the GR20 is joined again. There are signposts for Usciolu, Asinau and Zicavo, as well as for Monte Alcudina. Walkers should reach the track about 1½ hours after leaving the Chapelle San Petru, and the altitude is 1480m (4855ft). Refer to the map on p.184.

Cross over the track, just to cut a loop out of it, then turn right and follow it as marked. Turn left after a short while and walk down to a river, the **Ruisseau de Furcinchesu**, which is well wooded with beech. Walk upstream to reach a wobbly suspension **footbridge** and cross it. The path doubles back downstream a little, then rises up a **bouldery slope** covered in beech trees. There are some open areas, then the path reaches a much wider expanse of spiny broom and juniper scrub. There are signs for **I Pedinieddi Aire de Bivouac** off to the right.

I PEDINIEDDI AIRE DE BIVOUAC

The PNRC Refuge d' I Pedinieddi was destroyed by a lightning strike in 1981 and never rebuilt. Bear this in mind if storms are forecast, as the summit of Monte Alcudina is more than 500m (1640ft) higher than this site! Masonry from the ruins has been used to mark out a number of camping spaces, and this is the only place along the whole of the GR20 where you can legally pitch a tent for the night away from a refuge or *gîte*. A water source is signposted, and this is the only facility available, so if planning to use the bivouac area, remember to carry all other food and drink supplies with you.

Continue following the course of the GR20, which rises from the bivouac area of scrub onto another slope of beech trees. A **water source** is located just to the left of the path. As it climbs higher on the slope and crosses a flowery scrub, the

A fairly easy path traverses the high and sprawling slopes of Monte Alcudina before making a steep descent.

path is either on **bare rock** or has a stony surface. There is plenty of juniper scrub on the way to a broad, gently sloping gap on the **Crête de la Foce Aperta**, at an altitude of 1805m (5920ft). This gap should be reached 1¼ hours after leaving the track on the Plateau du Cuscione.

Look up to the summit of Monte Alcudina from the gap, and follow the path steadily as it rises along the **crest**. The ascent poses no problems, though the path drifts away from the crest to cross a **rugged slope** to the right, then after turning a corner the summit is much closer to hand. The path keeps away from the **rocky crest**, yet still crosses plenty of bare rock and weaves between boulders and alder scrub.

When the summit of **Monte Alcudina** is gained, pass the monumental **cross** that stands on a bare dome of granite at 2134m (7001ft). Walkers should reach the summit within an hour of leaving the Crête de la Foce Aperta, and can spend a while enjoying the view, looking back along the course of the GR20, and ahead to the exciting rocky spires and towers of the Aiguilles de Bavella.

A signboard gives directions for Usciolu and Asinau. Follow the **rocky ridge** southwest for the descent to the Refuge d'Asinau. Walk across **bare rock** and scramble around immense boulders to reach a **gap** at 2025m (6645ft), where there is a signpost pointing left for Asinau. Walk downhill and swing to the left, then pick a way across the **rocky face** of the mountain. Watch carefully for markers, as the route zigzags down more **rocky slopes** and weaves in and out of patches of alder scrub. Although the refuge is often plainly in view below, and looks quite close, getting down to it is slow and difficult. Take your time and tread carefully, especially if the rock underfoot is wet.

A few slender sycamore trees rise above the alder scrub, and the path continues zigzagging downhill on rock, boulders or loose stones. Eventually, and with some relief, walkers reach the **Refuge d'Asinau**, at an altitude of 1530m (5020ft), about 1½ hours after leaving the summit of Monte Alcudina.

REFUGE D'ASINAU

The PNRC Refuge d'Asinau is a simple stone *bergerie* style building clinging to a steep and rugged slope below Monte Alcudina. It has a dormitory with 30 beds, a kitchen/dining room and the *gardien's* quarters. A fine terrace looks across the valley to the spiky crest of the Aiguilles de Bavella. A shower and toilets are located in a small building near the refuge, along with a water supply. There are small camping spaces located downhill from the refuge and in the direction of the shower block. Meals, basic foodstuffs and drinks are on sale. The Bergeries d'Asinau, plainly in view below the refuge, operates a very basic *gîte d'étape* with 20 beds, meals, toilet and a primitive shower.

STAGE 14

Refuge d'Asinau to Village de Bavella (low-level)

There are two routes from the Refuge d'Asinau to the Village de Bavella. The low-level route is described here, but walkers interested in the Alpine Variant should refer to the next section. The low-level route is the main route of the GR20, clinging to the well-wooded slopes of the Asinau valley, turning round the mountainside to approach the Village de Bavella. On the map it looks relatively easy, and indeed many parts are easy, but sometimes the path is rough and narrow, and there is more ascent and descent than might be imagined. The final climb to the Village de Bavella is quite rocky. Those with an interest in flowers should take this route, as there is a wealth of species not noted on the route so far. Walkers looking for excitement and superb scenery, however, should take the Alpine Variant.

Distance	11km (6¾ miles)
Total Ascent	380m (1250 feet)
Total Descent	695m (2280 feet)
Time	4¾ hours
Map	IGN 4253 ET
Terrain	Mostly forest and woodland, though there are plenty of open areas along the way. The route is mostly along narrow paths clinging to steep slopes, and some parts can be quite rocky, especially towards the end.
Shelter	The trees on the valley sides provide good shade and shelter.
Food and Drink	Water is available from streams and signposted sources. There are a couple of bar–restaurants and a shop at the Village de Bavella.

Leave the **Refuge d'Asinau** as signposted for Paliri, following a rugged path across a well-vegetated and well-watered bouldery slope. Continue across a slope of spiny broom and boulders, noting a spur path to the left leading only to the

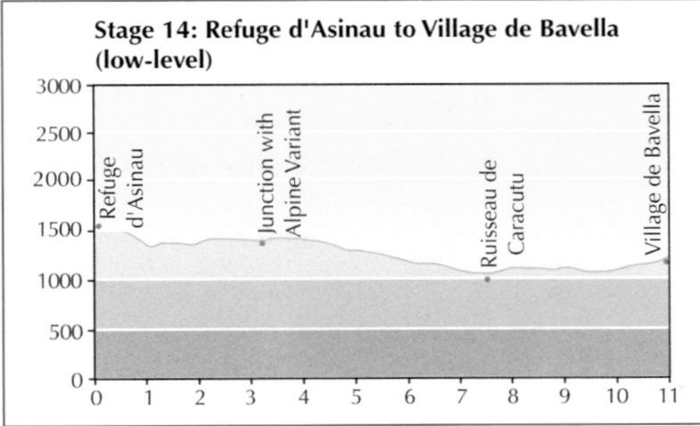

Bergeries d'Asinau, which offer accommodation, food and drink. However, continue downhill to reach a **stand of pines**. There are signposts here for the Refuge d' I Paliri, as well as a waymarked link with the village of Quenza.

The GR20 goes down among the pines and fords the bouldery bed of the **Ruisseau d'Asinau**. A bouldery path rises above the river and wanders across a slope covered in pines. It passes some big boulders and continues through a couple of clearings of spiny broom and juniper scrub. While in the clearings, look up at the rocky pinnacles of the Aiguilles de Bavella.

The path climbs to a signpost for a **water source** in an area of pines and slender birch trees. An easy stretch of well-engineered path contours across a slope, touching 1400m (4590ft), though it becomes narrower and rougher later. The path descends and is quite rugged in places, crossing a couple of streambeds. Again, there are clearings and views of the Aiguilles de Bavella high above.

Reach a **signpost** where the Alpine Variant is marked uphill to the left, waymarked with yellow flashes of paint. This point is reached about 1¼ hours after leaving the Refuge d'Asinau, at 1320m (4330ft). (Walkers who suddenly decide to walk the Alpine Variant should refer to the next section for a route description.)

The main course of the GR20 continues round the slope, as signposted for the Col de Bavella. The path descends to cross the open, rocky slopes of the **Ravin du Pargulu**, then continues through the forest. Watch out for a **rocky viewpoint** off to the right, which overlooks the valley, allows a view back to Monte Alcudina, and takes in some of the rocky pinnacles of the Aiguilles de Bavella. The path contours across the slope, then climbs, with tall heather becoming more noticeable. Reach another prominent **rocky outcrop** and again study the pinnacles high above.

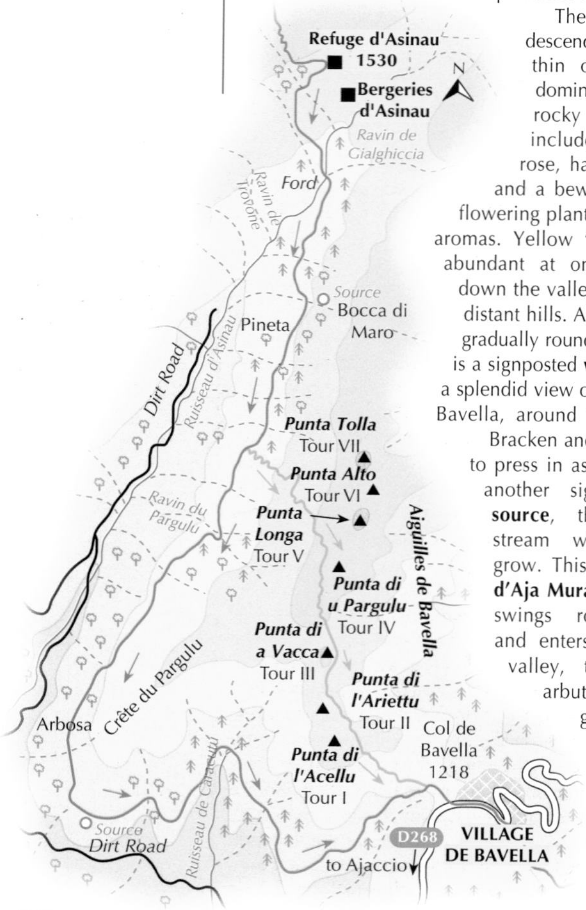

The path starts to descend, and as the pines thin out, tall heather dominates the steep and rocky slopes. Shrubs include holm oak, wild rose, hawthorn, arbutus, and a bewildering array of flowering plants with wonderful aromas. Yellow 'everlastings' are abundant at one point. Views down the valley lead the eye to distant hills. As the path swings gradually round to the left, there is a signposted **water source** and a splendid view of the Aiguilles de Bavella, around 1050m (3445ft). Bracken and brambles begin to press in as the path passes another signposted **water source**, then crosses a stream where hollyoaks grow. This is the **Ruisseau d'Aja Murata**. As the route swings round a ridge and enters the next little valley, the holm oak, arbutus and heather grow densely and obscure the sun and views.

Massive buttresses and towers of rock are a feature of the amazing crest of the Aiguilles de Bavella.

The path descends, then climbs, and water can be heard in the **Ruisseau de Caracutu** long before it is seen. Cross the bouldery stream, taking care if the boulders are greasy.

The path is again among tall laricio pines at this point. Follow it up another slope and the pines thin out, so that the heather and holm oak dominate again. After a bouldery stretch the path descends to cross a rocky slope and reaches the bed of the **Ruisseau de Donicelli**. Rocky pinnacles again tower high above.

The path is narrow as it leaves the streambed, and is flanked by scrub and pines. Watch carefully for **small cairns** that mark the route as it climbs up and around a **rocky corner** at 1055m (3460ft). There are good views up towards the Col de Bavella as it makes the turn, but the path becomes quite **rough and rocky** in its final stages. There are a few pines on the slope, as well as more heather scrub. Some parts of the path are easy, while others are stony or cross **bare rock**, picking out lines of weakness that require some short scrambles. It is almost like climbing an uneven **rocky stairway**.

A bouldery path passes a couple of solitary pines, aiming for the denser cover of laricio pines on the Col de

The white statue of Notre Dame des Neiges is perched on a large cairn on top of the Col de Bavella.

Bavella. There is a steep slope of grass, and from high above the voices of climbers might be heard, negotiating some of the pitches on the rock walls. It is possible to pick out some of the climbing routes by looking for signs bolted to the rock.

When the D268 is reached on the **Col de Bavella**, there is a cross and a statue of Notre Dame des Neiges, as well as plenty of parked cars. Walkers should reach this point, at an altitude of 1218m (3996ft), about 3½ hours after leaving the junction with the Alpine Variant route. Turn left to enter the **Village de Bavella** and choose a place to stay for the night, unless you wish to continue towards the Refuge d' I Paliri. Those who choose to continue to the Refuge d' I Paliri should refer to Stage 15 for the route description, and remember to buy food to take with you as there is none available at the refuge.

VILLAGE DE BAVELLA

The Village de Bavella is a ramshackle collection of wooden and stone huts, mostly with corrugated iron roofs, in various states of repair. Some are in a ruined state, while others are being rebuilt and even have satellite dishes. Traditionally, the Village de Bavella is the 'summer village' for distant Conca – a name that suggests the end is drawing very close at this stage. Some walkers actually prefer to finish at this point, while some commercial groups omit the entire stretch between Bavella and Conca from their itineraries.

Accommodation The first building reached on the Col de Bavella is *Les Aiguilles de Bavella,* tel 04 95 72 01 88, which has 18 beds in its *gîte d'etape,* as well as an additional mobile home. The road runs downhill to reach a hairpin bend and the Auberge du Col de Bavella, tel 04 95 72 09 87, which has 24 beds in its *gîte d'etape*. Camping is not permitted in the area, so those wishing to camp should continue along the GR20 to the Refuge d' I Paliri.

Food and Drink Both Les Aiguilles de Bavella and the Auberge du Col de Bavella have bar–restaurants. Just a short way further downhill is Le Refuge, which is a bar–restaurant–pizzeria. Despite its name it does not operate as a refuge. Walkers can stock up on food at the Alimentation du Col de Bavella. This is the last place to buy food and drink before Conca, and you are reminded that there is no food store or meals service at the Refuge d' I Paliri.

Transport A bus service is operated by Balesi Evasion, tel 04 95 70 15 55 or 04 95 70 59 32, to Ajaccio and Porto Vecchio, daily except Sundays through July and August, and from Monday to Friday through the rest of the year. Another bus service is operated by Autocars Ricci, tel 04 95 51 08 19, 04 95 78 81 45 or 04 95 76 25 59, to Ajaccio, daily through July and August, but not on Sundays through the rest of the year. Taxi services are operated by Jean Francois Crispi Levie, tel 04 95 78 41 26, mobile 06 07 58 17 98 or Taxi Station Zonza, mobile 06 14 69 84 66.

STAGE 14

Refuge d'Asinau to Village de Bavella (high-level)

The main route of the GR20 between the Refuge d'Asinau and Col de Bavella is essentially a low-level route. However, there is also a high-level alternative called the Alpine Variant available. This route branches away from the main route and climbs towards the pinnacles and towers of the Aiguilles de Bavella. It is highly recommended for those who want to experience a bit of excitement, and in terms of overall effort it is probably only a little more difficult than the low-level route. Although it involves a higher climb, the route to the Village de Bavella is shorter, so the two probably balance out. The Alpine Variant is highly recommended in clear weather in order to make the most of the views, which are quite remarkable. It is also helpful if the rock is dry, because at one point walkers have to climb up a short slab of rock with the aid of a chain. Those reaching the Col de Bavella early in the day may wish to continue to the Refuge d' I Paliri and so shorten the final day's walk. (See map on p.204.)

Distance	8km (5 miles)
Total Ascent	550m (1805 feet)
Total Descent	865m (2840 feet)
Time	4¼ hours
Map	IGN 4253 ET
Terrain	Mostly forest and woodland at first, then a steep climb up to the Aiguilles de Bavella. Paths can be steep and stony, but are not too difficult, though one short stretch up a rock slab has a chain for protection. The descent is steep and rocky. The Alpine Variant is recommended only in clear weather.
Shelter	There is shade and shelter in the trees at first, but the higher parts of the mountains are more exposed to sun, wind and rain.
Food and Drink	Use a water source before starting the Alpine Variant, as no water is available on the higher mountains. There are a couple of bar–restaurants and a shop at the Village de Bavella.

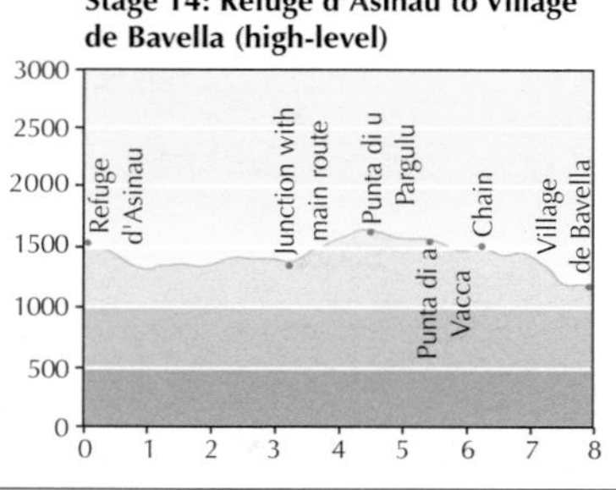

Leave the **Refuge d'Asinau** as signposted for Paliri, following a rugged path across a well-vegetated and well-watered bouldery slope. Continue across a slope of spiny broom and boulders, noting a spur path to the left leading only to the **Bergeries d'Asinau**, which offers accommodation, food and drink. However, continue downhill to reach a **stand of pines**. There are signposts here for the Refuge d' I Paliri, as well as a waymarked link with the village of Quenza. The GR20 goes down among the pines and fords the bouldery bed of the **Ruisseau d'Asinau**.

A bouldery path rises above the river and wanders across a slope covered in pines. It passes some big boulders and continues through a couple of clearings of spiny broom and juniper scrub. While in the clearings, look up at the rocky pinnacles of the Aiguilles de Bavella.

The path climbs to a signpost for a **water source** in an area of pines and slender birch trees. An easy stretch of well-engineered path contours across a slope, touching 1400m (4590ft), though it becomes narrower and rougher later. The path descends and is quite rugged in places, crossing a couple of streambeds. Again, there are clearings and views of the Aiguilles de Bavella high above. Reach a **signpost** where the Alpine Variant is marked uphill to the left, waymarked with yellow flashes of paint. This point is reached about 1¼ hours after leaving the Refuge d'Asinau, at 1320m (4330ft). (Walkers who suddenly decide they are not going to walk this route should refer to the previous chapter for the low-level route description.)

Zigzag steeply uphill, following the **stony path** up through the forest. The path swings to the right as the trees thin out on a slope littered with boulders, where the ground is clothed in juniper scrub. The yellow paint flashes and **small cairns** lead faultlessly uphill. There are towers and sheer walls of rock above and it all looks quite intimidating, but around 1690m (5545ft) the path swings right and levels out, then drops down a short way to reach an easy crest at the foot of an immense tower of rock. This tower is the **Punta**

The Alpine Variant passes Punta di u Pargulu, or Tour IV, as it crosses the crest of the Aiguilles de Bavella.

di u Pargulu, also known as Tour IV. Take a break at this point and simply gaze in awe and wonder at the surrounding scenery. Apart from the towers and pinnacles clustered along the ridge, there is also a view down the Ravin du Pargulu to the low-level route of the GR20, and a fine view up the valley to Monte Alcudina.

The path running down from the crest is broad and stony, but not too steep, and flanked by spiny broom and juniper scrub. Follow the path down to a gap where the **Punta di a Vacca**, also known as Tour III, rises as a conical mass of rock. The summit can be reached by scrambling, for those who fancy a short diversion, otherwise head off to the left across a bouldery slope, passing a few pines to reach another **rocky gap** on the side of the mountain.

Looking ahead, two tall and rather intimidating towers of rock are visible. These are the Punta di l'Ariettu, or Tour II, and the Punta di l'Acellu, or Tour I. There is obviously no way to walk over these two towers, but other people might be seen picking their way along a rugged path on their eastern flanks. You will soon be walking along that same path.

Follow a stony, bouldery path down towards the gap between the **Punta di a Vacca** and Punta di l'Ariettu. The path doesn't actually reach this gap, but drifts away to the left and keeps below it. Pass a few pines and walk beneath the rocky face of the **Punta di l'Ariettu**, basically outflanking this monstrous obstacle. The path then leads up to a sloping **slab of rock** surmounted by an enormous jammed boulder, forcing walkers out onto the exposed, tilted slope. Fortunately, there is a **chain** raised on posts, rather like a short fence, for protection. Most walkers are happy to heave-ho their way up, hand over hand on the chain, shuffling their feet up the slab**. In wet weather take care, as the rock can be slippery**.

At the top, squeeze between the rocks, then walk down a rocky stairway and along a rugged path towards the **Punta di l'Acellu**. Again, keep well to the left of the tower, picking a way along a **rocky terrace** with a slight overhang above. Follow the yellow flashes carefully beyond, across a bouldery slope and up through a stand of pines to reach a rocky little **gap** on the crest.

Descend through a rock-walled **gully**, which is grassy and bouldery at first, with a zigzag path overlooked by a **tower of rock**. There are plenty of laricio pines further down the slope, and tall heather too, but not enough to obscure the view towards the Bavella road and the mountains beyond. The path in the gully is rather more rugged for a while, then the markers direct walkers off to the left, more directly towards the Col de Bavella.

Cut across a more open, **rocky slope**, then descend again on a rough and bouldery slope where pines and heather grow. Plaques are bolted to rockfaces off to the left, giving the names of popular climbs, and there may well be several climbers picking their way up the faces. Entering a denser stand of laricio pines, pass a sign announcing the end of the Alpine Variant, and the path joins the main course of the GR20 again. Keep left to follow the GR20 a short way up the slope of grass and pines.

When the D268 is reached on the **Col de Bavella,** there is a cross and a statue of Notre Dame des Neiges, as well as plenty of parked cars. Walkers should reach this point, at an altitude of 1218m (3996ft), about 3 hours after beginning the Alpine Variant route. Turn left to enter the **Village de Bavella** and choose a place to stay for the night, unless you wish to continue towards the Refuge d' I Paliri. Those who choose to continue to the Refuge d' I Paliri should refer to Stage 15 for the route description, and remember to buy food to take with you, as there is none available at the refuge.

VILLAGE DE BAVELLA

The Village de Bavella is a ramshackle collection of wooden and stone huts, mostly with corrugated iron roofs, in various states of repair. Some are in a ruined state, while others are being rebuilt and even have satellite dishes. Traditionally, the Village de Bavella is the 'summer village' for distant Conca – a name that suggests the end is drawing very close at this stage. Some walkers actually prefer to finish at this point, while some commercial groups omit the entire stretch between Bavella and Conca from their itineraries.

Accommodation The first building reached on the Col de Bavella is Les Aiguilles de Bavella, tel 04 95 72 01 88, which has 18 beds in its *gîte d'etape*, as well as an additional mobile home. The road runs downhill to reach a hairpin bend and the Auberge du Col de Bavella, tel 04 95 72 09 87, which has 24 beds in its *gîte d'etape*. Camping is not permitted in the area, so those wishing to camp should continue along the GR20 to the Refuge d' I Paliri.

Food and Drink Both Les Aiguilles de Bavella and the Auberge du Col de Bavella have bar–restaurants. Just a short way further downhill is Le Refuge, which is a bar–restaurant–pizzeria. Despite its name it does not operate as a refuge. Walkers can stock up on food at the Alimentation du Col de Bavella. This is the last place to buy food and drink before Conca, and you are reminded that there is no food store or meals service at the Refuge d'I Paliri.

Transport A bus service is operated by Balesi Evasion, tel 04 95 70 15 55 or 04 95 70 59 32, to Ajaccio and Porto Vecchio, daily except Sundays through July and August, and from Monday to Friday through the rest of the year. Another bus service is operated by Autocars Ricci, tel 04 95 51 08 19, 04 95 78 81 45 or 04 95 76 25 59, to Ajaccio, daily through July and August, but not on Sundays through the rest of the year. Taxi services are operated by Jean Francois Crispi Levie, tel 04 95 78 41 26, mobile 06 07 58 17 98 or Taxi Station Zonza, mobile 06 14 69 84 66.

A short length of chain assists on the ascent of a rock slab between wedged boulders on the Punta di l'Ariettu

STAGE 15

Village de Bavella to Conca

The final stage of the GR20 looks quite long on the map, even for those who take the option of spending a night at the Refuge d' I Paliri. Apart from a few steep and rugged climbs, however, it is mostly quite an easy walk, and some parts of the path are level and pose no problems. The mountain scenery is remarkably good throughout the first half of the walk, and the surroundings remain quite rugged even to the end. However, there is a definite feeling that height is being lost – the vegetation becomes more exotic, the temperature rises, and ultimately walkers see the little village of Conca beckoning, with the sea beyond. You can reflect on your journey through the mountains of Corsica, unravelling the path in your mind, but you also need to think about how you are going to leave Conca and return home.

Distance	19km (12 miles)
Total Ascent	700m (2295 feet)
Total Descent	1670m (5480 feet)
Time	7 hours
Map	IGN 4253 ET
Terrain	Well forested at the start, but later the forests thin out. There are some steep and rugged slopes, but these are quite limited, though much of the terrain is rough and rocky. There is good woodland cover on the final descent to Conca. On the whole, it is mostly downhill to the end.
Shelter	The trees provide some shade and shelter. The Refuge d' I Paliri is encountered in the early part of the day's walk, but later, most areas are open, and it can be very hot on the lower parts.
Food and Drink	Water can be obtained before the Refuge d' I Paliri, before the Bocca di u Sordu, near the ruins of the Bergeries de Capeddu, and from the Ruisseau de Punta Pinzuta. There are a couple of bars and restaurants available in Conca.

To leave the **Village de Bavella**, follow the D268 downhill from Les Aiguilles de Bavella to the Auberge du Col de

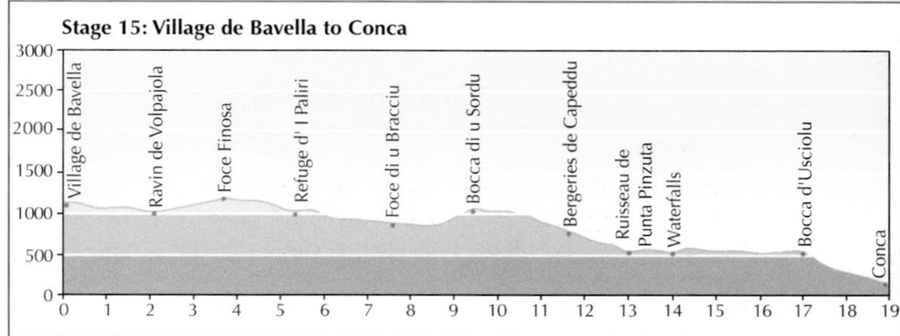

Bavella. Turn right off the **hairpin bend** in the road and walk along a clear **track** signposted for the GR20 and Paliri. Turn right again at another signpost reading the same, and follow a broad **dirt road** across a slope of laricio pines. There are a couple of signs erected by businesses in Conca, already anticipating your arrival!

Watch out for a **path** heading down to the left, which is signposted after a while for the Refuge d' I Paliri. Walk down the path, which is quite rough and stony in places, crossing a **streambed** and passing through bracken on the forest floor. On landing on another **track**, turn right, and enjoy a view of rugged mountains while walking to a concrete ford in the **Ravin de Volpajola**.

Walk a little further along the track amid tall pines, then a sign on the right indicates a **narrow path** climbing uphill. Follow the path as it cuts up across the slope, passing pines and tall heather, before zigzagging more steeply and over rockier terrain to reach a gap called **Foce Finosa** at 1206m (3957ft). Climb a little higher on the rocks behind a sign for a fine view back to the Aiguilles de Bavella, unobscured by pines. In the other direction, note the prominent peak of the Punta di l'Anima Damnata.

Follow the path downhill from from **Foce Finosa**, zigzagging on a steep and rocky slope. This is an old mule path that has been pitched in places with carefully laid stonework. Go up through a **rocky notch** next to a tower of rock, noting holm oak and arbutus growing amid the laricio and maritime pines. Continue walking down the path, then an easier stretch leads across a slope covered in pines where views through the trees are of remarkably jagged mountains.

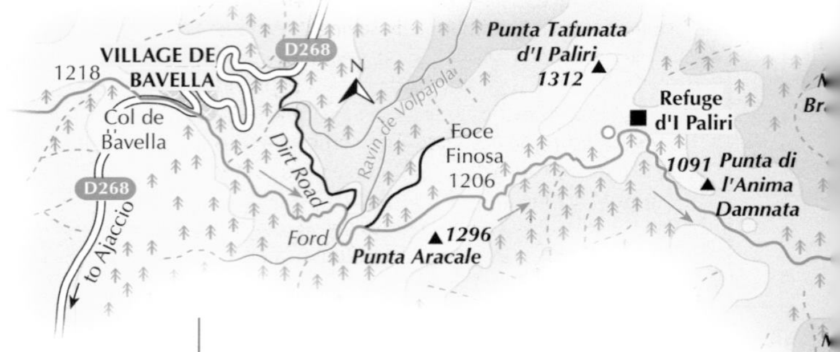

Map continues p.219

There is a fairly easy ascent for a short way, passing a **water source** and a sign for a shower before reaching the **Refuge d' I Paliri**. The refuge is situated at 1055m (3460ft), and is reached about two hours after leaving the Village de Bavella.

REFUGE D' I PALIRI

The PNRC Refuge d' I Paliri is built in the *bergerie* style and features a small dormitory and an even smaller dormitory, with 20 beds altogether. There is a kitchen/dining room in between, and the *gardien* lives in a small building nearby. The toilet is out at the back of the refuge, while the shower and water source are signposted off the GR20 nearby. Camping spaces are located in the forest in the direction signposted for Conca.

There is no food store or meals service at the refuge, so you should bring your own food and drink. However, some walkers unburden themselves and leave excess supplies at the refuge for anyone else to use. The refuge sits at the foot of the Punta Tafunata d' I Paliri, which has a hole known as the Trou de la Bombe pierced through the rock near the top – it often looks like a huge blue eye. Heart-shaped stones marked with poetry and prose have been positioned in the forest around the refuge.

Leave the **campsite** and descend along a rather **rocky path**, enjoying the variety of flowers and shrubs alongside. The path enters a pine forest where a number of trees have toppled, but becomes easier later, and is quite level as it passes through a denser part of the forest where bracken grows quite deeply. Walkers pass the prominent peak of the **Punta di l'Anima Damnata** without really seeing it. As they emerge into the open, however, it becomes more clearly visible. The path climbs towards a **gap**, and there is plenty of evidence that the forest suffered a severe burning in the past. The scrub contains arbutus, tall heather, rock rose and other flowering plants.

As the path contours easily across the slope, notice the blue eye of Punta Tafunata d' I Paliri watching walkers' progress, and the pinnacles of nearby Monte Bracchiutu. The path eventually crosses a broad gap, called the **Foce di u Bracciu**, where it is important to keep an eye on the paint flashes, as there are other paths converging on this point, around 915m (3000ft).

The path descends through pines, arbutus and tall heather as it swings to the right into the next valley. Cross a bouldery slab of granite, look out for a tiny **water source**, enjoy views across the valley, and continue descending with more tree cover.

All of a sudden the route starts climbing, sometimes on bare rock or on a rugged, **stony path**. There is still good shade from the trees, but the ascent, although fairly short, can be tiring. There are steep zigzags towards the top, where the route passes through a **gap of bare granite and boulders. This is the Bocca di u Sordu**, around 1040m (3410ft). Look up to the right while crossing the gap to see a lone olive tree leaning out from the rock. You may not have seen an olive tree since leaving Calenzana!

The GR20 heads off to the left, clambering over **rocks and boulders**, going through a small stand of pines and down a **grooved channel** on a slope of granite. The path leading

Looking southwards from the Refuge d' I Paliri, where the mountains may be lower, but remain impressive.

onwards is almost level, quite **narrow and sandy**, passing though pines and tall heather scrub. There is a descent on bulbous masses of **bare granite**, and plenty of evidence of a severe fire in the past. However, some of the trees grow from the bare rock, and have doubtless survived because there was no ground vegetation to carry the fire towards them.

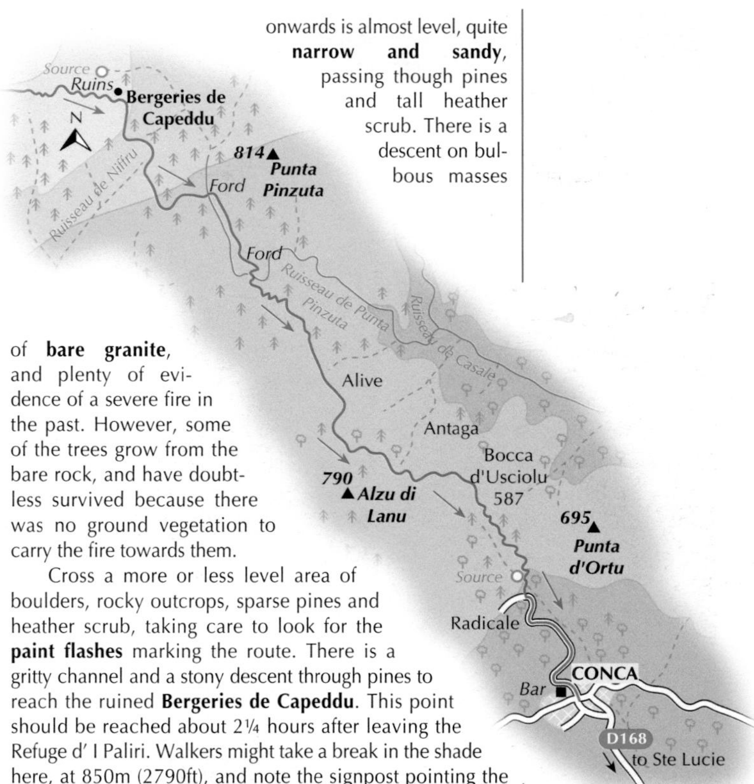

Cross a more or less level area of boulders, rocky outcrops, sparse pines and heather scrub, taking care to look for the **paint flashes** marking the route. There is a gritty channel and a stony descent through pines to reach the ruined **Bergeries de Capeddu**. This point should be reached about 2¼ hours after leaving the Refuge d' I Paliri. Walkers might take a break in the shade here, at 850m (2790ft), and note the signpost pointing the way to a handy little **water source**. There is also a skip full of rubbish nearby that seems incongruous in this sylvan setting.

Signposts point the way back to the Refuge d' I Paliri and Col de Bavella, ahead to Conca, and off-route to the Village de Sari. Sticky leaved cistus grows under the tree cover – a plant of the *maquis* not really seen since leaving Calenzana. All the signs indicate that the end of the walk is close.

Follow the path out of the shade near the **ruins** and walk down a slope of tall *maquis* and scrub. The area used to be tall forest, but was devastated by fire in 1985. A few tall

The striking rock tower of the Punta di l'Anima Damnata, or the Point of the Damned Soul.

laricio pines have survived, their bark still scorched black, and only small tufts of green at the tops of their trunks, while the scrub has taken advantage of the light and grown into remarkably dense thickets. The **narrow path** is awkward and stony for a while, with the scrub pressing on both sides. Later it is wider, more gently graded and easier to follow. Swing to the right through arbutus and heather scrub, passing a **tower of rock**, with a good view of Punta Batarchione at the head of the valley.

Swing left down to the **Ruisseau de Punta Pinzuta**. The tall pines near the river survived the forest fire in the past due to their higher water content, but they are still scorched along their trunks. Cross the river and turn right to walk between the pines as the route heads downstream. An excellent **mule path** develops, which has been well engineered on a steep and rugged slope, but walkers have to leave it to continue down a more **rugged path** and cross back over the river. A couple of inviting **pools** demand a break, and at 550m (1805ft) you can bet it will be lukewarm water on a hot day. It is advisable to treat the water if it is used for drinking, as it is popular with bathers.

Turn left after crossing the river and follow the path uphill. A series of steep zigzags climb alongside a **rock wall** in the shade of a stand of pine trees. The path reaches a **notch** in a little ridge and continues onwards. It climbs more gently to cross another notch, then rises even more gently across a scrubby slope high on the side of a valley. The **stony path** reaches a few pines, then there is a gradual descent until it reaches a rocky **ravine**. Drop down into the ravine to cross it, then climb uphill a short way through some thorny scrub.

The path descends a little, contours across the slope, then a rocky stairway leads uphill a short way to reach the **Bocca d'Usciolu**. This is a curious, narrow, crooked cleft in a rocky rib, reached at 587m (1926ft). The cleft is reached about 2 hours after leaving the ruined Bergeries de Capeddu. Turn around and take one last long look back at the mountains before they pass from sight.

You are finally leaving the mountains, and on starting the descent the village of Conca comes into view, nestling at the foot of the slope. The bells in the church tower will strike the quarter hours on the descent – it should take ¾ hour, so three strikes and you're out!

Most walkers who finish the GR20 are happy to take a celebratory drink at the Bar Le Soleil Levant in Conca.

The **narrow path** is quite stony, so tread carefully where heather, broom and cistus scrub press on both sides. On the descent, the arbutus grows taller and taller, with a few pines and gnarled cork oak trees offering more and more shade. There is a **water source** at the bottom for walkers who can't wait to reach the village to quench their thirst, and it will be quite warm now that the route has left the mountains.

The path quickly leads to a **minor road**, where a left turn leads down in loops to the village of **Conca** at 250m (820ft). Note the cork oak trees stripped of their bark along the way. On reaching a **road junction**, you have to decide whether to hit the **Bar Le Soleil Levant** for a celebratory drink or go directly to their accommodation. Whatever choice is made, the walk is over and you have completed the GR20!

Conca and the End of the GR20

You made it – well done!

No one in Conca seems impressed that you've just walked all the way through the mountains of Corsica to reach their little village, but all the same, they'll be happy to provide you with food, drink and accommodation. If you want to share a few tales of the trail, then do that with other walkers. Local folk have heard it all before, many times over!

Some walkers will want to dash away and catch a bus, but it is probably better if you take a break and spend at least one night in Conca. It is a quiet, unassuming little place, where you can quietly savour the feeling of satisfaction at completing the GR20. Think ahead about how you are going to leave Conca and make your way home.

Accommodation Little signs direct walkers to the Hôtel San Pasquale, tel. 04 95 71 56 13, a small hotel and the only one in the village. Walk down past the church, passing a monument to an ancient chapel and a number of family tombs, then turn left for the Gîte d'Étape La Tonnelle, tel. 04 95 71 46 55, which is opposite a cemetery. There is dormitory accommodation with 30 beds, as well as a campsite. A *navette* service is provided to take walkers to the buses on the main N198 at Sainte Lucie de Porto Vecchio.

Gentle countryside and olive groves are seen around the quiet and unassuming little village of Conca.

Food and Drink On entering Conca, the Bar Le Soleil Levant is on the right, offering food and drink, and they can organise a taxi down to the main road. The Restaurant Bar U Chjosu is off to the left and also provides food and drink. The Gîte d'Étape La Tonnelle has its own bar and restaurant. There is a basic *alimentation* opposite the post office in the village, for those who wish to buy food and cook their own meals.

Transport Having left Conca to link with bus services on the main road at Ste Lucie de Porto Vecchio, there is a choice of two main destinations – Bastia and Ajaccio. To reach Bastia, check the timetables of Les Rapides Bleus Corsicatours, tel. 04 95 31 03 79 or 04 95 70 96 52. Services run daily, except Sundays, for most of the year, but run every day through July to the middle of September. To reach Ajaccio, travel with Les Rapides Bleus Corsicatours, to Porto Vecchio, then switch to Eurocorse Voyages, tel. 04 95 70 13 83 or 04 95 21 06 30. Services run daily, except Sundays, for most of the year, but run every day through July to the middle of September. Autocars Balesi Evasion, tel. 04 95 70 15 55, also runs between Porto Vecchio and Ajaccio, including the Village de Bavella, daily except Sundays through July and August, and from Monday to Friday through the rest of the year.

At Bastia and Ajaccio it is possible to link with bus services to other parts of Corsica, or to switch to the CFC/SNCF railway to reach Vizzavona, Corte and Calvi. Railway timetables can be picked up at the main stations, or tel. 04 95 32 80 61, 04 95 23 11 03, 04 95 65 00 61 or 04 95 46 00 97. Those hoping to link with a particular ferry or flight to leave Corsica should check all timetable details carefully.

Transport can be rather slow and delays are normal. It is a good idea to allow a whole day, and maybe an extra night, to make a long transfer around Corsica. For example, it can take as long as 10½ hours to travel by bus from Sainte Lucie to Calvi, changing at Bastia, but coming the other way the trip can be accomplished in only 4¼ hours by changing buses at Casamozza. Obtain and carefully study up-to-date timetables in advance. If you call for a taxi to make a long journey in Corsica, it will be prove to be very expensive.

APPENDIX 1
Summary of GR20 Walking Times and Facilities

The timings below are the ones generally quoted for the sections of the route given in this table. Walkers should adapt them to suit their own performance, and plan ahead on that basis. The timings do not take into account any breaks whatsoever for lunch, rests, taking pictures, and so on.

The facilities listed are all available in July and August. Some are available from June to September. Few are available through the winter. Note that the refuges have *gardiens* in residence from June to September, but are left open throughout the rest of the year. Camping is available only at the refuges and at a couple of other designated sites.

Shops where walkers can stock up on food and drink are rare, but basic supplies of food and drink can be obtained at nearly all the refuges. Some of the *bergeries* also offer basic food and drink supplies. Transport links with the route are limited, and some bus services operate only through July and August. Road access for back-up vehicles is available at Calenzana, Haut Asco, Hôtel Castel di Vergio, Vizzavona, Bergeries d' E Capanelle, Bocca di Verdi, Village de Bavella and Conca.

Place	Time	Facilities
Calenzana (start of GR20)	0hr 00min	Hotels, *gîte,* camping, restaurants, bars, shops, bus, taxi
GR20/TMM junction	1hr 00min	
Arghioa	1hr 30min	
Bocca a u Saltu	1hr 30min	
Bocca a u Bassiguellu	1hr 30min	
Refuge d'Ortu di u Piobbu	1hr 30min	Refuge, camping, meals, supplies
Ruisseau de la Mandriaccia	1hr 00min	
Bocca Piccaia	2hr 30min	
Bocca d'Avartol	1hr 00min	
Bocca Carozzu	0hr 45min	
Refuge de Carozzu	1hr 15min	Refuge, camping, meals, supplies
Lac de la Muvrella	3hr 00min	
Bocca a i Stagni	1hr 00min	
Haut Asco	1hr 30min	Hotel, *gîte,* refuge, camping, restaurant, bar, supplies, bus
Altore (old refuge site)	2hr 00min	
Col Perdu	0hr 30min	

Place	Time	Facilities
Bocca Minuta	2hr 00min	
Refuge de Tighjettu	1hr 30min	Refuge, camping, meals supplies
Auberges U Vallone	0hr 30min	Basic *gîte*, camping, meals, supplies
Refuge de Ciottulu di I Mori	3hr 15min	Refuge, camping, meals, supplies
Bergeries de Radule	1hr 30min	Cheese
Hôtel Castel di Vergio	1hr 15min	Hotel, *gîte*, camping, restaurant, bar, supplies, bus
Bocca San Petru	1hr 30min	
Lac du Ninu	2hr 00min	
Bergeries de Vaccaghja	1hr 30min	Camping, supplies
Refuge de Manganu	0hr 45min	Refuge, camping, meals, supplies
Brèche de Capitellu	3hr 00min	
Bocca a Soglia	1hr 15min	
Bocca Muzella	1hr 45min	
Refuge de Petra Piana	1hr 00min	Refuge, camping, meals, supplies
Bergeries de Gialgo	0hr 30min	Cheese
Bergeries de Tolla	2hr 30min	Meals, supplies
Passerelle de Tolla	0hr 15min	
Refuge de l'Onda	1hr 45min	Refuge, camping, meals, supplies
Punta Muratello	2hr 30min	
Cascade des Anglais	2hr 30min	Bar–restaurant
Vizzavona (midpoint of GR20)	1hr 00min	Hotel, refuge, camping, restaurants, bars, shop, bus, train
Bocca Palmento	2hr 45min	
Bergeries d' E Capanelle	2hr 45min	*Gîtes*, refuge, camping, bar–restaurants, supplies
Pont de Casacchie	0hr 30min	
Plateau de Gialgone	3hr 00min	
Bocca di Verdi	1hr 30min	Refuge, camping, bar–restaurant, supplies
Bocca d'Oru	1hr 45 min	
Refuge de Prati	0hr 15min	Refuge, camping, meals, supplies
Punta Capella	1hr 00min	
Bocca di Laparo	1hr 30min	Refuge nearby
Refuge d'Usciolu	2hr 45min	Refuge, camping, meals, supplies
Bocca di l'Agnonu	2hr 30min	
Aire Bivouac I Pedinieddi	1hr 45min	Camping
Crête de Foce Aperta	0hr 30min	
Monte Alcudina	1hr 00min	
Refuge d'Asinau	1hr 30min	Refuge, camping, meals, supplies
GR20/Alpine Variant junction	1hr 15min	

Place	Time	Facilities
Village de Bavella	3hr 30min	*Gîtes,* bar–restaurants, shop, bus, taxi
Refuge d' I Paliri	2hr 00min	Refuge, camping
Bergeries de Capeddu	2hr 15min	
Bocca d'Usciolu	2hr 00min	
Conca (end of GR20)	0hr 45min	Hotel, *gîte,* camping, bar–restaurants, shop, taxi

The white flowers of cistus bushes are common among the lowland maquis, but absent on the high mountains.

A linear rocky dyke acts as a rugged stairway leading deep down into the awesome Cirque de la Solitude (Stage 4).

APPENDIX 2
Reverse Route Summary

There are some who prefer to walk the GR20 from south to north. The route descriptions in this guidebook can be reversed without difficulty, but it can become tedious changing all the starts and finishes, lefts and rights, ascents and descents. The red and white flashes that mark the route are just as easy to follow one way as the other, and most walkers are happy to rely on the waymarking, no matter what maps and guides they carry.

Below is a reverse route summary, which indicates the approximate length of time it takes to walk between short stages. Those walking south to north should not simply reverse each and every stage as described in this book. The first day's walk, from Conca, would be best concluded at the Refuge d' I Paliri, rather than the Village de Bavella. The last day's walk, downhill to Calenzana, proves remarkably easy when compared with the ascent from Calenzana. Adapt and amend the route to suit your own individual requirements.

Place	Time	Facilities
Conca (start of GR20)	0hr 00min	Hotel, *gîte,* camping, bar–restaurants, shop, taxi
Bocca d'Usciolu	1hr 15min	
Bergeries de Capeddu	2hr 30min	
Refuge d' I Paliri	2hr 45min	Refuge, camping
Village de Bavella	2hr 15min	*Gîtes,* bar–restaurants, shop, bus, taxi
GR20/Alpine Variant junction	3hr 30min	
Refuge d'Asinau	1hr 30min	Refuge, camping, meals, supplies
Monte Alcudina	2hr 30min	
Crête de Foce Aperta	0hr 45min	
Aire Bivouac I Pedinieddi	0hr 15min	Camping
Bocca di l'Agnonu	2hr 00min	
Refuge d'Usciolu	3hr 00min	Refuge, camping, meals, supplies
Bocca di Laparo	2hr 30min	Water, nearby refuge, camping
Punta Capella	2hr 30min	
Refuge de Prati	1hr 00min	Refuge, camping, meals, supplies

Place	Time	Facilities
Bocca d'Oru	0hr 15 min	
Bocca di Verdi	1hr 15min	Refuge, camping, bar–restaurant, supplies
Plateau de Gialgone	1hr 45min	
Pont de Casacchie	2hr 15min	
Bergeries d' E Capanelle	0hr 45min	*Gîtes,* refuge, camping, bar–restaurants, supplies
Bocca Palmento	2hr 45min	
Vizzavona (midpoint of GR20)	2hr 00min	Hotel, refuge, camping, restaurants, bars, shop, bus, train
Cascade des Anglais	1hr 00min	Bar–restaurant
Punta Muratello	3hr 15min	
Refuge de l'Onda	2hr 00min	Refuge, camping, meals, supplies
Passerelle de Tolla	1hr 30min	
Bergeries de Tolla	0hr 15min	Meals, supplies
Bergeries de Gialgo	2hr 45min	Cheese
Refuge de Petra Piana	0hr 45min	Refuge, camping, meals, supplies
Bocca Muzella	1hr 30min	
Bocca a Soglia	1hr 30min	
Brèche de Capitellu	1hr 45min	
Refuge de Manganu	2hr 00min	Refuge, camping, meals, supplies
Bergeries de Vaccaghja	0hr 45min	Camping, supplies
Lac du Ninu	1hr 45min	
Bocca San Petru	1hr 45min	
Hôtel Castel di Vergio	1hr 15min	Hotel, *gîte,* camping, restaurant, bar, supplies, bus
Bergeries de Radule	1hr 00min	Cheese
Refuge de Ciottulu di I Mori	2hr 00min	Refuge, camping, meals, supplies
Auberge U Vallone	2hr 45min	Basic *gîte,* camping, meals, supplies
Refuge de Tighjettu	0hr 45min	Refuge, camping, meals supplies
Bocca Minuta	2hr 00min	
Col Perdu	2hr 00min	
Altore (old refuge site)	0hr 30min	

Place	Time	Facilities
Haut Asco	1hr 30min	Hotel, *gîte,* refuge, camping, restaurant, bar, supplies, bus
Bocca a i Stagni	2hr 15min	
Lac de la Muvrella	1hr 00min	
Refuge de Carozzu	2hr 15min	Refuge, camping, meals, supplies
Bocca Carozzu	1hr 45min	
Bocca d'Avartoli	0hr 45min	
Bocca Piccaia	1hr 15min	
Ruisseau de la Mandriaccia	1hr 45min	
Refuge d'Ortu di u Piobbu	1hr 00min	Refuge, camping, meals, supplies
Bocca a u Bassiguellu	1hr 15min	
Bocca a u Saltu	1hr 00min	
Arghioa	1hr 00min	
GR20/TMM junction	1hr 00min	
Calenzana (end of GR20)	0hr 45min	Hotels, *gîte,* camping, restaurants, bars, shops, bus, taxi

The Auberge Gîte Bergerie de Basseta offers chalets, a dortoir *and camping, as well as a bar-restaurant (Link from Bocca di l'Agnonu).*

At a higher level on Paglia Orba, steep and exposed scrambling is required, needing great care (Ascent of Paglia Orba).

APPENDIX 3
Basic French for the GR20

Arrival in Corsica

Hello!/good evening/how are you?	*Bonjour!/bonsoir/ça va?*
Where can I get a taxi?	*Où puis-je trouver un taxi?*
Take me to . . .	*Conduisez-moi à . . .*
. . . The railway station/the hotel/this address . . .	*La gare/l'hôtel/cette adresse*
How much is it?	*C'est combien?*
Where is the bus stop/train station?	*Où se-trouve l'arrêt de bus/la gare?*
Tourist information office	*L'office de tourisme*
Post office/grocery	*La poste/alimentation*
I'd like a single/return ticket to . . .	*Je voudrais un billet aller simple/aller-retour à . . .*
Can I have a timetable?	*Puis-je avoir un horaire?*
Information/open/closed	*Reseignements/ouvert/fermé*

Staying the Night

Rooms available/no vacancies	*Chambres libres/complet*
I'd like a single/double room	*Je voudrais une chambre pour une personne/deux personnes*
How much does it cost per night?	*Quel est le prix par nuit?*
How much does it cost for bed and breakfast?	*Quel est le prix avec petit déjeuner?*
Is there hot water/a toilet/a shower?	*Y-a-t-il l'eau chaude/une toilette/un douche?*
Where is the dining room/bar?	*Où est la salle à manger/bar?*

Walking the GR20

Where is the GR20?	*Où est le GR20?* (pronounced jairvan)
The path/the waymarks/rucksack	*Le sentier/les balisés/sac à dos*
Where are you going?	*Vous allez où?*
I'm going to . . .	*Je vais à . . .*
Right/left/straight ahead	*À droit/à gauche/tout droit*
Can you show me on the map?	*Est-ce-que vous pouver me le montrer sur la carte?*
Camping/fire prohibited	*Camping/feu interdit*

At the Refuge

Guardian	*Gardien (male)/gardienne (female)*
Can I stay in the refuge?	*Puis-je reste dans le refuge?*
Dormitory/bed/sleeping bag	*Dortoir/lit/sac à couchage*
Can I camp here?	*Puis-je camper ici?*
Tent/camping space/campsite	*Tente/emplacement/aire de bivouac*
Where are the toilets/showers?	*Où sont les toilettes/douches?*
Can I have a meal/a beer/breakfast?	*Puis-je avoir un repas/une bière/petit déjeuner?*
What is the weather forecast for tomorrow?	*Quel est le météo demain?*
Hot/cold/rain/snow/storm	*Chaud/froid/pluie/neige/orage*

When It All Goes Wrong

Help me!	*Aidez-moi!*
I feel sick	*Je suis malade*
There has been an accident	*Il y a eu un accident*

Last Resort

I don't understand	*Je ne comprends pas*
Do you speak English?	*Parlez-vous anglais?*

Common Food and Drink Terms

Ail	Garlic
Beurre	Butter
Bière	Beer
Boissons(froid/chaud)	Drinks (cold/hot)
Brocciu	Goats' or sheeps' cheese, in main courses and desserts
Café/café au lait	Black/white coffee
Champignons	Mushrooms
Charcuterie	Cured pork meats served cold
Châtaigne	Chestnut, used in main courses, desserts and even beer
Chocolat	Chocolate
Confiture	Jam
Coppa	Smoked pork shoulder
Crudités	Chopped raw vegetables or salad
Figatellu	Pork liver sausage
Flan	An egg custard dessert
Fromage	Cheese
Gâteau	Cake
Haricots	Beans

Huile	Oil
Jambon	Ham
Jus d'orange	Orange juice
Légumes	Vegetables
Lentilles	Lentils
Miel	Honey
Oeufs	Eggs
Omelette	Omelette
Pain (chaud)	Bread (hot)
Panini	Filled bread rolls, often toasted
Pâtes	Pasta
Poivre	Pepper
Pomme de terre	Potato
Ravitaillement	Food store
Riz	Rice
Sanglier	Wild boar
Saucisson	Sausage
Sel	Salt
Soup Corse	Thick or thin soup, with or without meat, anything goes!
Sucre	Sugar
Thé/thé au lait	Black/white tea
Thon	Tuna
Vin blanc/rouge	White/red wine

LAZY WALKER'S FRENCH

'Bonjour', 'merci' and *'s'il vous plaît'* will get you a long way!
Hello *Bonjour*! (A standard greeting, which is useful everywhere you go. For instance, on entering a refuge or bar, greet all present with this.)
Please, a bed/a meal/a beer *S'il vous plaît, un lit/un repas/une bière* (the simplest and politest way of dealing with requests and needs)
How much? Thank you! *Combien? Merci!* (keep it polite and simple!)
Goodbye *Au revoir*
See you later *À tout à l'heure* (as English 'toodleloo'!)
The bigger the word is in English, the more likely the French word is to be similar!

APPENDIX 4
Topographical Glossary

Corsican	French	English
Bocca/foce	*col*	gap/saddle
Caminu	*sentier*	path
Capu	*sommet*	summit
Furesta	*forêt*	forest
Funtana	*source*	spring
Lavu	*lac*	lake
Monte	*mont/montagne*	mountain
Pianu	*plateau*	plateau
Pozzi	*puits*	pools
Punta	*pointe*	peak
Serra	*crête*	ridge/crest
Valdu	*vallée*	valley

NOTES

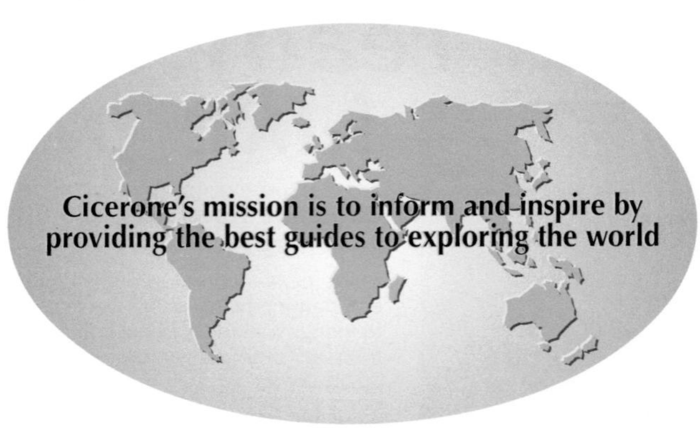

Since its foundation over 30 years ago, Cicerone has specialised in publishing guidebooks and has built a reputation for quality and reliability. It now publishes nearly 300 guides to the major destinations for outdoor enthusiasts, including Europe, UK and the rest of the world.

Written by leading and committed specialists, Cicerone guides are recognised as the most authoritative. They are full of information, maps and illustrations so that the user can plan and complete a successful and safe trip or expedition – be it a long face climb, a walk over Lakeland fells, an alpine traverse, a Himalayan trek or a ramble in the countryside.

With a thorough introduction to assist planning, clear diagrams, maps and colour photographs to illustrate the terrain and route, and accurate and detailed text, Cicerone guides are designed for ease of use and access to the information.

If the facts on the ground change, or there is any aspect of a guide that you think we can improve, we are always delighted to hear from you.

Cicerone Press
2 Police Square Milnthorpe Cumbria LA7 7PY
Tel:01539 562 069 Fax:01539 563 417
e-mail:info@cicerone.co.uk web:www.cicerone.co.uk